SEPT. 2012

Test Results for Digital Data Acquisition Tool:
ASR Data SMART version 2010-11-03

NCJ 238994

John Laub

Director, National Institute of Justice

This report was prepared for the National Institute of Justice, U.S. Department of Justice, by the Office of Law Enforcement Standards of the National Institute of Standards and Technology under Interagency Agreement 2003–IJ–R–029.

The National Institute of Justice is a component of the Office of Justice Programs, which also includes the Bureau of Justice Assistance, the Bureau of Justice Statistics, the Office of Juvenile Justice and Delinquency Prevention, and the Office for Victims of Crime.

Contents

Introduction

The Computer Forensics Tool Testing (CFTT) program is a joint project of the National Institute of Justice (NIJ), the Department of Homeland Security (DHS), and the National Institute of Standards and Technology's (NIST's) Law Enforcement Standards Office (OLES) and Information Technology Laboratory (ITL). CFTT is supported by other organizations, including the Federal Bureau of Investigation, the U.S. Department of Defense Cyber Crime Center, the U.S. Internal Revenue Service Criminal Investigation Division Electronic Crimes Program, the Bureau of Immigration and Customs Enforcement and the U.S. Secret Service. The objective of the CFTT program is to provide measurable assurance to practitioners, researchers and other applicable users that the tools used in computer forensics investigations provide accurate results. Accomplishing this requires the development of specifications and test methods for computer forensics tools and subsequent testing of specific tools against those specifications.

Test results provide the information necessary for developers to improve tools, users to make informed choices, and the legal community and others to understand the tools' capabilities. The CFTT approach to testing computer forensic tools is based on well-recognized methodologies for conformance and quality testing. The specifications and test methods are posted on the CFTT Web site (http://www.cftt.nist.gov/) for review and comment by the computer forensics community.

This document reports the results from testing ASR Data SMART version 2010-11-03 against the *Digital Data Acquisition Tool Assertions and Test Plan Version 1.0*, available at the CFTT Web site (http://www.cftt.nist.gov/DA-ATP-pc-01.pdf).

Test results from other tools and the CFTT tool methodology can be found on NIJ's CFTT Web page, http://www.nij.gov/nij/topics/forensics/evidence/digital/standards/cftt.htm.

How to Read This Report

This report is divided into five sections. The first section is a summary of the results from the test runs. This section is sufficient for most readers to assess the suitability of the tool for its intended use. The remaining sections of the report describe how the tests were conducted, discuss any anomalies that were encountered and provide documentation of test case run details that support the report summary. Section 2 gives justification for the selection of test cases from the set of possible cases defined in the test plan for Digital Data Acquisition tools. The test cases are selected, in general, based on features offered by the tool. Section 3 describes in more depth any anomalies summarized in the first section. Section 4 lists hardware and software used to run the test cases with links to additional information about the items used. Section 5 contains a description of each test case run. The description of each test run lists all test assertions used in the test case, the expected result and the actual result. Please refer to the vendor's owner manual for guidance on using the tool.

Test Results for Digital Data Acquisition Tool

Tool Tested:	SMART
Software Version:	2010-11-03
Execution Environment:	SMART Linux live CD version 2011-01
Supplier:	ASR Data, Data Acquisition and Analysis, LLC.
Address:	3505 Cumberland Gap Cedar Park, Texas 78613
Tel:	(512) 918-9227
Fax:	(512) 918-9393
Web:	http://www.asrdata.com

1 Results Summary

The tool, SMART, acquired visible and hidden sectors from the test media completely and accurately with the exception of the following cases: DA-08-DCO and DA-09. In both test cases the test results document tool features and not errors in the tool.

It was also observed that the execution environment, the SMART Linux live CD version 2011-01, modified a particular source drive containing an NTFS partition that was used in three cases: DA-02-F12, DA-02-F32, and DA-06-ATA28. CFTT has verified that the problem with NTFS partitions has been fixed in the current release of SMART Linux (August 2011). Upgrading the version of the SMART Linux live CD from the version shipped to NIST by the vendor resulted in an environment that appeared to be SMART Linux, but where the treatment of Linux swap files was misconfigured. Such an environment can under certain conditions manifest anomalies with acquiring Linux swap partitions. This Linux environment displayed anomalies with the following cases: DA-02-SWAP, DA-02-SWAP-ALT, DA-07-SWAP, and DA-14-SWAP. CFTT has verified that these swap anomalies are not present in either the original version of the SMART Linux live CD shipped to NIST by the vendor (May 6, 2010) or the current version of SMART Linux (August 2011).

The following anomalies were observed:

- The sectors hidden by a *device configuration overlay* (DCO) were not acquired (DA-08-DCO).
- Some readable sectors that were near faulty sectors on the test drive were replaced by zeros in the clone that was created in test case DA-09. The number of readable sectors missed varied between 6 and 206 sectors.

- The SMART Linux live CD execution environment modified 88 sectors of the NTFS file system on the source drive used in test cases DA-02-F12, DA-02-F32, and DA-06-ATA28. In DA-06-ATA28 this resulted in 88 sectors differing between the image file created by the tool and the original unaltered source.
- In test case DA-02-SWAP, when cloning a source swap partition to a destination swap partition of the same size, the clone operation aborted without copying the last seven sectors of the source partition.
- When restoring the image of a swap partition to a destination partition that was the same size as the source, the restore operation aborted and did not copy the last seven sectors (DA-14-SWAP).
- When a source swap partition was cloned to a larger destination swap partition in test case DA-02-SWAP-ALT, the clone differed from the source by seven sectors.
- Seven sectors of the image file differed from the source when a swap partition was acquired to an image file (DA-07-SWAP).

2 Test Case Selection

Test cases used to test disk imaging tools are defined in *Digital Data Acquisition Tool Assertions and Test Plan Version 1.0*. To test a tool, test cases are selected from the *Test Plan* document based on the features offered by the tool. Not all test cases or test assertions are appropriate for all tools. There is a core set of base cases (DA-06, DA-07 and DA-08) that are executed for every tool tested. Tool features guide the selection of additional test cases. If a given tool implements a given feature then the test cases linked to that feature are run. Table 1 lists the features available in SMART and the linked test cases selected for execution. Table 2 lists the features not available in SMART and the test cases not executed.

Table 1. Selected Test Cases

Supported Optional Feature	Cases selected for execution
Create a clone during acquisition	01
Create an unaligned clone from a digital source	02
Create a truncated clone from a physical device	04
Base Cases	06, 07 and 08
Read error during acquisition	09
Create an image file in more than one format	10
Insufficient space for image file	12
Destination Device Switching	13
Create a clone from an image file	14 and 17
Create a clone from a subset of an image file	16
Detect a corrupted (or changed) image file	24 and 25
Convert an image file from one format to another	26

Table 2. Omitted Test Cases

Unsupported Optional Feature	Cases omitted (not executed)
Create cylinder aligned clones	03, 15, 21 and 23
Device I/O error generator available	05, 11 and 18
Fill excess sectors on a clone acquisition	19
Fill excess sectors on a clone device	20, 21, 22 and 23

Some test cases have different forms to accommodate parameters within test assertions. These variations cover the acquisition interface to the source drive, the type of digital object acquired, image file format, and the way that sectors are hidden on a drive. Additional parameters that were varied between test cases were number of target devices (one device or two), interface to destination device(s), type(s) of hash algorithm calculated, method for segmenting image files, and media drive file system type.

The following source access interfaces were tested: ATA28, ATA48, SATA28, SATA48, ESATA, SCSI, FW, and USB. These are noted as variations on test cases DA-01, DA-06, and DA-08.

The following digital source types were tested: partitions (EXT2, Linux swap, FAT12, FAT16, FAT32, FAT32X, NTFS, OSX or HFS, OSXC or HFS+ case sensitive, OSXCJ or HFS+ case sensitive journaled, OSXJ or HFS+ journaled, and OSXU or UFS), compact flash (CF), and thumb drive (Thumb). There are two FAT 32 variations testing acquisition of both FAT 32 partition codes 0x0B (FAT32) and 0x0C (FAT32X). These digital source types are noted as variations on test cases DA-02 and DA-07.

The following types of image file compression are supported by the tool: bzip2, gzip, and Ewcompress. These were tested as alternate image file formats and are noted as variations on test case DA-10.

Four methods for segmenting image files were available: Standard, Partition Aligned, Fixed Size, and Transport Media. These were tested and varied across test cases DA-06, DA-07, and DA-12.

The SMART tool allows a source drive to be acquired to more than one target clone device or image file set at a time. Except for two instances, all acquisitions and restores involved the use of one target device or image file set. Test cases DA-01-ATA28 and DA-01-ATA28-CLONE2 document the acquisition of an ATA28 device to two target clone devices. Test cases DA-06-SATA28 and DA-06-SATA28-IMAGE2 document the acquisition of a SATA28 device to two destination image file sets.

The following hash algorithms were used in testing: md5 and sha1.

3 Results by Test Assertion

A test assertion is a verifiable statement about a single condition after an action is performed by the tool under test. A test case usually checks a group of assertions after the action of a single execution of the tool under test. Test assertions are defined and linked to test cases in *Digital Data Acquisition Tool Assertions and Test Plan Version 1.0*. Table 3 summarizes the test results for all the test cases by assertion. The column labeled **Assertions Tested** gives the text of each assertion. The column labeled **Tests** gives the number of test cases that use the given assertion. The column labeled **Anomaly** gives the section number in this report where any observed anomalies are discussed.

See section 2 for a discussion of source access interface and digital source. See section 4 for more information on execution environment.

Table 3. Assertions Tested

Assertions Tested	Tests	Anomaly
AM-01 The tool uses access interface SRC-AI to access the digital source.	63	
AM-02 The tool acquires digital source DS.	63	
AM-03 The tool executes in execution environment XE.	104	
AM-04 If clone creation is specified, the tool creates a clone of the digital source.	27	
AM-05 If image file creation is specified, the tool creates an image file on file system type FS.	36	
AM-06 All visible sectors are acquired from the digital source.	60	3.1 and 3.4
AM-07 All hidden sectors are acquired from the digital source.	3	3.3
AM-08 All sectors acquired from the digital source are acquired accurately.	60	3.1 and 1.1
AM-09 If unresolved errors occur while reading from the selected digital source, the tool notifies the user of the error type and location within the digital source.	1	
AM-10 If unresolved errors occur while reading from the selected digital source, the tool uses a benign fill in the destination object in place of the inaccessible data.	1	
AO-01 If the tool creates an image file, the data represented by the image file are the same as the data acquired by the tool.	33	
AO-02 If an image file format is specified, the tool creates an image file in the specified format.	3	
AO-04 If the tool is creating an image file and there is insufficient space on the image destination device to contain the image file, the tool shall notify the user.	4	
AO-05 If the tool creates a multifile image of a requested size then all the individual files shall be no larger than the requested size.	33	
AO-06 If the tool performs an image file integrity check on an image file that has not been changed since the file was created, the tool shall notify the user that the image file has not been changed.	2	
AO-07 If the tool performs an image file integrity check on an image file that has been changed since	2	

Assertions Tested	Tests	Anomaly
the file was created, the tool shall notify the user that the image file has been changed.		
AO-08 If the tool performs an image file integrity check on an image file that has been changed since the file was created, the tool shall notify the user of the affected locations.	2	
AO-09 If the tool converts a source image file from one format to a target image file in another format, the acquired data represented in the target image file are the same as the acquired data in the source image file.	6	
AO-10 If there is insufficient space to contain all files of a multifile image and if destination device switching is supported, the image is continued on another device.	1	
AO-11 If requested, a clone is created during an acquisition of a digital source.	27	
AO-12 If requested, a clone is created from an image file.	31	3.1
AO-13 A clone is created using access interface DST-AI to write to the clone device.	58	
AO-14 If an unaligned clone is created, each sector written to the clone is accurately written to the same disk address on the clone that the sector occupied on the digital source.	56	3.1
AO-16 If a subset of an image or acquisition is specified, all the subset is cloned.	1	
AO-17 If requested, any excess sectors on a clone destination device are not modified.	28	
AO-19 If there is insufficient space to create a complete clone, a truncated clone is created using all available sectors of the clone device.	2	
AO-20 If a truncated clone is created, the tool notifies the user.	2	
AO-22 If requested, the tool calculates block hashes for a specified block size during an acquisition for each block acquired from the digital source.	8	
AO-23 If the tool logs any log significant information, the information is accurately recorded in the log file.	104	3.1
AO-24 If the tool executes in a forensically safe execution environment, the digital source is unchanged by the acquisition process.	63	1.1

Two test assertions only apply in special circumstances. The assertion AO-22 is checked only for tools that create block hashes. The assertion AO-24 is only checked if the tool is executed in a runtime environment that does not modify attached storage devices, such as MS-DOS. In normal operation, an imaging tool is used in conjunction with a write block device to protect the source drive; however, a blocker was not used during the tests so that assertion AO-24 could be checked (note: in several test cases the test environment was observed to have modified the source. These cases were rerun with the use of a write blocker). Table 4 lists the assertions that were not tested, usually due to the tool not supporting some optional feature, e.g., creation of cylinder-aligned clones.

Table 4. Assertions Not Tested

Assertions Not Tested
AO-03 If there is an error while writing the image file, the tool notifies the user.
AO-15 If an aligned clone is created, each sector within a contiguous span of sectors from the source is accurately written to the same disk address on the clone device relative to the start of the span as the sector occupied on the original digital source. A span of sectors is defined to be either a mountable partition or a contiguous sequence of sectors not part of a mountable partition. Extended partitions, which may contain both mountable partitions and unallocated sectors, are not mountable partitions.
AO-18 If requested, a benign fill is written to excess sectors of a clone.
AO-21 If there is a write error during clone creation, the tool notifies the user.

3.1 Swap Partitions

Upgrading the version of the SMART Linux live CD from the version shipped to NIST by the vendor resulted in an environment that appeared to be SMART Linux, but where the treatment of Linux swap files was misconfigured. Such an environment can under certain conditions manifest anomalies with acquiring Linux swap partitions. This Linux environment displayed anomalies with the following cases: DA-02-SWAP, DA-02-SWAP-ALT, DA-07-SWAP, and DA-14-SWAP. CFTT has verified that these swap anomalies are not present in either the original version of the SMART Linux live CD shipped to NIST by the vendor (May 6, 2010) or the current version of SMART Linux (August 2011).

Test cases DA-02-SWAP and DA-14-SWAP both involved creating a clone of a swap partition on a destination swap partition that was the same size as the source. In both cases, the clone operations aborted without copying the last seven sectors of the source partition.

In test case DA-02-SWAP-ALT, which acquired a source swap partition to a larger destination swap partition, and test case DA-07-SWAP, where a swap partition was acquired to an image file, the clone and imaging operations completed without error. However, the last seven sectors of the clone (DA-02-SWAP-ALT) and the image file (DA-07-SWAP) differed from the source. The tool wrote zeros for these last seven sectors in place of the appropriate source drive content.

These behaviors related to swap seemed to be connected to the execution environment, the SMART Linux live CD version 2011-01, mounting available swap partitions. These behaviors were not observed in alternate execution environments that had been configured to disable mounting of swap.

3.2 Source Media Modified by Test Environment

The execution environment, the SMART Linux live CD version 2011-01, not the tool, modified the source drive in test cases DA-02-F12, DA-02-F32, and DA-06-ATA28. The source drive, 01-IDE, contained an NTFS and several other file systems. In each case 88 sectors belonging to the NTFS file system journal were changed. Since the execution environment's changes were limited to the NTFS partition, the accuracy of the DA-02-F12 and DA-02-F32 acquisitions (acquisitions of the drive's FAT 12 and FAT 32 partitions) were not affected. However, in DA-06-ATA28 this resulted in 88 sectors differing between the image file created by the tool and the original unaltered source. When the test cases were rerun with the source attached via hardware write block (DA-02-F12-WB, DA-02-F32-WB and DA-06-ATA28-WB), the tests completed without anomaly.

It should be noted that in testing SMART, other drives that contained NTFS file systems were imaged but were not modified by the SMART Linux environment. This behavior of SMART Linux changing the source was only seen with the NTFS file system on drive 01-IDE.

3.3 Acquisition of HPA and DCO

The tool does not remove either *Host Protected Areas* (HPAs) or DCOs. However, the Linux test environment automatically removed the HPA on the test drives, allowing the tool to image sectors hidden by an HPA. The tool did not acquire sectors hidden by a DCO (DA-08-DCO).

3.4 Readable Sectors Near Faulty Sectors

In test case DA-09 the tool was used to image a hard drive with 35 faulty sectors to a clone. In the clone, faulty sectors were replaced with zeros, as were some readable sectors near the faulty sectors. The number of readable sectors missed varied between 6 and 206 sectors.

4 Testing Environment

The tests were run in the NIST CFTT lab. This section describes the selected test execution environment, test computers available for testing, using the support software, and notes on other test hardware.

4.1 Execution Environment

SMART executes in the Linux environment. All test cases were executed with the SMART Linux live CD version 2011-01 as the test execution environment.

4.2 Test Computers

Three test computers were used. Bold lettering indicates the computer name (unique identifier), and is followed by the computer's configuration.

WoFat and **McGarrett** have the following configuration:
Intel® Desktop Motherboard DX48BT2
BIOS Version BTX3810J.86A.1554.2008.0501.1628
Intel® Core™ 2 Extreme QX9770 CPU 3.20Ghz
4GB DDR3 RAM
Diamond Radeon™ HD3450 PCI-E graphics card
SIIG® 3-Port IEEE1395 PCI-E card
LG Blu-Ray Super multi drive BD/HD-DVD/DVD/CD
Three slots for removable SATA hard disk drives
Two slots for removable IDE hard disk drives

Max has the following configuration:
Intel Desktop Motherboard D865GB/D865PERC (with ATA-6 IDE on board controller)
BIOS Version BF86510A.86A.0053.P13
Adaptec SCSI BIOS V3.10.0
Intel® Pentium™ 4 CPU 3.4Ghz
2577972KB RAM
SONY DVD RW DRU-530A, ATAPI CD/DVD-ROM drive
1.44 MB floppy drive
Two slots for removable IDE hard disk drives
Two slots for removable SATA hard disk drives
Two slots for removable SCSI hard disk drives

4.3 Support Software

A package of programs to support test analysis, FS-TST Release 2.0, was used. The software can be obtained from: http://www.cftt.nist.gov/diskimaging/fs-tst20.zip.

4.4 Test Drive Creation

There are three ways that a hard drive may be used in a tool test case: as a source drive that is imaged by the tool, as a media drive that contains image files created by the tool under test, or as a destination drive on which the tool under test creates a clone of the source drive. In addition to the operating system drive formatting tools, some tools (**diskwipe** and **diskhash**) from the FS-TST package are used to setup test drives.

To setup a media drive, the drive is formatted with one of the supported file systems. A media drive may be used in several test cases.

The setup of most source drives follows the same general procedure, but there are several steps that may be varied depending on the needs of the test case.
   1. The drive is filled with known data by the **diskwipe** program from FS-TST. The **diskwipe** program writes the sector address to each sector in both C/H/S and LBA

format. The remainder of the sector bytes is set to a constant fill value unique for each drive. The fill value is noted in the **diskwipe** tool log file.
2. The drive may be formatted with partitions as required for the test case.
3. An operating system may optionally be installed.
4. A set of reference hashes is created by the FS-TST **diskhash** tool. These include both SHA1 and MD5 hashes. In addition to full drive hashes, hashes of each partition may also be computed.
5. If the drive is intended for hidden area tests (DA-08), an HPA, a DCO or both may be created. The **diskhash** tool is then used to calculate reference hashes of just the visible sectors of the drive.

The source drives for DA-09 are created such that there is a consistent set of faulty sectors on the drive. Each of these source drives is initialized with **diskwipe** and then their faulty sectors are activated. For each of these source drives, a second drive of the same size with the same content as the faulty sector drive, but with no faulty sectors serves as a reference drive for images made from the faulty drive.

To setup a destination drive, the drive is filled with known data by the **diskwipe** program from FS-TST. Partitions may be created if the test case involves restoring from the image of a logical acquire.

4.5 Test Drive Analysis

For test cases that create a clone of a physical device, e.g., DA-01, DA-04, etc., the destination drive is compared to the source drive with the **diskcmp** program from the FS-TST package; for test cases that create a clone of a logical device, i.e., a partition, e.g., DA-02, DA-20, etc., the destination partition is compared to the source partition with the **partcmp** program. For a destination created from an image file, e.g., DA-14, the destination is compared, using either **diskcmp** (for physical device clones) or **partcmp** (for partition clones), to the source that was acquired to create the image file. Both **diskcmp** and **partcmp** note differences between the source and destination. If the destination is larger than the source it is scanned and the excess destination sectors are categorized as either, undisturbed (still containing the fill pattern written by **diskwipe**), zero filled or changed to something else.

For test case DA-09, imaging a drive with known faulty sectors, the program **anabad** is used to compare the faulty sector reference drive to a cloned version of the faulty sector drive.

For test cases such as DA-06 and DA-07 any acquisition hash computed by the tool under test is compared to the reference hash of the source to check that the source is completely and accurately acquired.

4.6 Note on Test Drives

The testing uses several test drives from a variety of vendors. The drives are identified by an external label that consists of a two digit hexadecimal value and an optional tag, e.g., 25-SATA. The combination of hex value and tag serves as a unique identifier for each drive. The two digit hex value is used by the FS-TST **diskwipe** program as a sector fill value. The FS-TST compare tools, **diskcmp** and **partcmp,** count sectors that are filled with the source and destination fill values on a destination that is larger than the original source.

5 Test Results

The main item of interest for interpreting the test results is determining the conformance of the device with the test assertions. Conformance with each assertion tested by a given test case is evaluated by examining the **Log Highlights** box of the test case details.

5.1 Test Results Report Key

A summary of the actual test results is presented in this report. The following table presents a description of each section of the test report summary. The Tester Name, Test Host, Test Date, Drives, Source Setup and Log Highlights sections for each test case are populated by excerpts taken from the log files produced by the tool under test and the FS-TST tools that were executed in support of test case setup and analysis.

Heading	Description
First Line:	Test case ID, name, and version of tool tested.
Case Summary:	Test case summary from *Digital Data Acquisition Tool Assertions and Test Plan Version 1.0.*
Assertions:	The test assertions applicable to the test case, selected from *Digital Data Acquisition Tool Assertions and Test Plan Version 1.0.*
Tester Name:	Name or initials of person executing test procedure.
Test Host:	Host computer executing the test.
Test Date:	Time and date that test was started.
Drives:	Source drive (the drive acquired), destination drive (if a clone is created) and media drive (to contain a created image).
Source Setup:	Layout of partitions on the source drive and the expected hash of the drive.
Log Highlights:	Information extracted from various log files to illustrate conformance or non-conformance to the test assertions.
Results:	Expected and actual results for each assertion tested.
Analysis:	Whether or not the expected results were achieved.

5.2 Test Details

5.2.1 DA-01-ATA28

Test Case DA-01-ATA28 Smart Version 2010/11/03	
Case Summary:	DA-01 Acquire a physical device using access interface AI to an unaligned clone.
Assertions:	AM-01 The tool uses access interface SRC-AI to access the digital source. AM-02 The tool acquires digital source DS. AM-03 The tool executes in execution environment XE.

AM-04 If clone creation is specified, the tool creates a clone of the digital source.
AM-06 All visible sectors are acquired from the digital source.
AM-08 All sectors acquired from the digital source are acquired accurately.
AO-11 If requested, a clone is created during an acquisition of a digital source.
AO-13 A clone is created using access interface DST-AI to write to the clone device.
AO-14 If an unaligned clone is created, each sector written to the clone is accurately written to the same disk address on the clone that the sector occupied on the digital source.
AO-17 If requested, any excess sectors on a clone destination device are not modified.
AO-22 If requested, the tool calculates block hashes for a specified block size during an acquisition for each block acquired from the digital source.
AO-23 If the tool logs any log significant information, the information is accurately recorded in the log file.
AO-24 If the tool executes in a forensically safe execution environment, the digital source is unchanged by the acquisition process.

Tester Name:	brl
Test Host:	McGarrett
Test Date:	Tue Feb 1 14:10:45 2011
Drives:	src(41) dst (02-IDE) other (none)

Source Setup:	src hash (SHA1): < 15CAA1A307271160D8372668BF8A03FC45A51CC9 >
	 src hash (MD5): < 0A6A8EF78BDC14E2026710D8CCB5607C >
	 78125000 total sectors (40000000000 bytes)
	 65534/015/63 (max cyl/hd values)
	 65535/016/63 (number of cyl/hd)
	 IDE disk: Model (WDC WD400BB-75JHC0) serial # (WD-WMAMC4658355)
	  N Start LBA Length Start C/H/S End C/H/S boot Partition type
	  1 P 000000063 078107967 0000/001/01 1023/254/63 Boot 07 NTFS
	  2 P 000000000 000000000 0000/000/00 0000/000/00 00 empty entry
	  3 P 000000000 000000000 0000/000/00 0000/000/00 00 empty entry
	  4 P 000000000 000000000 0000/000/00 0000/000/00 00 empty entry
	 1 078107967 sectors 39991279104 bytes

Log Highlights:	====== Destination drive setup ====== 78165360 sectors wiped with 2 ====== Comparison of original to clone drive ====== Sectors compared: 78125000 Sectors match: 78125000 Sectors differ: 0 Bytes differ: 0 Diffs range Source (78125000) has 40360 fewer sectors than destination (78165360) Zero fill: 0 Src Byte fill (41): 0 Dst Byte fill (02): 40360 Other fill: 0 Other no fill: 0 Zero fill range: Src fill range: Dst fill range: 78125000-78165359 Other fill range: Other not filled range: 0 source read errors, 0 destination read errors ====== Tool Settings: ====== dst-interface ATA28 OS: Linux ubuntu 2.6.32-21-generic #32-Ubuntu SMP Fri Apr 16 08:10:02 UTC 2010 i686 GNU/Linux ======== Excerpt from SMART log ========

```
                    MD5 Span Hashes
                     total span hash: 0a6a8ef78bdc14e2026710d8ccb5607c

                    IO Summary:(Time: Tue Feb 1 14:52:44 2011)
                    Bytes Read: 40,000,000,000
                    40,000,000,000 bytes written to /dev/sdb
                    40,000,000,000 bytes written to /dev/sde
                    ======== End of Excerpt from SMART log ========


                    ====== Source drive rehash ======
                    Rehash (SHA1) of source: 15CAA1A307271160D8372668BF8A03FC45A51CC9
```

Results:

Assertion and Expected Result	Actual Result
AM-01 Source acquired using interface AI.	as expected
AM-02 Source is type DS.	as expected
AM-03 Execution environment is XE.	as expected
AM-04 A clone is created.	as expected
AM-06 All visible sectors acquired.	as expected
AM-08 All sectors accurately acquired.	as expected
AO-11 A clone is created during acquisition.	as expected
AO-13 Clone created using interface AI.	as expected
AO-14 An unaligned clone is created.	as expected
AO-17 Excess sectors are unchanged.	as expected
AO-22 Tool calculates hashes by block.	option not tested
AO-23 Logged information is correct.	as expected
AO-24 Source is unchanged by acquisition.	as expected

Analysis: Expected results achieved

5.2.2 DA-01-ATA28-CLONE2

Test Case DA-01-ATA28-CLONE2 Smart Version 2010/11/03	
Case Summary:	DA-01 Acquire a physical device using access interface AI to an unaligned clone.
Assertions:	AM-01 The tool uses access interface SRC-AI to access the digital source. AM-02 The tool acquires digital source DS. AM-03 The tool executes in execution environment XE. AM-04 If clone creation is specified, the tool creates a clone of the digital source. AM-06 All visible sectors are acquired from the digital source. AM-08 All sectors acquired from the digital source are acquired accurately. AO-11 If requested, a clone is created during an acquisition of a digital source. AO-13 A clone is created using access interface DST-AI to write to the clone device. AO-14 If an unaligned clone is created, each sector written to the clone is accurately written to the same disk address on the clone that the sector occupied on the digital source. AO-17 If requested, any excess sectors on a clone destination device are not modified. AO-22 If requested, the tool calculates block hashes for a specified block size during an acquisition for each block acquired from the digital source. AO-23 If the tool logs any log significant information, the information is accurately recorded in the log file. AO-24 If the tool executes in a forensically safe execution environment, the digital source is unchanged by the acquisition process.
Tester Name:	brl
Test Host:	McGarrett
Test Date:	Tue Feb 1 14:12:17 2011
Drives:	src(41) dst (4E-SATA) other (none)
Source Setup:	src hash (SHA1): < 15CAA1A307271160D8372668BF8A03FC45A51CC9 > src hash (MD5): < 0A6A8EF78BDC14E2026710D8CCB5607C > 78125000 total sectors (40000000000 bytes) 65534/015/63 (max cyl/hd values) 65535/016/63 (number of cyl/hd) IDE disk: Model (WDC WD400BB-75JHC0) serial # (WD-WMAMC4658355) N Start LBA Length Start C/H/S End C/H/S boot Partition type 1 P 000000063 078107967 0000/001/01 1023/254/63 Boot 07 NTFS 2 P 000000000 000000000 0000/000/00 0000/000/00 00 empty entry 3 P 000000000 000000000 0000/000/00 0000/000/00 00 empty entry 4 P 000000000 000000000 0000/000/00 0000/000/00 00 empty entry 1 078107967 sectors 39991279104 bytes
Log Highlights:	====== Destination drive setup ====== 156301488 sectors wiped with 4E ====== Comparison of original to clone drive ====== Sectors compared: 78125000 Sectors match: 78125000 Sectors differ: 0 Bytes differ: 0 Diffs range Source (78125000) has 78176488 fewer sectors than destination (156301488) Zero fill: 0 Src Byte fill (41): 0 Dst Byte fill (4E): 78176488 Other fill: 0 Other no fill: 0 Zero fill range: Src fill range: Dst fill range: 78125000-156301487 Other fill range: Other not filled range: 0 source read errors, 0 destination read errors ====== Tool Settings: ====== dst-interface ESATA

```
Test Case DA-01-ATA28-CLONE2 Smart Version 2010/11/03
```

OS: Linux ubuntu 2.6.32-21-generic #32-Ubuntu SMP Fri Apr 16 08:10:02 UTC
2010 i686 GNU/Linux

======== Excerpt from SMART log ========

MD5 Span Hashes
 total span hash: 0a6a8ef78bdc14e2026710d8ccb5607c

IO Summary:(Time: Tue Feb 1 14:52:44 2011)
Bytes Read: 40,000,000,000
40,000,000,000 bytes written to /dev/sdb
40,000,000,000 bytes written to /dev/sde
======== End of Excerpt from SMART log ========

====== Source drive rehash ======
Rehash (SHA1) of source: 15CAA1A307271160D8372668BF8A03FC45A51CC9

Results:

Assertion and Expected Result	Actual Result
AM-01 Source acquired using interface AI.	as expected
AM-02 Source is type DS.	as expected
AM-03 Execution environment is XE.	as expected
AM-04 A clone is created.	as expected
AM-06 All visible sectors acquired.	as expected
AM-08 All sectors accurately acquired.	as expected
AO-11 A clone is created during acquisition.	as expected
AO-13 Clone created using interface AI.	as expected
AO-14 An unaligned clone is created.	as expected
AO-17 Excess sectors are unchanged.	as expected
AO-22 Tool calculates hashes by block.	option not tested
AO-23 Logged information is correct.	as expected
AO-24 Source is unchanged by acquisition.	as expected

Analysis: Expected results achieved

5.2.3 DA-01-ATA48

Test Case DA-01-ATA48 Smart Version 2010/11/03	
Case Summary:	DA-01 Acquire a physical device using access interface AI to an unaligned clone.
Assertions:	AM-01 The tool uses access interface SRC-AI to access the digital source. AM-02 The tool acquires digital source DS. AM-03 The tool executes in execution environment XE. AM-04 If clone creation is specified, the tool creates a clone of the digital source. AM-06 All visible sectors are acquired from the digital source. AM-08 All sectors acquired from the digital source are acquired accurately. AO-11 If requested, a clone is created during an acquisition of a digital source. AO-13 A clone is created using access interface DST-AI to write to the clone device. AO-14 If an unaligned clone is created, each sector written to the clone is accurately written to the same disk address on the clone that the sector occupied on the digital source. AO-17 If requested, any excess sectors on a clone destination device are not modified. AO-22 If requested, the tool calculates block hashes for a specified block size during an acquisition for each block acquired from the digital source. AO-23 If the tool logs any log significant information, the information is accurately recorded in the log file. AO-24 If the tool executes in a forensically safe execution environment, the digital source is unchanged by the acquisition process.
Tester Name:	brl
Test Host:	WoFat
Test Date:	Tue Feb 1 08:37:39 2011
Drives:	src(4C) dst (32-IDE) other (none)
Source Setup:	src hash (SHA1): < 8FF620D2BEDCCAFE8412EDAAD56C8554F872EFBF > src hash (MD5): < D10F763B56D4CEBA2D1311C61F9FB382 > 390721968 total sectors (200049647616 bytes) 24320/254/63 (max cyl/hd values) 24321/255/63 (number of cyl/hd) IDE disk: Model (WDC WD2000JB-00KFA0) serial # (WD-WMAMR1031111) N Start LBA Length Start C/H/S End C/H/S boot Partition type 1 P 000000063 390700737 0000/001/01 1023/254/63 Boot 07 NTFS 2 P 000000000 000000000 0000/000/00 0000/000/00 00 empty entry 3 P 000000000 000000000 0000/000/00 0000/000/00 00 empty entry 4 P 000000000 000000000 0000/000/00 0000/000/00 00 empty entry 1 390700737 sectors 200038777344 bytes
Log Highlights:	====== Destination drive setup ====== 488397168 sectors wiped with 32 ====== Comparison of original to clone drive ====== Sectors compared: 390721968 Sectors match: 390721968 Sectors differ: 0 Bytes differ: 0 Diffs range Source (390721968) has 97675200 fewer sectors than destination (488397168) Zero fill: 0 Src Byte fill (4C): 0 Dst Byte fill (32): 97675200 Other fill: 0 Other no fill: 0 Zero fill range: Src fill range: Dst fill range: 390721968-488397167 Other fill range: Other not filled range: 0 source read errors, 0 destination read errors ====== Tool Settings: ====== dst-interface ATA48

```
OS: Linux ubuntu 2.6.32-21-generic #32-Ubuntu SMP Fri Apr 16 08:10:02 UTC
2010 i686 GNU/Linux

======== Excerpt from SMART log ========


SHA1 Span Hashes
 total span hash: 8ff620d2 bedccafe 8412edaa d56c8554 f872efbf

IO Summary:(Time: Tue Feb 1 13:07:38 2011)
Bytes Read: 200,049,647,616
200,049,647,616 bytes written to /dev/sdb
======== End of Excerpt from SMART log ========


====== Source drive rehash ======
Rehash (SHA1) of source: 8FF620D2BEDCCAFE8412EDAAD56C8554F872EFBF
```

Results:		
	Assertion and Expected Result	**Actual Result**
	AM-01 Source acquired using interface AI.	as expected
	AM-02 Source is type DS.	as expected
	AM-03 Execution environment is XE.	as expected
	AM-04 A clone is created.	as expected
	AM-06 All visible sectors acquired.	as expected
	AM-08 All sectors accurately acquired.	as expected
	AO-11 A clone is created during acquisition.	as expected
	AO-13 Clone created using interface AI.	as expected
	AO-14 An unaligned clone is created.	as expected
	AO-17 Excess sectors are unchanged.	as expected
	AO-22 Tool calculates hashes by block.	option not tested
	AO-23 Logged information is correct.	as expected
	AO-24 Source is unchanged by acquisition.	as expected
Analysis:	Expected results achieved	

5.2.4 DA-01-ESATA

Test Case DA-01-ESATA Smart Version 2010/11/03	
Case Summary:	DA-01 Acquire a physical device using access interface AI to an unaligned clone.
Assertions:	AM-01 The tool uses access interface SRC-AI to access the digital source. AM-02 The tool acquires digital source DS. AM-03 The tool executes in execution environment XE. AM-04 If clone creation is specified, the tool creates a clone of the digital source. AM-06 All visible sectors are acquired from the digital source. AM-08 All sectors acquired from the digital source are acquired accurately. AO-11 If requested, a clone is created during an acquisition of a digital source. AO-13 A clone is created using access interface DST-AI to write to the clone device. AO-14 If an unaligned clone is created, each sector written to the clone is accurately written to the same disk address on the clone that the sector occupied on the digital source. AO-17 If requested, any excess sectors on a clone destination device are not modified. AO-22 If requested, the tool calculates block hashes for a specified block size during an acquisition for each block acquired from the digital source. AO-23 If the tool logs any log significant information, the information is accurately recorded in the log file. AO-24 If the tool executes in a forensically safe execution environment, the digital source is unchanged by the acquisition process.
Tester Name:	brl
Test Host:	McGarrett
Test Date:	Mon Jan 31 11:15:56 2011
Drives:	src(07-SATA) dst (50-IDE) other (none)

Source Setup:	src hash (SHA1): < 655E9BDDB36A3F9C5C4CC8BF32B8C5B41AF9F52E >
	 src hash (MD5): < 2EAF712DAD80F66E30DEA00365B4579B >
	 156301488 total sectors (80026361856 bytes)
	 Model (WDC WD800JD-32HK) serial # (WD-WMAJ91510044)
	  N Start LBA Length Start C/H/S End C/H/S boot Partition type
	  1 P 000000063 156280257 0000/001/01 1023/254/63 Boot 07 NTFS
	  2 P 000000000 000000000 0000/000/00 0000/000/00 00 empty entry
	  3 P 000000000 000000000 0000/000/00 0000/000/00 00 empty entry
	  4 P 000000000 000000000 0000/000/00 0000/000/00 00 empty entry
	 1 156280257 sectors 80015491584 bytes

Log Highlights:	====== Destination drive setup ======
	 156301488 sectors wiped with 50
	
	 ====== Comparison of original to clone drive ======
	 Sectors compared: 156301488
	 Sectors match: 156301488
	 Sectors differ: 0
	 Bytes differ: 0
	 Diffs range
	 0 source read errors, 0 destination read errors
	
	 ====== Tool Settings: ======
	 dst-interface ATA28
	
	 OS: Linux ubuntu 2.6.32-21-generic #32-Ubuntu SMP Fri Apr 16 08:10:02 UTC 2010 i686 GNU/Linux
	
	 ======== Excerpt from SMART log ========
	
	 SHA1 Span Hashes
	  total span hash: 655e9bdd b36a3f9c 5c4cc8bf 32b8c5b4 1af9f52e
	 MD5 Span Hashes
	  total span hash: 2eaf712dad80f66e30dea00365b4579b
	
	 IO Summary:(Time: Mon Jan 31 15:21:43 2011)

Test Case DA-01-ESATA Smart Version 2010/11/03		
	Bytes Read: 80,026,361,856 80,026,361,856 bytes written to /dev/sda ======== End of Excerpt from SMART log ======== ====== Source drive rehash ====== Rehash (SHA1) of source: 655E9BDDB36A3F9C5C4CC8BF32B8C5B41AF9F52E	
Results:		

Assertion and Expected Result	Actual Result
AM-01 Source acquired using interface AI.	as expected
AM-02 Source is type DS.	as expected
AM-03 Execution environment is XE.	as expected
AM-04 A clone is created.	as expected
AM-06 All visible sectors acquired.	as expected
AM-08 All sectors accurately acquired.	as expected
AO-11 A clone is created during acquisition.	as expected
AO-13 Clone created using interface AI.	as expected
AO-14 An unaligned clone is created.	as expected
AO-17 Excess sectors are unchanged.	as expected
AO-22 Tool calculates hashes by block.	option not tested
AO-23 Logged information is correct.	as expected
AO-24 Source is unchanged by acquisition.	as expected

Analysis:	Expected results achieved

5.2.5 DA-01-FW

Test Case DA-01-FW Smart Version 2010/11/03	
Case Summary:	DA-01 Acquire a physical device using access interface AI to an unaligned clone.
Assertions:	AM-01 The tool uses access interface SRC-AI to access the digital source. AM-02 The tool acquires digital source DS. AM-03 The tool executes in execution environment XE. AM-04 If clone creation is specified, the tool creates a clone of the digital source. AM-06 All visible sectors are acquired from the digital source. AM-08 All sectors acquired from the digital source are acquired accurately. AO-11 If requested, a clone is created during an acquisition of a digital source. AO-13 A clone is created using access interface DST-AI to write to the clone device. AO-14 If an unaligned clone is created, each sector written to the clone is accurately written to the same disk address on the clone that the sector occupied on the digital source. AO-17 If requested, any excess sectors on a clone destination device are not modified. AO-22 If requested, the tool calculates block hashes for a specified block size during an acquisition for each block acquired from the digital source. AO-23 If the tool logs any log significant information, the information is accurately recorded in the log file. AO-24 If the tool executes in a forensically safe execution environment, the digital source is unchanged by the acquisition process.
Tester Name:	brl
Test Host:	Max
Test Date:	Fri Jan 28 10:02:20 2011
Drives:	src(63-FU2) dst (84-FU2) other (none)
Source Setup:	src hash (SHA1): < F7069EDCBEAC863C88DECED82159F22DA96BE99B > src hash (MD5): < EE217BC4FA4F3D1B4021D29B065AA9EC > 117304992 total sectors (60060155904 bytes) Model (SP0612N) serial # () N Start LBA Length Start C/H/S End C/H/S boot Partition type 1 P 000000063 004192902 0000/001/01 0260/254/63 Boot 06 Fat16 2 X 004192965 113097600 0261/000/01 1023/254/63 0F extended 3 S 000000063 113097537 0261/001/01 1023/254/63 0B Fat32 4 S 000000000 000000000 0000/000/00 0000/000/00 00 empty entry 5 P 000000000 000000000 0000/000/00 0000/000/00 00 empty entry 6 P 000000000 000000000 0000/000/00 0000/000/00 00 empty entry 1 004192902 sectors 2146765824 bytes 3 113097537 sectors 57905938944 bytes
Log Highlights:	====== Destination drive setup ====== 160836480 sectors wiped with 84 ====== Comparison of original to clone drive ====== Sectors compared: 117304992 Sectors match: 117304992 Sectors differ: 0 Bytes differ: 0 Diffs range Source (117304992) has 43531488 fewer sectors than destination (160836480) Zero fill: 0 Src Byte fill (63): 0 Dst Byte fill (84): 43531488 Other fill: 0 Other no fill: 0 Zero fill range: Src fill range: Dst fill range: 117304992-160836479 Other fill range: Other not filled range: 0 source read errors, 0 destination read errors ====== Tool Settings: ======

```
dst-interface FW

OS: Linux ubuntu 2.6.32-21-generic #32-Ubuntu SMP Fri Apr 16 08:10:02 UTC
2010 i686 GNU/Linux

======== Excerpt from SMART log ========


SHA1 Span Hashes
 total span hash: f7069edc beac863c 88deced8 2159f22d a96be99b

IO Summary:(Time: Fri Jan 28 15:40:49 2011)
Bytes Read: 60,060,155,904
60,060,155,904 bytes written to /dev/sdg
======== End of Excerpt from SMART log ========

====== Source drive rehash ======
Rehash (SHA1) of source: F7069EDCBEAC863C88DECED82159F22DA96BE99B
```

Results:

Assertion and Expected Result	Actual Result
AM-01 Source acquired using interface AI.	as expected
AM-02 Source is type DS.	as expected
AM-03 Execution environment is XE.	as expected
AM-04 A clone is created.	as expected
AM-06 All visible sectors acquired.	as expected
AM-08 All sectors accurately acquired.	as expected
AO-11 A clone is created during acquisition.	as expected
AO-13 Clone created using interface AI.	as expected
AO-14 An unaligned clone is created.	as expected
AO-17 Excess sectors are unchanged.	as expected
AO-22 Tool calculates hashes by block.	option not tested
AO-23 Logged information is correct.	as expected
AO-24 Source is unchanged by acquisition.	as expected

Analysis: Expected results achieved

5.2.6 DA-01-SATA28

Test Case DA-01-SATA28 Smart Version 2010/11/03	
Case Summary:	DA-01 Acquire a physical device using access interface AI to an unaligned clone.
Assertions:	AM-01 The tool uses access interface SRC-AI to access the digital source. AM-02 The tool acquires digital source DS. AM-03 The tool executes in execution environment XE. AM-04 If clone creation is specified, the tool creates a clone of the digital source. AM-06 All visible sectors are acquired from the digital source. AM-08 All sectors acquired from the digital source are acquired accurately. AO-11 If requested, a clone is created during an acquisition of a digital source. AO-13 A clone is created using access interface DST-AI to write to the clone device. AO-14 If an unaligned clone is created, each sector written to the clone is accurately written to the same disk address on the clone that the sector occupied on the digital source. AO-17 If requested, any excess sectors on a clone destination device are not modified. AO-22 If requested, the tool calculates block hashes for a specified block size during an acquisition for each block acquired from the digital source. AO-23 If the tool logs any log significant information, the information is accurately recorded in the log file. AO-24 If the tool executes in a forensically safe execution environment, the digital source is unchanged by the acquisition process.
Tester Name:	brl
Test Host:	WoFat
Test Date:	Fri Jan 28 09:22:17 2011
Drives:	src (07-SATA) dst (04-SATA) other (none)
Source Setup:	src hash (SHA1): < 655E9BDDB36A3F9C5C4CC8BF32B8C5B41AF9F52E > src hash (MD5): < 2EAF712DAD80F66E30DEA00365B4579B > 156301488 total sectors (80026361856 bytes) Model (WDC WD800JD-32HK) serial # (WD-WMAJ91510044) N Start LBA Length Start C/H/S End C/H/S boot Partition type 1 P 000000063 156280257 0000/001/01 1023/254/63 Boot 07 NTFS 2 P 000000000 000000000 0000/000/00 0000/000/00 00 empty entry 3 P 000000000 000000000 0000/000/00 0000/000/00 00 empty entry 4 P 000000000 000000000 0000/000/00 0000/000/00 00 empty entry 1 156280257 sectors 80015491584 bytes
Log Highlights:	====== Destination drive setup ====== 156301488 sectors wiped with 4 ====== Comparison of original to clone drive ====== Sectors compared: 156301488 Sectors match: 156301488 Sectors differ: 0 Bytes differ: 0 Diffs range 0 source read errors, 0 destination read errors ====== Tool Settings: ====== dst-interface SATA28 OS: Linux ubuntu 2.6.32-21-generic #32-Ubuntu SMP Fri Apr 16 08:10:02 UTC 2010 i686 GNU/Linux ======== Excerpt from SMART log ======== SHA1 Span Hashes total span hash: 655e9bdd b36a3f9c 5c4cc8bf 32b8c5b4 1af9f52e IO Summary:(Time: Fri Jan 28 12:13:04 2011) Bytes Read: 80,026,361,856 80,026,361,856 bytes written to /dev/sdb

```
======== End of Excerpt from SMART log ========

====== Source drive rehash ======
Rehash (SHA1) of source: 655E9BDDB36A3F9C5C4CC8BF32B8C5B41AF9F52E
```

Results:

Assertion and Expected Result	Actual Result
AM-01 Source acquired using interface AI.	as expected
AM-02 Source is type DS.	as expected
AM-03 Execution environment is XE.	as expected
AM-04 A clone is created.	as expected
AM-06 All visible sectors acquired.	as expected
AM-08 All sectors accurately acquired.	as expected
AO-11 A clone is created during acquisition.	as expected
AO-13 Clone created using interface AI.	as expected
AO-14 An unaligned clone is created.	as expected
AO-17 Excess sectors are unchanged.	as expected
AO-22 Tool calculates hashes by block.	option not tested
AO-23 Logged information is correct.	as expected
AO-24 Source is unchanged by acquisition.	as expected

Analysis: Expected results achieved

5.2.7 DA-01-SATA48

Test Case DA-01-SATA48 Smart Version 2010/11/03	
Case Summary:	DA-01 Acquire a physical device using access interface AI to an unaligned clone.
Assertions:	AM-01 The tool uses access interface SRC-AI to access the digital source. AM-02 The tool acquires digital source DS. AM-03 The tool executes in execution environment XE. AM-04 If clone creation is specified, the tool creates a clone of the digital source. AM-06 All visible sectors are acquired from the digital source. AM-08 All sectors acquired from the digital source are acquired accurately. AO-11 If requested, a clone is created during an acquisition of a digital source. AO-13 A clone is created using access interface DST-AI to write to the clone device. AO-14 If an unaligned clone is created, each sector written to the clone is accurately written to the same disk address on the clone that the sector occupied on the digital source. AO-17 If requested, any excess sectors on a clone destination device are not modified. AO-22 If requested, the tool calculates block hashes for a specified block size during an acquisition for each block acquired from the digital source. AO-23 If the tool logs any log significant information, the information is accurately recorded in the log file. AO-24 If the tool executes in a forensically safe execution environment, the digital source is unchanged by the acquisition process.
Tester Name:	brl
Test Host:	WoFat
Test Date:	Mon Jan 31 09:15:59 2011
Drives:	src(0D-SATA) dst (46-SATA) other (none)

Source Setup:	src hash (SHA1): < BAAD80E8781E55F2E3EF528CA73BD41D228C1377 >
	 src hash (MD5): < 1FA7C3CBE60EB9E89863DED2411E40C9 >
	 488397168 total sectors (250059350016 bytes)
	 30400/254/63 (max cyl/hd values)
	 30401/255/63 (number of cyl/hd)
	 Model (WDC WD2500JD-22F) serial # (WD-WMAEH2678216)
	  N Start LBA Length Start C/H/S End C/H/S boot Partition type
	  1 P 000000063 488375937 0000/001/01 1023/254/63 Boot 07 NTFS
	  2 P 000000000 000000000 0000/000/00 0000/000/00 00 empty entry
	  3 P 000000000 000000000 0000/000/00 0000/000/00 00 empty entry
	  4 P 000000000 000000000 0000/000/00 0000/000/00 00 empty entry
	 1 488375937 sectors 250048479744 bytes

Log Highlights:	====== Destination drive setup ====== 488397168 sectors wiped with 46 ====== Comparison of original to clone drive ====== Sectors compared: 488397168 Sectors match: 488397168 Sectors differ: 0 Bytes differ: 0 Diffs range 0 source read errors, 0 destination read errors ====== Tool Settings: ====== dst-interface SATA48 OS: Linux ubuntu 2.6.32-21-generic #32-Ubuntu SMP Fri Apr 16 08:10:02 UTC 2010 i686 GNU/Linux ======== Excerpt from SMART log ======== SHA1 Span Hashes total span hash: baad80e8 781e55f2 e3ef528c a73bd41d 228c1377 IO Summary:(Time: Mon Jan 31 15:22:19 2011)

Test Case DA-01-SATA48 Smart Version 2010/11/03	
	Bytes Read: 250,059,350,016 250,059,350,016 bytes written to /dev/sdb ======== End of Excerpt from SMART log ======== ====== Source drive rehash ====== Rehash (SHA1) of source: BAAD80E8781E55F2E3EF528CA73BD41D228C1377
Results:	

Assertion and Expected Result	Actual Result
AM-01 Source acquired using interface AI.	as expected
AM-02 Source is type DS.	as expected
AM-03 Execution environment is XE.	as expected
AM-04 A clone is created.	as expected
AM-06 All visible sectors acquired.	as expected
AM-08 All sectors accurately acquired.	as expected
AO-11 A clone is created during acquisition.	as expected
AO-13 Clone created using interface AI.	as expected
AO-14 An unaligned clone is created.	as expected
AO-17 Excess sectors are unchanged.	as expected
AO-22 Tool calculates hashes by block.	option not tested
AO-23 Logged information is correct.	as expected
AO-24 Source is unchanged by acquisition.	as expected

Analysis:	Expected results achieved

5.2.8 DA-01-SCSI

Test Case DA-01-SCSI Smart Version 2010/11/03	
Case Summary:	DA-01 Acquire a physical device using access interface AI to an unaligned clone.
Assertions:	AM-01 The tool uses access interface SRC-AI to access the digital source. AM-02 The tool acquires digital source DS. AM-03 The tool executes in execution environment XE. AM-04 If clone creation is specified, the tool creates a clone of the digital source. AM-06 All visible sectors are acquired from the digital source. AM-08 All sectors acquired from the digital source are acquired accurately. AO-11 If requested, a clone is created during an acquisition of a digital source. AO-13 A clone is created using access interface DST-AI to write to the clone device. AO-14 If an unaligned clone is created, each sector written to the clone is accurately written to the same disk address on the clone that the sector occupied on the digital source. AO-17 If requested, any excess sectors on a clone destination device are not modified. AO-22 If requested, the tool calculates block hashes for a specified block size during an acquisition for each block acquired from the digital source. AO-23 If the tool logs any log significant information, the information is accurately recorded in the log file. AO-24 If the tool executes in a forensically safe execution environment, the digital source is unchanged by the acquisition process.
Tester Name:	brl
Test Host:	Max
Test Date:	Mon Jan 31 09:36:19 2011
Drives:	src(E0) dst (CC) other (none)
Source Setup:	src hash (SHA1): < 4A6941F1337A8A22B10FC844B4D7FA6158BECB82 > src hash (MD5): < A97C8F36B7AC9D5233B90AC09284F938 > 17938985 total sectors (9184760320 bytes) Model (ATLAS10K2-TY092J) serial # (169028142436)
Log Highlights:	====== Destination drive setup ====== 71687370 sectors wiped with CC ====== Comparison of original to clone drive ====== Sectors compared: 17938985 Sectors match: 17938985 Sectors differ: 0 Bytes differ: 0 Diffs range Source (17938985) has 53748385 fewer sectors than destination (71687370) Zero fill: 0 Src Byte fill (E0): 0 Dst Byte fill (CC): 53748385 Other fill: 0 Other no fill: 0 Zero fill range: Src fill range: Dst fill range: 17938985-71687369 Other fill range: Other not filled range: 0 source read errors, 0 destination read errors ====== Tool Settings: ====== dst-interface SCSI OS: Linux ubuntu 2.6.32-21-generic #32-Ubuntu SMP Fri Apr 16 08:10:02 UTC 2010 i686 GNU/Linux ======== Excerpt from SMART log ======== SHA1 Span Hashes

```
total span hash: 4a6941f1 337a8a22 b10fc844 b4d7fa61 58becb82

IO Summary:(Time: Mon Jan 31 11:52:46 2011)
Bytes Read: 9,184,760,320
9,184,760,320 bytes written to /dev/sdf
======== End of Excerpt from SMART log ========

====== Source drive rehash ======
Rehash (SHA1) of source: 4A6941F1337A8A22B10FC844B4D7FA6158BECB82
```

Results:

Assertion and Expected Result	Actual Result
AM-01 Source acquired using interface AI.	as expected
AM-02 Source is type DS.	as expected
AM-03 Execution environment is XE.	as expected
AM-04 A clone is created.	as expected
AM-06 All visible sectors acquired.	as expected
AM-08 All sectors accurately acquired.	as expected
AO-11 A clone is created during acquisition.	as expected
AO-13 Clone created using interface AI.	as expected
AO-14 An unaligned clone is created.	as expected
AO-17 Excess sectors are unchanged.	as expected
AO-22 Tool calculates hashes by block.	option not tested
AO-23 Logged information is correct.	as expected
AO-24 Source is unchanged by acquisition.	as expected

Analysis: Expected results achieved

5.2.9 DA-01-USB

Test Case DA-01-USB Smart Version 2010/11/03	
Case Summary:	DA-01 Acquire a physical device using access interface AI to an unaligned clone.
Assertions:	AM-01 The tool uses access interface SRC-AI to access the digital source. AM-02 The tool acquires digital source DS. AM-03 The tool executes in execution environment XE. AM-04 If clone creation is specified, the tool creates a clone of the digital source. AM-06 All visible sectors are acquired from the digital source. AM-08 All sectors acquired from the digital source are acquired accurately. AO-11 If requested, a clone is created during an acquisition of a digital source. AO-13 A clone is created using access interface DST-AI to write to the clone device. AO-14 If an unaligned clone is created, each sector written to the clone is accurately written to the same disk address on the clone that the sector occupied on the digital source. AO-17 If requested, any excess sectors on a clone destination device are not modified. AO-22 If requested, the tool calculates block hashes for a specified block size during an acquisition for each block acquired from the digital source. AO-23 If the tool logs any log significant information, the information is accurately recorded in the log file. AO-24 If the tool executes in a forensically safe execution environment, the digital source is unchanged by the acquisition process.
Tester Name:	brl
Test Host:	Max
Test Date:	Tue Feb 1 09:05:07 2011
Drives:	src(63-FU2) dst (84-FU2) other (none)
Source Setup:	src hash (SHA1): < F7069EDCBEAC863C88DECED82159F22DA96BE99B > src hash (MD5): < EE217BC4FA4F3D1B4021D29B065AA9EC > 117304992 total sectors (60060155904 bytes) Model (SP0612N) serial # () N Start LBA Length Start C/H/S End C/H/S boot Partition type 1 P 000000063 004192902 0000/001/01 0260/254/63 Boot 06 Fat16 2 X 004192965 113097600 0261/000/01 1023/254/63 0F extended 3 S 000000063 113097537 0261/001/01 1023/254/63 0B Fat32 4 S 000000000 000000000 0000/000/00 0000/000/00 00 empty entry 5 P 000000000 000000000 0000/000/00 0000/000/00 00 empty entry 6 P 000000000 000000000 0000/000/00 0000/000/00 00 empty entry 1 004192902 sectors 2146765824 bytes 3 113097537 sectors 57905938944 bytes
Log Highlights:	====== Destination drive setup ====== 160836480 sectors wiped with 84 ====== Comparison of original to clone drive ====== Sectors compared: 117304992 Sectors match: 117304992 Sectors differ: 0 Bytes differ: 0 Diffs range Source (117304992) has 43531488 fewer sectors than destination (160836480) Zero fill: 0 Src Byte fill (63): 0 Dst Byte fill (84): 43531488 Other fill: 0 Other no fill: 0 Zero fill range: Src fill range: Dst fill range: 117304992-160836479 Other fill range: Other not filled range: 0 source read errors, 0 destination read errors ====== Tool Settings: ======

```
dst-interface USB

OS: Linux ubuntu 2.6.32-21-generic #32-Ubuntu SMP Fri Apr 16 08:10:02 UTC
2010 i686 GNU/Linux

======== Excerpt from SMART log ========


SHA1 Span Hashes
 total span hash: f7069edc beac863c 88deced8 2159f22d a96be99b

IO Summary:(Time: Tue Feb 1 12:27:14 2011)
Bytes Read: 60,060,155,904
60,060,155,904 bytes written to /dev/sdg
======== End of Excerpt from SMART log ========

====== Source drive rehash ======
Rehash (SHA1) of source: F7069EDCBEAC863C88DECED82159F22DA96BE99B
```

Results:

Assertion and Expected Result	Actual Result
AM-01 Source acquired using interface AI.	as expected
AM-02 Source is type DS.	as expected
AM-03 Execution environment is XE.	as expected
AM-04 A clone is created.	as expected
AM-06 All visible sectors acquired.	as expected
AM-08 All sectors accurately acquired.	as expected
AO-11 A clone is created during acquisition.	as expected
AO-13 Clone created using interface AI.	as expected
AO-14 An unaligned clone is created.	as expected
AO-17 Excess sectors are unchanged.	as expected
AO-22 Tool calculates hashes by block.	option not tested
AO-23 Logged information is correct.	as expected
AO-24 Source is unchanged by acquisition.	as expected

Analysis: Expected results achieved

5.2.10   DA-02-CF

Test Case DA-02-CF Smart Version 2010/11/03	
Case Summary:	DA-02 Acquire a digital source of type DS to an unaligned clone.
Assertions:	AM-01 The tool uses access interface SRC-AI to access the digital source. AM-02 The tool acquires digital source DS. AM-03 The tool executes in execution environment XE. AM-04 If clone creation is specified, the tool creates a clone of the digital source. AM-06 All visible sectors are acquired from the digital source. AM-08 All sectors acquired from the digital source are acquired accurately. AO-11 If requested, a clone is created during an acquisition of a digital source. AO-13 A clone is created using access interface DST-AI to write to the clone device. AO-14 If an unaligned clone is created, each sector written to the clone is accurately written to the same disk address on the clone that the sector occupied on the digital source. AO-17 If requested, any excess sectors on a clone destination device are not modified. AO-22 If requested, the tool calculates block hashes for a specified block size during an acquisition for each block acquired from the digital source. AO-23 If the tool logs any log significant information, the information is accurately recorded in the log file. AO-24 If the tool executes in a forensically safe execution environment, the digital source is unchanged by the acquisition process.
Tester Name:	brl
Test Host:	Max
Test Date:	Wed Feb 2 12:27:40 2011
Drives:	src(C1-CF) dst (C2-CF) other (none)
Source Setup:	src hash (SHA1): < 5B8235178DF99FA307430C088F81746606638A0B > src hash (MD5): < 776DF8B4D2589E21DEBCF589EDC16D78 > 503808 total sectors (257949696 bytes) Model (CF) serial # () N Start LBA Length Start C/H/S End C/H/S boot Partition type 1 P 778135908 1141509631 0357/116/40 0357/032/45 Boot 72 other 2 P 168689522 1936028240 0288/115/43 0367/114/50 Boot 65 other 3 P 1869881465 1936028192 0366/032/33 0357/032/43 Boot 79 other 4 P 2885681152 000055499 0372/097/50 0000/010/00 Boot 0D other 1 1141509631 sectors 584452931072 bytes 2 1936028240 sectors 991246458880 bytes 3 1936028192 sectors 991246434304 bytes 4 000055499 sectors 28415488 bytes
Log Highlights:	====== Destination drive setup ====== 503808 sectors wiped with C2 ====== Comparison of original to clone drive ====== Sectors compared: 503808 Sectors match: 503808 Sectors differ: 0 Bytes differ: 0 Diffs range 0 source read errors, 0 destination read errors ====== Tool Settings: ====== dst-interface USB OS: Linux ubuntu 2.6.32-21-generic #32-Ubuntu SMP Fri Apr 16 08:10:02 UTC 2010 i686 GNU/Linux ======== Excerpt from SMART log ======== SHA1 Span Hashes total span hash: 5b823517 8df99fa3 07430c08 8f817466 06638a0b

Test Case DA-02-CF Smart Version 2010/11/03	
	IO Summary:(Time: Wed Feb 2 13:28:33 2011) Bytes Read: 257,949,696 257,949,696 bytes written to /dev/sde ======== End of Excerpt from SMART log ======== ====== Source drive rehash ====== Rehash (SHA1) of source: 5B8235178DF99FA307430C088F81746606638A0B
Results:	

Assertion and Expected Result	Actual Result
AM-01 Source acquired using interface AI.	as expected
AM-02 Source is type DS.	as expected
AM-03 Execution environment is XE.	as expected
AM-04 A clone is created.	as expected
AM-06 All visible sectors acquired.	as expected
AM-08 All sectors accurately acquired.	as expected
AO-11 A clone is created during acquisition.	as expected
AO-13 Clone created using interface AI.	as expected
AO-14 An unaligned clone is created.	as expected
AO-17 Excess sectors are unchanged.	as expected
AO-22 Tool calculates hashes by block.	option not tested
AO-23 Logged information is correct.	as expected
AO-24 Source is unchanged by acquisition.	as expected

Analysis:	Expected results achieved

5.2.11   DA-02-EXT2

Test Case DA-02-EXT2 Smart Version 2010/11/03	
Case Summary:	DA-02 Acquire a digital source of type DS to an unaligned clone.
Assertions:	AM-01 The tool uses access interface SRC-AI to access the digital source. AM-02 The tool acquires digital source DS. AM-03 The tool executes in execution environment XE. AM-04 If clone creation is specified, the tool creates a clone of the digital source. AM-06 All visible sectors are acquired from the digital source. AM-08 All sectors acquired from the digital source are acquired accurately. AO-11 If requested, a clone is created during an acquisition of a digital source. AO-13 A clone is created using access interface DST-AI to write to the clone device. AO-14 If an unaligned clone is created, each sector written to the clone is accurately written to the same disk address on the clone that the sector occupied on the digital source. AO-17 If requested, any excess sectors on a clone destination device are not modified. AO-22 If requested, the tool calculates block hashes for a specified block size during an acquisition for each block acquired from the digital source. AO-23 If the tool logs any log significant information, the information is accurately recorded in the log file. AO-24 If the tool executes in a forensically safe execution environment, the digital source is unchanged by the acquisition process.
Tester Name:	brl
Test Host:	WoFat
Test Date:	Thu Feb 3 15:46:46 2011
Drives:	src(43) dst (49-SATA) other (none)
Source Setup:	src hash (SHA1): < 888E2E7F7AD237DC7A732281DD93F325065E5871 > src hash (MD5): < BC39C3F7EE7A50E77B9BA1E65A5AEEF7 > 78125000 total sectors (40000000000 bytes) Model (0BB-75JHC0) serial # (WD-WMAMC46588) N Start LBA Length Start C/H/S End C/H/S boot Partition type 1 P 000000063 020980827 0000/001/01 1023/254/63 0C Fat32X 2 X 020980890 057143205 1023/000/01 1023/254/63 0F extended 3 S 000000063 000032067 1023/001/01 1023/254/63 01 Fat12 4 x 000032130 002104515 1023/000/01 1023/254/63 05 extended 5 S 000000063 002104452 1023/001/01 1023/254/63 06 Fat16 6 x 002136645 004192965 1023/000/01 1023/254/63 05 extended 7 S 000000063 004192902 1023/001/01 1023/254/63 16 other 8 x 006329610 008401995 1023/000/01 1023/254/63 05 extended 9 S 000000063 008401932 1023/001/01 1023/254/63 0B Fat32 10 x 014731605 010490445 1023/000/01 1023/254/63 05 extended 11 S 000000063 010490382 1023/001/01 1023/254/63 83 Linux 12 x 025222050 004209030 1023/000/01 1023/254/63 05 extended 13 S 000000063 004208967 1023/001/01 1023/254/63 82 Linux swap 14 x 029431080 027712125 1023/000/01 1023/254/63 05 extended 15 S 000000063 027712062 1023/001/01 1023/254/63 07 NTFS 16 S 000000000 000000000 0000/000/00 0000/000/00 00 empty entry 17 P 000000000 000000000 0000/000/00 0000/000/00 00 empty entry 18 P 000000000 000000000 0000/000/00 0000/000/00 00 empty entry 1 020980827 sectors 10742183424 bytes 3 000032067 sectors 16418304 bytes 5 002104452 sectors 1077479424 bytes 7 004192902 sectors 2146765824 bytes 9 008401932 sectors 4301789184 bytes 11 010490382 sectors 5371075584 bytes 13 004208967 sectors 2154991104 bytes 15 027712062 sectors 14188575744 bytes 43ext2-md5sum 5371075583 C7A84DE9ACBCB05463604CE8823D0874 43ext2-sha1sum 5371075583 283BCC32DE892C12C37698AF7E38703619E57F57 Excess destination partition sectors hash: SHA1 5371075584 - 5872817663 = 58344A633C5DF644ECC51E253BBC26E29BECF224 -
Log Highlights:	====== Destination drive setup ====== 156301488 sectors wiped with 49

```
====== Comparison of original to clone drive ======
Sectors compared: 10490382
Sectors match: 10490382
Sectors differ: 0
Bytes differ: 0
Diffs range:
Source (10490382) has 979965 fewer sectors than destination (11470347)
Zero fill: 30839
Src Byte fill (43): 0
Dst Byte fill (49): 946245
Other fill: 61
Other no fill: 2820
Zero fill range: 10502147, 10502193, 10502196-10502707,
10518531, 10518577, 10518580-10519091, 10534915, 10534961,
10534964-10535475, 10551299, 10551345, 10551348-10551859,
10567683, 10567729, 10567732-10568243, 10584067, 10584113,
10584116-10584627, 10600451, 10600497. . . + 27753 more
Src fill range:
Dst fill range: 10490382-10502145, 10502708-10518529,
10519092-10534913, 10535476-10551297, 10551860-10567681,
10568244-10584065, 10584628-10600449, 10601012-10616833,
10617396-10633217, 10633780-10649601, 10650164-10665985,
10666548-10682369, 10682932-10698753, 10699316-10715137,
10715700-10731521, 10732084-10747905, 10748468-10764289,
10764852-10780673, 10781236-10797057, 10797620-10813441. . . + 633863 more
Other fill range: 10502195, 10518579, 10534963, 10551347,
10567731, 10584115, 10600499, 10616883, 10633267, 10649651,
10666035, 10682419, 10698803, 10715187, 10731571, 10747955,
10764339, 10780723, 10797107, 10813491. . . + 41 more
Other not filled range: 10502146, 10502148-10502192,
10502194, 10518530, 10518532-10518576, 10518578, 10534914,
10534916-10534960, 10534962, 10551298, 10551300-10551344,
10551346, 10567682, 10567684-10567728, 10567730, 10584066,
10584068-10584112, 10584114, 10600450, 10600452-10600496. . . + 2492 more
run start Thu Feb 3 16:23:38 2011
run finish Thu Feb 3 16:27:23 2011
elapsed time 0:3:45
Normal exit


====== Tool Settings: ======
dst-interface SATA28

OS: Linux ubuntu 2.6.32-21-generic #32-Ubuntu SMP Fri Apr 16 08:10:02 UTC
2010 i686 GNU/Linux

======== Excerpt from SMART log ========


SHA1 Span Hashes
 total span hash: 283bcc32 de892c12 c37698af 7e387036 19e57f57

IO Summary:(Time: Thu Feb 3 16:04:12 2011)
Bytes Read: 5,371,075,584
5,371,075,584 bytes written to /dev/sda9
======== End of Excerpt from SMART log ========

Excess destination partition sectors hash:
SHA1 5371075584 - 5872817663 = 58344A633C5DF644ECC51E253BBC26E29BECF224 -

====== Source drive rehash ======
Rehash (SHA1) of source: 888E2E7F7AD237DC7A732281DD93F325065E5871
```

Results:

Assertion and Expected Result	Actual Result
AM-01 Source acquired using interface AI.	as expected
AM-02 Source is type DS.	as expected
AM-03 Execution environment is XE.	as expected

Test Case DA-02-EXT2 Smart Version 2010/11/03		
	AM-04 A clone is created.	as expected
	AM-06 All visible sectors acquired.	as expected
	AM-08 All sectors accurately acquired.	as expected
	AO-11 A clone is created during acquisition.	as expected
	AO-13 Clone created using interface AI.	as expected
	AO-14 An unaligned clone is created.	as expected
	AO-17 Excess sectors are unchanged.	as expected
	AO-22 Tool calculates hashes by block.	option not tested
	AO-23 Logged information is correct.	as expected
	AO-24 Source is unchanged by acquisition.	as expected
Analysis:	Expected results achieved	

5.2.12 DA-02-F12

Case Summary:	DA-02 Acquire a digital source of type DS to an unaligned clone.
Assertions:	AM-01 The tool uses access interface SRC-AI to access the digital source. AM-02 The tool acquires digital source DS. AM-03 The tool executes in execution environment XE. AM-04 If clone creation is specified, the tool creates a clone of the digital source. AM-06 All visible sectors are acquired from the digital source. AM-08 All sectors acquired from the digital source are acquired accurately. AO-11 If requested, a clone is created during an acquisition of a digital source. AO-13 A clone is created using access interface DST-AI to write to the clone device. AO-14 If an unaligned clone is created, each sector written to the clone is accurately written to the same disk address on the clone that the sector occupied on the digital source. AO-17 If requested, any excess sectors on a clone destination device are not modified. AO-22 If requested, the tool calculates block hashes for a specified block size during an acquisition for each block acquired from the digital source. AO-23 If the tool logs any log significant information, the information is accurately recorded in the log file. AO-24 If the tool executes in a forensically safe execution environment, the digital source is unchanged by the acquisition process.
Tester Name:	brl
Test Host:	McGarrett
Test Date:	Thu Feb 3 11:20:53 2011
Drives:	src (01-IDE) dst (4D-SATA) other (none)
Source Setup:	src hash (SHA1): < A48BB5665D6DC57C22DB68E2F723DA9AA8DF82B9 > src hash (MD5): < F458F673894753FA6A0EC8B8EC63848E > 78165360 total sectors (40020664320 bytes) Model (0BB-00JHC0) serial # (WD-WMAMC74171) N Start LBA Length Start C/H/S End C/H/S boot Partition type 1 P 000000063 020980827 0000/001/01 1023/254/63 0C Fat32X 2 X 020980890 057175335 1023/000/01 1023/254/63 0F extended 3 S 000000063 000032067 1023/001/01 1023/254/63 01 Fat12 4 x 000032130 002104515 1023/000/01 1023/254/63 05 extended 5 S 000000063 002104452 1023/001/01 1023/254/63 06 Fat16 6 x 002136645 004192965 1023/000/01 1023/254/63 05 extended 7 S 000000063 004192902 1023/001/01 1023/254/63 16 other 8 x 006329610 008401995 1023/000/01 1023/254/63 05 extended 9 S 000000063 008401932 1023/001/01 1023/254/63 0B Fat32 10 x 014731605 010490445 1023/000/01 1023/254/63 05 extended 11 S 000000063 010490382 1023/001/01 1023/254/63 83 Linux 12 x 025222050 004209030 1023/000/01 1023/254/63 05 extended 13 S 000000063 004208967 1023/001/01 1023/254/63 82 Linux swap 14 x 029431080 027744255 1023/000/01 1023/254/63 05 extended 15 S 000000063 027744192 1023/001/01 1023/254/63 07 NTFS 16 S 000000000 000000000 0000/000/00 0000/000/00 00 empty entry 17 P 000000000 000000000 0000/000/00 0000/000/00 00 empty entry 18 P 000000000 000000000 0000/000/00 0000/000/00 00 empty entry 1 020980827 sectors 10742183424 bytes 3 000032067 sectors 16418304 bytes 5 002104452 sectors 1077479424 bytes 7 004192902 sectors 2146765824 bytes 9 008401932 sectors 4301789184 bytes 11 010490382 sectors 5371075584 bytes 13 004208967 sectors 2154991104 bytes 15 027744192 sectors 14205026304 bytes 01F12-md5 16418303 E20E3CFEA80BF6F2D2AA75E829CC8CD9 01F12-sha1 16418303 F8B72B65436DE3BD394ACFF71D405D0389C0E9B7
Log Highlights:	====== Destination drive setup ====== 156301488 sectors wiped with 4D ====== Comparison of original to clone drive ======

```
Sectors compared: 32067
Sectors match: 32067
Sectors differ: 0
Bytes differ: 0
Diffs range:
run start Thu Feb 3 15:08:39 2011
run finish Thu Feb 3 15:08:41 2011
elapsed time 0:0:2
Normal exit


====== Tool Settings: ======
dst-interface SATA28

OS: Linux ubuntu 2.6.32-21-generic #32-Ubuntu SMP Fri Apr 16 08:10:02 UTC
2010 i686 GNU/Linux

======== Excerpt from SMART log ========


SHA1 Span Hashes
 total span hash: f8b72b65 436de3bd 394acff7 1d405d03 89c0e9b7

IO Summary:(Time: Thu Feb 3 14:50:10 2011)
Bytes Read: 16,418,304
16,418,304 bytes written to /dev/sda5
======== End of Excerpt from SMART log ========

====== Source drive rehash ======
Rehash (SHA1) of source: A96A7193E1D9C270587B2BE7098638AC048221D1
```

	Assertion and Expected Result	Actual Result
Results:	AM-01 Source acquired using interface AI.	as expected
	AM-02 Source is type DS.	as expected
	AM-03 Execution environment is XE.	as expected
	AM-04 A clone is created.	as expected
	AM-06 All visible sectors acquired.	as expected
	AM-08 All sectors accurately acquired.	as expected
	AO-11 A clone is created during acquisition.	as expected
	AO-13 Clone created using interface AI.	as expected
	AO-14 An unaligned clone is created.	as expected
	AO-17 Excess sectors are unchanged.	as expected
	AO-22 Tool calculates hashes by block.	option not tested
	AO-23 Logged information is correct.	as expected
	AO-24 Source is unchanged by acquisition.	source changed

Analysis:	Expected results not achieved

5.2.13 DA-02-F12-WB

Test Case DA-02-F12-WB Smart Version 2010/11/03	
Case Summary:	DA-02 Acquire a digital source of type DS to an unaligned clone.
Assertions:	AM-01 The tool uses access interface SRC-AI to access the digital source. AM-02 The tool acquires digital source DS. AM-03 The tool executes in execution environment XE. AM-04 If clone creation is specified, the tool creates a clone of the digital source. AM-06 All visible sectors are acquired from the digital source. AM-08 All sectors acquired from the digital source are acquired accurately. AO-11 If requested, a clone is created during an acquisition of a digital source. AO-13 A clone is created using access interface DST-AI to write to the clone device. AO-14 If an unaligned clone is created, each sector written to the clone is accurately written to the same disk address on the clone that the sector occupied on the digital source. AO-17 If requested, any excess sectors on a clone destination device are not modified. AO-22 If requested, the tool calculates block hashes for a specified block size during an acquisition for each block acquired from the digital source. AO-23 If the tool logs any log significant information, the information is accurately recorded in the log file. AO-24 If the tool executes in a forensically safe execution environment, the digital source is unchanged by the acquisition process.
Tester Name:	brl
Test Host:	WoFat
Test Date:	Mon Mar 14 11:13:53 2011
Drives:	src(01-IDE) dst (46-SATA) other (none)
Source Setup:	src hash (SHA1): < A48BB5665D6DC57C22DB68E2F723DA9AA8DF82B9 > src hash (MD5): < F458F673894753FA6A0EC8B8EC63848E > 78165360 total sectors (40020664320 bytes) Model (0BB-00JHC0) serial # (WD-WMAMC74171) N Start LBA Length Start C/H/S End C/H/S boot Partition type 1 P 000000063 020980827 0000/001/01 1023/254/63 0C Fat32X 2 X 020980890 057175335 1023/000/01 1023/254/63 0F extended 3 S 000000063 000032067 1023/001/01 1023/254/63 01 Fat12 4 x 000032130 002104515 1023/000/01 1023/254/63 05 extended 5 S 000000063 002104452 1023/001/01 1023/254/63 06 Fat16 6 x 002136645 004192965 1023/000/01 1023/254/63 05 extended 7 S 000000063 004192902 1023/001/01 1023/254/63 16 other 8 x 006329610 008401995 1023/000/01 1023/254/63 05 extended 9 S 000000063 008401932 1023/001/01 1023/254/63 0B Fat32 10 x 014731605 010490445 1023/000/01 1023/254/63 05 extended 11 S 000000063 010490382 1023/001/01 1023/254/63 83 Linux 12 x 025222050 004209030 1023/000/01 1023/254/63 05 extended 13 S 000000063 004208967 1023/001/01 1023/254/63 82 Linux swap 14 x 029431080 027744255 1023/000/01 1023/254/63 05 extended 15 S 000000063 027744192 1023/001/01 1023/254/63 07 NTFS 16 S 000000000 000000000 0000/000/00 0000/000/00 00 empty entry 17 P 000000000 000000000 0000/000/00 0000/000/00 00 empty entry 18 P 000000000 000000000 0000/000/00 0000/000/00 00 empty entry 1 020980827 sectors 10742183424 bytes 3 000032067 sectors 16418304 bytes 5 002104452 sectors 1077479424 bytes 7 004192902 sectors 2146765824 bytes 9 008401932 sectors 4301789184 bytes 11 010490382 sectors 5371075584 bytes 13 004208967 sectors 2154991104 bytes 15 027744192 sectors 14205026304 bytes 01F12-md5 16418303 E20E3CFEA80BF6F2D2AA75E829CC8CD9 01F12-sha1 16418303 F8B72B65436DE3BD394ACFF71D405D0389C0E9B7
Log Highlights:	====== Destination drive setup ====== 40397168 sectors wiped with 46 ====== Comparison of original to clone drive ======

```
Sectors compared: 32067
Sectors match: 32067
Sectors differ: 0
Bytes differ: 0
Diffs range:
run start Mon Mar 14 10:40:57 2011
run finish Mon Mar 14 10:41:11 2011
elapsed time 0:0:14
Normal exit


====== Tool Settings: ======
dst-interface SATA28

Write Block: 3 FastBloc IDE

OS: Linux ubuntu 2.6.32-21-generic #32-Ubuntu SMP Fri Apr 16 08:10:02 UTC
2010 i686 GNU/Linux

======== Excerpt from SMART log ========


SHA1 Span Hashes
 total span hash: f8b72b65 436de3bd 394acff7 1d405d03 89c0e9b7

IO Summary:(Time: Mon Mar 14 11:23:08 2011)
Bytes Read: 16,418,304
16,418,304 bytes written to /dev/sda5
======== End of Excerpt from SMART log ========
```

Results:

Assertion and Expected Result	Actual Result
AM-01 Source acquired using interface AI.	as expected
AM-02 Source is type DS.	as expected
AM-03 Execution environment is XE.	as expected
AM-04 A clone is created.	as expected
AM-06 All visible sectors acquired.	as expected
AM-08 All sectors accurately acquired.	as expected
AO-11 A clone is created during acquisition.	as expected
AO-13 Clone created using interface AI.	as expected
AO-14 An unaligned clone is created.	as expected
AO-17 Excess sectors are unchanged.	as expected
AO-22 Tool calculates hashes by block.	option not tested
AO-23 Logged information is correct.	as expected
AO-24 Source is unchanged by acquisition.	not checked

Analysis: | Expected results achieved

5.2.14 DA-02-F16

Test Case DA-02-F16 Smart Version 2010/11/03	
Case Summary:	DA-02 Acquire a digital source of type DS to an unaligned clone.
Assertions:	AM-01 The tool uses access interface SRC-AI to access the digital source. AM-02 The tool acquires digital source DS. AM-03 The tool executes in execution environment XE. AM-04 If clone creation is specified, the tool creates a clone of the digital source. AM-06 All visible sectors are acquired from the digital source. AM-08 All sectors acquired from the digital source are acquired accurately. AO-11 If requested, a clone is created during an acquisition of a digital source. AO-13 A clone is created using access interface DST-AI to write to the clone device. AO-14 If an unaligned clone is created, each sector written to the clone is accurately written to the same disk address on the clone that the sector occupied on the digital source. AO-17 If requested, any excess sectors on a clone destination device are not modified. AO-22 If requested, the tool calculates block hashes for a specified block size during an acquisition for each block acquired from the digital source. AO-23 If the tool logs any log significant information, the information is accurately recorded in the log file. AO-24 If the tool executes in a forensically safe execution environment, the digital source is unchanged by the acquisition process.
Tester Name:	brl
Test Host:	WoFat
Test Date:	Thu Feb 3 11:32:04 2011
Drives:	src(43) dst (49-SATA) other (none)
Source Setup:	src hash (SHA1): < 888E2E7F7AD237DC7A732281DD93F325065E5871 > src hash (MD5): < BC39C3F7EE7A50E77B9BA1E65A5AEEF7 > 78125000 total sectors (40000000000 bytes) Model (0BB-75JHC0) serial # (WD-WMAMC46588) N Start LBA Length Start C/H/S End C/H/S boot Partition type 1 P 000000063 020980827 0000/001/01 1023/254/63 0C Fat32X 2 X 020980890 057143205 1023/000/01 1023/254/63 0F extended 3 S 000000063 000032067 1023/001/01 1023/254/63 01 Fat12 4 x 000032130 002104515 1023/000/01 1023/254/63 05 extended 5 S 000000063 002104452 1023/001/01 1023/254/63 06 Fat16 6 x 002136645 004192965 1023/000/01 1023/254/63 05 extended 7 S 000000063 004192902 1023/001/01 1023/254/63 16 other 8 x 006329610 008401995 1023/000/01 1023/254/63 05 extended 9 S 000000063 008401932 1023/001/01 1023/254/63 0B Fat32 10 x 014731605 010490445 1023/000/01 1023/254/63 05 extended 11 S 000000063 010490382 1023/001/01 1023/254/63 83 Linux 12 x 025222050 004209030 1023/000/01 1023/254/63 05 extended 13 S 000000063 004208967 1023/001/01 1023/254/63 82 Linux swap 14 x 029431080 027712125 1023/000/01 1023/254/63 05 extended 15 S 000000063 027712062 1023/001/01 1023/254/63 07 NTFS 16 S 000000000 000000000 0000/000/00 0000/000/00 00 empty entry 17 P 000000000 000000000 0000/000/00 0000/000/00 00 empty entry 18 P 000000000 000000000 0000/000/00 0000/000/00 00 empty entry 1 020980827 sectors 10742183424 bytes 3 000032067 sectors 16418304 bytes 5 002104452 sectors 1077479424 bytes 7 004192902 sectors 2146765824 bytes 9 008401932 sectors 4301789184 bytes 11 010490382 sectors 5371075584 bytes 13 004208967 sectors 2154991104 bytes 15 027712062 sectors 14188575744 bytes 43F16-md5sum 1077479423 37E81FFB31C3CB38AA48B2237500908E 43F16-sha1sum 1077479423 443CCEC9A22F726DAF6CE384817151C83B3EBC8B 43F16-sha1sum 1077479423 443CCEC9A22F726DAF6CE384817151C83B3EBC8B
Log Highlights:	====== Destination drive setup ====== 156301488 sectors wiped with 49

```
====== Comparison of original to clone drive ======
Sectors compared: 2104452
Sectors match: 2104452
Sectors differ: 0
Bytes differ: 0
Diffs range:
Source (2104452) has 208845 fewer sectors than destination (2313297)
Zero fill: 0
Src Byte fill (43): 0
Dst Byte fill (49): 208845
Other fill: 0
Other no fill: 0
Zero fill range:
Src fill range:
Dst fill range: 2104452-2313296
Other fill range:
Other not filled range:
run start Fri Feb 4 11:11:47 2011
run finish Fri Feb 4 11:12:32 2011
elapsed time 0:0:45
Normal exit


====== Tool Settings: ======
dst-interface SATA28

OS: Linux ubuntu 2.6.32-21-generic #32-Ubuntu SMP Fri Apr 16 08:10:02 UTC
2010 i686 GNU/Linux

======== Excerpt from SMART log ========


SHA1 Span Hashes
 total span hash: 443ccec9 a22f726d af6ce384 817151c8 3b3ebc8b

IO Summary:(Time: Fri Feb 4 10:56:16 2011)
Bytes Read: 1,077,479,424
1,077,479,424 bytes written to /dev/sda6
======== End of Excerpt from SMART log ========

====== Source drive rehash ======
Rehash (SHA1) of source: 888E2E7F7AD237DC7A732281DD93F325065E5871
```

Results:		
	Assertion and Expected Result	**Actual Result**
	AM-01 Source acquired using interface AI.	as expected
	AM-02 Source is type DS.	as expected
	AM-03 Execution environment is XE.	as expected
	AM-04 A clone is created.	as expected
	AM-06 All visible sectors acquired.	as expected
	AM-08 All sectors accurately acquired.	as expected
	AO-11 A clone is created during acquisition.	as expected
	AO-13 Clone created using interface AI.	as expected
	AO-14 An unaligned clone is created.	as expected
	AO-17 Excess sectors are unchanged.	as expected
	AO-22 Tool calculates hashes by block.	option not tested
	AO-23 Logged information is correct.	as expected
	AO-24 Source is unchanged by acquisition.	as expected
Analysis:	Expected results achieved	

5.2.15 DA-02-F32

Case Summary:	DA-02 Acquire a digital source of type DS to an unaligned clone.
Assertions:	AM-01 The tool uses access interface SRC-AI to access the digital source. AM-02 The tool acquires digital source DS. AM-03 The tool executes in execution environment XE. AM-04 If clone creation is specified, the tool creates a clone of the digital source. AM-06 All visible sectors are acquired from the digital source. AM-08 All sectors acquired from the digital source are acquired accurately. AO-11 If requested, a clone is created during an acquisition of a digital source. AO-13 A clone is created using access interface DST-AI to write to the clone device. AO-14 If an unaligned clone is created, each sector written to the clone is accurately written to the same disk address on the clone that the sector occupied on the digital source. AO-17 If requested, any excess sectors on a clone destination device are not modified. AO-22 If requested, the tool calculates block hashes for a specified block size during an acquisition for each block acquired from the digital source. AO-23 If the tool logs any log significant information, the information is accurately recorded in the log file. AO-24 If the tool executes in a forensically safe execution environment, the digital source is unchanged by the acquisition process.
Tester Name:	brl
Test Host:	McGarrett
Test Date:	Fri Feb 4 13:59:45 2011
Drives:	src(01-IDE) dst (4D-SATA) other (none)
Source Setup:	src hash (SHA1): < A48BB5665D6DC57C22DB68E2F723DA9AA8DF82B9 > src hash (MD5): < F458F673894753FA6A0EC8B8EC63848E > 78165360 total sectors (40020664320 bytes) Model (0BB-00JHC0) serial # (WD-WMAMC74171) N Start LBA Length Start C/H/S End C/H/S boot Partition type 1 P 000000063 020980827 0000/001/01 1023/254/63 0C Fat32X 2 X 020980890 057175335 1023/000/01 1023/254/63 0F extended 3 S 000000063 000032067 1023/001/01 1023/254/63 01 Fat12 4 x 000032130 002104515 1023/000/01 1023/254/63 05 extended 5 S 000000063 002104452 1023/001/01 1023/254/63 06 Fat16 6 x 002136645 004192965 1023/000/01 1023/254/63 05 extended 7 S 000000063 004192902 1023/001/01 1023/254/63 16 other 8 x 006329610 008401995 1023/000/01 1023/254/63 05 extended 9 S 000000063 008401932 1023/001/01 1023/254/63 0B Fat32 10 x 014731605 010490445 1023/000/01 1023/254/63 05 extended 11 S 000000063 010490382 1023/001/01 1023/254/63 83 Linux 12 x 025222050 004209030 1023/000/01 1023/254/63 05 extended 13 S 000000063 004208967 1023/001/01 1023/254/63 82 Linux swap 14 x 029431080 027744255 1023/000/01 1023/254/63 05 extended 15 S 000000063 027744192 1023/001/01 1023/254/63 07 NTFS 16 S 000000000 000000000 0000/000/00 0000/000/00 00 empty entry 17 P 000000000 000000000 0000/000/00 0000/000/00 00 empty entry 18 P 000000000 000000000 0000/000/00 0000/000/00 00 empty entry 1 020980827 sectors 10742183424 bytes 3 000032067 sectors 16418304 bytes 5 002104452 sectors 1077479424 bytes 7 004192902 sectors 2146765824 bytes 9 008401932 sectors 4301789184 bytes 11 010490382 sectors 5371075584 bytes 13 004208967 sectors 2154991104 bytes 15 027744192 sectors 14205026304 bytes 01F32-md5 4301789183 BFF7DC64C54339DA2A9D7972C076B514 01F32-sha1 4301789183 B861D9E999F39750B484FFB693FF69DEC090C6B8
Log Highlights:	====== Destination drive setup ====== 156301488 sectors wiped with 4D ====== Comparison of original to clone drive ======

```
                    Sectors compared: 8401932
                    Sectors match: 8401932
                    Sectors differ: 0
                    Bytes differ: 0
                    Diffs range:
                    run start Fri Feb 4 14:30:23 2011
                    run finish Fri Feb 4 14:33:13 2011
                    elapsed time 0:2:50
                    Normal exit


                    ====== Tool Settings: ======
                    dst-interface SATA28

                    OS: Linux ubuntu 2.6.32-21-generic #32-Ubuntu SMP Fri Apr 16 08:10:02 UTC
                    2010 i686 GNU/Linux

                    ======== Excerpt from SMART log ========


                    SHA1 Span Hashes
                     total span hash: b861d9e9 99f39750 b484ffb6 93ff69de c090c6b8

                    IO Summary:(Time: Fri Feb 4 14:16:24 2011)
                    Bytes Read: 4,301,789,184
                    4,301,789,184 bytes written to /dev/sda8
                    ======== End of Excerpt from SMART log ========

                    ====== Source drive rehash ======
                    Rehash (SHA1) of source: A96A7193E1D9C270587B2BE7098638AC048221D1
```

Results:		
	Assertion and Expected Result	**Actual Result**
	AM-01 Source acquired using interface AI.	as expected
	AM-02 Source is type DS.	as expected
	AM-03 Execution environment is XE.	as expected
	AM-04 A clone is created.	as expected
	AM-06 All visible sectors acquired.	as expected
	AM-08 All sectors accurately acquired.	as expected
	AO-11 A clone is created during acquisition.	as expected
	AO-13 Clone created using interface AI.	as expected
	AO-14 An unaligned clone is created.	as expected
	AO-17 Excess sectors are unchanged.	as expected
	AO-22 Tool calculates hashes by block.	option not tested
	AO-23 Logged information is correct.	as expected
	AO-24 Source is unchanged by acquisition.	source changed
Analysis:	Expected results not achieved	

5.2.16   DA-02-F32-WB

Test Case DA-02-F32-WB Smart Version 2010/11/03	
Case Summary:	DA-02 Acquire a digital source of type DS to an unaligned clone.
Assertions:	AM-01 The tool uses access interface SRC-AI to access the digital source. AM-02 The tool acquires digital source DS. AM-03 The tool executes in execution environment XE. AM-04 If clone creation is specified, the tool creates a clone of the digital source. AM-06 All visible sectors are acquired from the digital source. AM-08 All sectors acquired from the digital source are acquired accurately. AO-11 If requested, a clone is created during an acquisition of a digital source. AO-13 A clone is created using access interface DST-AI to write to the clone device. AO-14 If an unaligned clone is created, each sector written to the clone is accurately written to the same disk address on the clone that the sector occupied on the digital source. AO-17 If requested, any excess sectors on a clone destination device are not modified. AO-22 If requested, the tool calculates block hashes for a specified block size during an acquisition for each block acquired from the digital source. AO-23 If the tool logs any log significant information, the information is accurately recorded in the log file. AO-24 If the tool executes in a forensically safe execution environment, the digital source is unchanged by the acquisition process.
Tester Name:	brl
Test Host:	WoFat
Test Date:	Mon Mar 14 10:55:49 2011
Drives:	src(01-IDE) dst (46-SATA) other (none)
Source Setup:	src hash (SHA1): < A48BB5665D6DC57C22DB68E2F723DA9AA8DF82B9 > src hash (MD5): < F458F673894753FA6A0EC8B8EC63848E > 78165360 total sectors (40020664320 bytes) Model (0BB-00JHC0) serial # (WD-WMAMC74171) N Start LBA Length Start C/H/S End C/H/S boot Partition type 1 P 000000063 020980827 0000/001/01 1023/254/63 0C Fat32X 2 X 020980890 057175335 1023/000/01 1023/254/63 0F extended 3 S 000000063 000032067 1023/001/01 1023/254/63 01 Fat12 4 x 000032130 002104515 1023/000/01 1023/254/63 05 extended 5 S 000000063 002104452 1023/001/01 1023/254/63 06 Fat16 6 x 002136645 004192965 1023/000/01 1023/254/63 05 extended 7 S 000000063 004192902 1023/001/01 1023/254/63 16 other 8 x 006329610 008401995 1023/000/01 1023/254/63 05 extended 9 S 000000063 008401932 1023/001/01 1023/254/63 0B Fat32 10 x 014731605 010490445 1023/000/01 1023/254/63 05 extended 11 S 000000063 010490382 1023/001/01 1023/254/63 83 Linux 12 x 025222050 004209030 1023/000/01 1023/254/63 05 extended 13 S 000000063 004208967 1023/001/01 1023/254/63 82 Linux swap 14 x 029431080 027744255 1023/000/01 1023/254/63 05 extended 15 S 000000063 027744192 1023/001/01 1023/254/63 07 NTFS 16 S 000000000 000000000 0000/000/00 0000/000/00 00 empty entry 17 P 000000000 000000000 0000/000/00 0000/000/00 00 empty entry 18 P 000000000 000000000 0000/000/00 0000/000/00 00 empty entry 1 020980827 sectors 10742183424 bytes 3 000032067 sectors 16418304 bytes 5 002104452 sectors 1077479424 bytes 7 004192902 sectors 2146765824 bytes 9 008401932 sectors 4301789184 bytes 11 010490382 sectors 5371075584 bytes 13 004208967 sectors 2154991104 bytes 15 027744192 sectors 14205026304 bytes 01F32-md5 4301789183 BFF7DC64C54339DA2A9D7972C076B514 01F32-sha1 4301789183 B861D9E999F39750B484FFB693FF69DEC090C6B8
Log Highlights:	====== Destination drive setup ====== 40397168 sectors wiped with 46 ====== Comparison of original to clone drive ======

```
Sectors compared: 8401932
Sectors match: 8401932
Sectors differ: 0
Bytes differ: 0
Diffs range:
Source (8401932) has 1044225 fewer sectors than destination (9446157)
Zero fill: 0
Src Byte fill (01): 0
Dst Byte fill (46): 1044225
Other fill: 0
Other no fill: 0
Zero fill range:
Src fill range:
Dst fill range: 8401932-9446156
Other fill range:
Other not filled range:
run start Mon Mar 14 12:27:31 2011
run finish Mon Mar 14 12:30:47 2011
elapsed time 0:3:16
Normal exit


====== Tool Settings: ======
dst-interface SATA28

Write Block: 3 FastBloc IDE

OS: Linux ubuntu 2.6.32-21-generic #32-Ubuntu SMP Fri Apr 16 08:10:02 UTC
2010 i686 GNU/Linux

======== Excerpt from SMART log ========


SHA1 Span Hashes
 total span hash: b861d9e9 99f39750 b484ffb6 93ff69de c090c6b8

IO Summary:(Time: Mon Mar 14 11:07:58 2011)
Bytes Read: 4,301,789,184
4,301,789,184 bytes written to /dev/sdb6
======== End of Excerpt from SMART log ========
```

Results:

Assertion and Expected Result	Actual Result
AM-01 Source acquired using interface AI.	as expected
AM-02 Source is type DS.	as expected
AM-03 Execution environment is XE.	as expected
AM-04 A clone is created.	as expected
AM-06 All visible sectors acquired.	as expected
AM-08 All sectors accurately acquired.	as expected
AO-11 A clone is created during acquisition.	as expected
AO-13 Clone created using interface AI.	as expected
AO-14 An unaligned clone is created.	as expected
AO-17 Excess sectors are unchanged.	as expected
AO-22 Tool calculates hashes by block.	option not tested
AO-23 Logged information is correct.	as expected
AO-24 Source is unchanged by acquisition.	not checked

Analysis: Expected results achieved

5.2.17 DA-02-F32X

Test Case DA-02-F32X Smart Version 2010/11/03	
Case Summary:	DA-02 Acquire a digital source of type DS to an unaligned clone.
Assertions:	AM-01 The tool uses access interface SRC-AI to access the digital source. AM-02 The tool acquires digital source DS. AM-03 The tool executes in execution environment XE. AM-04 If clone creation is specified, the tool creates a clone of the digital source. AM-06 All visible sectors are acquired from the digital source. AM-08 All sectors acquired from the digital source are acquired accurately. AO-11 If requested, a clone is created during an acquisition of a digital source. AO-13 A clone is created using access interface DST-AI to write to the clone device. AO-14 If an unaligned clone is created, each sector written to the clone is accurately written to the same disk address on the clone that the sector occupied on the digital source. AO-17 If requested, any excess sectors on a clone destination device are not modified. AO-22 If requested, the tool calculates block hashes for a specified block size during an acquisition for each block acquired from the digital source. AO-23 If the tool logs any log significant information, the information is accurately recorded in the log file. AO-24 If the tool executes in a forensically safe execution environment, the digital source is unchanged by the acquisition process.
Tester Name:	brl
Test Host:	WoFat
Test Date:	Fri Feb 4 14:46:57 2011
Drives:	src(43) dst (49-SATA) other (none)
Source Setup:	src hash (SHA1): < 888E2E7F7AD237DC7A732281DD93F325065E5871 > src hash (MD5): < BC39C3F7EE7A50E77B9BA1E65A5AEEF7 > 78125000 total sectors (40000000000 bytes) Model (0BB-75JHC0) serial # (WD-WMAMC46588) N Start LBA Length Start C/H/S End C/H/S boot Partition type 1 P 000000063 020980827 0000/001/01 1023/254/63 0C Fat32X 2 X 020980890 057143205 1023/000/01 1023/254/63 0F extended 3 S 000000063 000032067 1023/001/01 1023/254/63 01 Fat12 4 x 000032130 002104515 1023/000/01 1023/254/63 05 extended 5 S 000000063 002104452 1023/001/01 1023/254/63 06 Fat16 6 x 002136645 004192965 1023/000/01 1023/254/63 05 extended 7 S 000000063 004192902 1023/001/01 1023/254/63 16 other 8 x 006329610 008401995 1023/000/01 1023/254/63 05 extended 9 S 000000063 008401932 1023/001/01 1023/254/63 0B Fat32 10 x 014731605 010490445 1023/000/01 1023/254/63 05 extended 11 S 000000063 010490382 1023/001/01 1023/254/63 83 Linux 12 x 025222050 004209030 1023/000/01 1023/254/63 05 extended 13 S 000000063 004208967 1023/001/01 1023/254/63 82 Linux swap 14 x 029431080 027712125 1023/000/01 1023/254/63 05 extended 15 S 000000063 027712062 1023/001/01 1023/254/63 07 NTFS 16 S 000000000 000000000 0000/000/00 0000/000/00 00 empty entry 17 P 000000000 000000000 0000/000/00 0000/000/00 00 empty entry 18 P 000000000 000000000 0000/000/00 0000/000/00 00 empty entry 1 020980827 sectors 10742183424 bytes 3 000032067 sectors 16418304 bytes 5 002104452 sectors 1077479424 bytes 7 004192902 sectors 2146765824 bytes 9 008401932 sectors 4301789184 bytes 11 010490382 sectors 5371075584 bytes 13 004208967 sectors 2154991104 bytes 15 027712062 sectors 14188575744 bytes 43F32x-md5sum 10742183424 5980CB0FA68E9862C65765DF50F00906 43F32x-sha1sum 10742183423 379C1AC47AF956FC8C80389C2A7427A7F8FB4E89 43F32x-sha1sum 10742183423 379C1AC47AF956FC8C80389C2A7427A7F8FB4E89
Log Highlights:	====== Destination drive setup ====== 156301488 sectors wiped with 49

```
====== Comparison of original to clone drive ======
Sectors compared: 20980827
Sectors match: 20980827
Sectors differ: 0
Bytes differ: 0
Diffs range:
Source (20980827) has 1558305 fewer sectors than destination (22539132)
Zero fill: 0
Src Byte fill (43): 0
Dst Byte fill (49): 1558305
Other fill: 0
Other no fill: 0
Zero fill range:
Src fill range:
Dst fill range: 20980827-22539131
Other fill range:
Other not filled range:
run start Fri Feb 4 15:42:28 2011
run finish Fri Feb 4 15:57:08 2011
elapsed time 0:14:40
Normal exit


====== Tool Settings: ======
dst-interface SATA28

OS: Linux ubuntu 2.6.32-21-generic #32-Ubuntu SMP Fri Apr 16 08:10:02 UTC
2010 i686 GNU/Linux

======== Excerpt from SMART log ========


SHA1 Span Hashes
 total span hash: 379c1ac4 7af956fc 8c80389c 2a7427a7 f8fb4e89

IO Summary:(Time: Fri Feb 4 15:21:36 2011)
Bytes Read: 10,742,183,424
10,742,183,424 bytes written to /dev/sda1
======== End of Excerpt from SMART log ========

====== Source drive rehash ======
Rehash (SHA1) of source: 888E2E7F7AD237DC7A732281DD93F325065E5871
```

Results:

Assertion and Expected Result	Actual Result
AM-01 Source acquired using interface AI.	as expected
AM-02 Source is type DS.	as expected
AM-03 Execution environment is XE.	as expected
AM-04 A clone is created.	as expected
AM-06 All visible sectors acquired.	as expected
AM-08 All sectors accurately acquired.	as expected
AO-11 A clone is created during acquisition.	as expected
AO-13 Clone created using interface AI.	as expected
AO-14 An unaligned clone is created.	as expected
AO-17 Excess sectors are unchanged.	as expected
AO-22 Tool calculates hashes by block.	option not tested
AO-23 Logged information is correct.	as expected
AO-24 Source is unchanged by acquisition.	as expected

Analysis: Expected results achieved

5.2.18 DA-02-NTFS

Test Case DA-02-NTFS Smart Version 2010/11/03	
Case Summary:	DA-02 Acquire a digital source of type DS to an unaligned clone.
Assertions:	AM-01 The tool uses access interface SRC-AI to access the digital source. AM-02 The tool acquires digital source DS. AM-03 The tool executes in execution environment XE. AM-04 If clone creation is specified, the tool creates a clone of the digital source. AM-06 All visible sectors are acquired from the digital source. AM-08 All sectors acquired from the digital source are acquired accurately. AO-11 If requested, a clone is created during an acquisition of a digital source. AO-13 A clone is created using access interface DST-AI to write to the clone device. AO-14 If an unaligned clone is created, each sector written to the clone is accurately written to the same disk address on the clone that the sector occupied on the digital source. AO-17 If requested, any excess sectors on a clone destination device are not modified. AO-22 If requested, the tool calculates block hashes for a specified block size during an acquisition for each block acquired from the digital source. AO-23 If the tool logs any log significant information, the information is accurately recorded in the log file. AO-24 If the tool executes in a forensically safe execution environment, the digital source is unchanged by the acquisition process.
Tester Name:	brl
Test Host:	McGarrett
Test Date:	Mon Feb 7 09:31:47 2011
Drives:	src(43) dst (4D-SATA) other (none)
Source Setup:	src hash (SHA1): < 888E2E7F7AD237DC7A732281DD93F325065E5871 > src hash (MD5): < BC39C3F7EE7A50E77B9BA1E65A5AEEF7 > 78125000 total sectors (40000000000 bytes) Model (0BB-75JHC0) serial # (WD-WMAMC46588) N Start LBA Length Start C/H/S End C/H/S boot Partition type 1 P 000000063 020980827 0000/001/01 1023/254/63 0C Fat32X 2 X 020980890 057143205 1023/000/01 1023/254/63 0F extended 3 S 000000063 000032067 1023/001/01 1023/254/63 01 Fat12 4 x 000032130 002104515 1023/000/01 1023/254/63 05 extended 5 S 000000063 002104452 1023/001/01 1023/254/63 06 Fat16 6 x 002136645 004192965 1023/000/01 1023/254/63 05 extended 7 S 000000063 004192902 1023/001/01 1023/254/63 16 other 8 x 006329610 008401995 1023/000/01 1023/254/63 05 extended 9 S 000000063 008401932 1023/001/01 1023/254/63 0B Fat32 10 x 014731605 010490445 1023/000/01 1023/254/63 05 extended 11 S 000000063 010490382 1023/001/01 1023/254/63 83 Linux 12 x 025222050 004209030 1023/000/01 1023/254/63 05 extended 13 S 000000063 004208967 1023/001/01 1023/254/63 82 Linux swap 14 x 029431080 027712125 1023/000/01 1023/254/63 05 extended 15 S 000000063 027712062 1023/001/01 1023/254/63 07 NTFS 16 S 000000000 000000000 0000/000/00 0000/000/00 00 empty entry 17 P 000000000 000000000 0000/000/00 0000/000/00 00 empty entry 18 P 000000000 000000000 0000/000/00 0000/000/00 00 empty entry 1 020980827 sectors 10742183424 bytes 3 000032067 sectors 16418304 bytes 5 002104452 sectors 1077479424 bytes 7 004192902 sectors 2146765824 bytes 9 008401932 sectors 4301789184 bytes 11 010490382 sectors 5371075584 bytes 13 004208967 sectors 2154991104 bytes 15 027712062 sectors 14188575744 bytes 43ntfs-md5sum 14188575744 5D42FA317C802ACFEF2D313092D7411E 43ntfs-sha1sum 14188575744 73eb2d27564b060db796efb78694a10e6b43d23f Excess destination partition sectors hash: SHA1 14188575744 - 14205026303 = 827CF7F19C380D204700B479398C184664C662AE -
Log Highlights:	====== Destination drive setup ====== 156301488 sectors wiped with 4D

```
====== Comparison of original to clone drive ======
Sectors compared: 27712062
Sectors match: 27712062
Sectors differ: 0
Bytes differ: 0
Diffs range:
Source (27712062) has 32130 fewer sectors than destination (27744192)
Zero fill: 0
Src Byte fill (43): 0
Dst Byte fill (4D): 32129
Other fill: 0
Other no fill: 1
Zero fill range:
Src fill range:
Dst fill range: 27712062-27744190
Other fill range:
Other not filled range: 27744191
run start Tue Feb 8 10:57:07 2011
run finish Tue Feb 8 11:06:31 2011
elapsed time 0:9:24
Normal exit


====== Tool Settings: ======
dst-interface SATA28

OS: Linux ubuntu 2.6.32-21-generic #32-Ubuntu SMP Fri Apr 16 08:10:02 UTC
2010 i686 GNU/Linux

======== Excerpt from SMART log ========


SHA1 Span Hashes
 total span hash: 73eb2d27 564b060d b796efb7 8694a10e 6b43d23f

IO Summary:(Time: Mon Feb 7 14:33:03 2011)
Bytes Read: 14,188,575,744
14,188,575,744 bytes written to /dev/sdb11
======== End of Excerpt from SMART log ========

Excess destination partition sectors hash:
SHA1 14188575744 - 14205026303 = 827CF7F19C380D204700B479398C184664C662AE -

====== Source drive rehash ======
Rehash (SHA1) of source: 888E2E7F7AD237DC7A732281DD93F325065E5871
```

Results:	

Assertion and Expected Result	Actual Result
AM-01 Source acquired using interface AI.	as expected
AM-02 Source is type DS.	as expected
AM-03 Execution environment is XE.	as expected
AM-04 A clone is created.	as expected
AM-06 All visible sectors acquired.	as expected
AM-08 All sectors accurately acquired.	as expected
AO-11 A clone is created during acquisition.	as expected
AO-13 Clone created using interface AI.	as expected
AO-14 An unaligned clone is created.	as expected
AO-17 Excess sectors are unchanged.	as expected
AO-22 Tool calculates hashes by block.	option not tested
AO-23 Logged information is correct.	as expected
AO-24 Source is unchanged by acquisition.	as expected

Analysis:	Expected results achieved

5.2.19　DA-02-OSX

Test Case DA-02-OSX Smart Version 2010/11/03	
Case Summary:	DA-02 Acquire a digital source of type DS to an unaligned clone.
Assertions:	AM-01 The tool uses access interface SRC-AI to access the digital source.
	AM-02 The tool acquires digital source DS.
	AM-03 The tool executes in execution environment XE.
	AM-04 If clone creation is specified, the tool creates a clone of the digital source.
	AM-06 All visible sectors are acquired from the digital source.
	AM-08 All sectors acquired from the digital source are acquired accurately.
	AO-11 If requested, a clone is created during an acquisition of a digital source.
	AO-13 A clone is created using access interface DST-AI to write to the clone device.
	AO-14 If an unaligned clone is created, each sector written to the clone is accurately written to the same disk address on the clone that the sector occupied on the digital source.
	AO-17 If requested, any excess sectors on a clone destination device are not modified.
	AO-22 If requested, the tool calculates block hashes for a specified block size during an acquisition for each block acquired from the digital source.
	AO-23 If the tool logs any log significant information, the information is accurately recorded in the log file.
	AO-24 If the tool executes in a forensically safe execution environment, the digital source is unchanged by the acquisition process.
Tester Name:	brl
Test Host:	WoFat
Test Date:	Thu Feb 24 09:46:22 2011
Drives:	src(4B-SATA) dst (1A-SATA) other (none)
Source Setup:	src hash (SHA1): < 70CC62B43F6A41CA4D6760AA0B9B4C415D3F48E2 >
	src hash (MD5): < 746B4C06CDD5FBD67C0820DB4325B40C >
	156301488 total sectors (80026361856 bytes)
	Model (ST380815AS) serial # (6QZ5C9V5)
	N Start LBA Length Start C/H/S End C/H/S boot Partition type
	1 P 000000063 020971520 0000/001/01 1023/254/63 AF other
	2 P 020971629 010485536 1023/254/63 1023/254/63 AF other
	3 P 031457223 006291456 1023/254/63 1023/254/63 A8 other
	4 X 037748679 008388694 1023/254/63 1023/254/63 05 extended
	5 S 000000039 004194304 1023/254/63 1023/254/63 AF other
	6 x 004194343 004194351 1023/254/63 1023/254/63 05 extended
	7 S 000000047 004194304 1023/254/63 1023/254/63 AF other
	8 S 000000000 000000000 0000/000/00 0000/000/00 00 empty entry
	1 020971520 sectors 10737418240 bytes
	2 010485536 sectors 5368594432 bytes
	3 006291456 sectors 3221225472 bytes
	5 004194304 sectors 2147483648 bytes
	7 004194304 sectors 2147483648 bytes
	4BOSX-sha1 5368594432 3DE70998AD136E66CD09B9B4F2F5164E77B3B705
	Excess destination partition sectors hash:
	SHA1 5368594432 - 5368709119 = 4E92C62451C88F7C744055796B6DA3110B34582E -
Log Highlights:	====== Destination drive setup ======
	234441648 sectors wiped with 1A
	====== Comparison of original to clone drive ======
	Sectors compared: 10485536
	Sectors match: 10485536
	Sectors differ: 0
	Bytes differ: 0
	Diffs range:
	Source (10485536) has 224 fewer sectors than destination (10485760)
	Zero fill: 7
	Src Byte fill (4B): 0
	Dst Byte fill (1A): 216
	Other fill: 0
	Other no fill: 1
	Zero fill range: 10485752-10485757, 10485759

```
                    Src fill range:
                    Dst fill range: 10485536-10485751
                    Other fill range:
                    Other not filled range: 10485758
                    run start Thu Feb 24 10:10:33 2011
                    run finish Thu Feb 24 10:14:24 2011
                    elapsed time 0:3:51
                    Normal exit



                    ====== Tool Settings: ======
                    dst-interface SATA28

                    OS: Linux ubuntu 2.6.32-21-generic #32-Ubuntu SMP Fri Apr 16 08:10:02 UTC
                    2010 i686 GNU/Linux

                    ======== Excerpt from SMART log ========


                    SHA1 Span Hashes
                     total span hash: 3de70998 ad136e66 cd09b9b4 f2f5164e 77b3b705

                    IO Summary:(Time: Thu Feb 24 09:56:37 2011)
                    Bytes Read: 5,368,594,432
                    5,368,594,432 bytes written to /dev/sdb2
                    ======== End of Excerpt from SMART log ========

                    Excess destination partition sectors hash:
                    SHA1 5368594432 - 5368709119 = 4E92C62451C88F7C744055796B6DA3110B34582E -

                    ====== Source drive rehash ======
                    Rehash (SHA1) of source: 70CC62B43F6A41CA4D6760AA0B9B4C415D3F48E2
```

Results:

Assertion and Expected Result	Actual Result
AM-01 Source acquired using interface AI.	as expected
AM-02 Source is type DS.	as expected
AM-03 Execution environment is XE.	as expected
AM-04 A clone is created.	as expected
AM-06 All visible sectors acquired.	as expected
AM-08 All sectors accurately acquired.	as expected
AO-11 A clone is created during acquisition.	as expected
AO-13 Clone created using interface AI.	as expected
AO-14 An unaligned clone is created.	as expected
AO-17 Excess sectors are unchanged.	as expected
AO-22 Tool calculates hashes by block.	option not tested
AO-23 Logged information is correct.	as expected
AO-24 Source is unchanged by acquisition.	as expected

Analysis: Expected results achieved

5.2.20   DA-02-OSXC

Test Case DA-02-OSXC Smart Version 2010/11/03	
Case Summary:	DA-02 Acquire a digital source of type DS to an unaligned clone.
Assertions:	AM-01 The tool uses access interface SRC-AI to access the digital source. AM-02 The tool acquires digital source DS. AM-03 The tool executes in execution environment XE. AM-04 If clone creation is specified, the tool creates a clone of the digital source. AM-06 All visible sectors are acquired from the digital source. AM-08 All sectors acquired from the digital source are acquired accurately. AO-11 If requested, a clone is created during an acquisition of a digital source. AO-13 A clone is created using access interface DST-AI to write to the clone device. AO-14 If an unaligned clone is created, each sector written to the clone is accurately written to the same disk address on the clone that the sector occupied on the digital source. AO-17 If requested, any excess sectors on a clone destination device are not modified. AO-22 If requested, the tool calculates block hashes for a specified block size during an acquisition for each block acquired from the digital source. AO-23 If the tool logs any log significant information, the information is accurately recorded in the log file. AO-24 If the tool executes in a forensically safe execution environment, the digital source is unchanged by the acquisition process.
Tester Name:	brl
Test Host:	WoFat
Test Date:	Fri Feb 25 10:39:59 2011
Drives:	src(4B-SATA) dst (1A-SATA) other (none)
Source Setup:	src hash (SHA1): < 70CC62B43F6A41CA4D6760AA0B9B4C415D3F48E2 > src hash (MD5): < 746B4C06CDD5FBD67C0820DB4325B40C > 156301488 total sectors (80026361856 bytes) Model (ST380815AS) serial # (6QZ5C9V5) N Start LBA Length Start C/H/S End C/H/S boot Partition type 1 P 000000063 020971520 0000/001/01 1023/254/63 AF other 2 P 020971629 010485536 1023/254/63 1023/254/63 AF other 3 P 031457223 006291456 1023/254/63 1023/254/63 A8 other 4 X 037748679 008388694 1023/254/63 1023/254/63 05 extended 5 S 000000039 004194304 1023/254/63 1023/254/63 AF other 6 x 004194343 004194351 1023/254/63 1023/254/63 05 extended 7 S 000000047 004194304 1023/254/63 1023/254/63 AF other 8 S 000000000 000000000 0000/000/00 0000/000/00 00 empty entry 1 020971520 sectors 10737418240 bytes 2 010485536 sectors 5368594432 bytes 3 006291456 sectors 3221225472 bytes 5 004194304 sectors 2147483648 bytes 7 004194304 sectors 2147483648 bytes 4BOSXC-sha1 2147483648 2D6303D74F9EDE617639643DCCF41EC2091D5F37
Log Highlights:	====== Destination drive setup ====== 234441648 sectors wiped with 1A ====== Comparison of original to clone drive ====== Sectors compared: 4194304 Sectors match: 4194304 Sectors differ: 0 Bytes differ: 0 Diffs range: run start Fri Feb 25 11:07:30 2011 run finish Fri Feb 25 11:09:00 2011 elapsed time 0:1:30 Normal exit ====== Tool Settings: ====== dst-interface SATA28

```
OS: Linux ubuntu 2.6.32-21-generic #32-Ubuntu SMP Fri Apr 16 08:10:02 UTC
2010 i686 GNU/Linux

======== Excerpt from SMART log ========


SHA1 Span Hashes
 total span hash: 2d6303d7 4f9ede61 7639643d ccf41ec2 091d5f37

IO Summary:(Time: Fri Feb 25 10:52:43 2011)
Bytes Read: 2,147,483,648
2,147,483,648 bytes written to /dev/sdb5
======== End of Excerpt from SMART log ========

====== Source drive rehash ======
Rehash (SHA1) of source: 70CC62B43F6A41CA4D6760AA0B9B4C415D3F48E2
```

Results:

Assertion and Expected Result	Actual Result
AM-01 Source acquired using interface AI.	as expected
AM-02 Source is type DS.	as expected
AM-03 Execution environment is XE.	as expected
AM-04 A clone is created.	as expected
AM-06 All visible sectors acquired.	as expected
AM-08 All sectors accurately acquired.	as expected
AO-11 A clone is created during acquisition.	as expected
AO-13 Clone created using interface AI.	as expected
AO-14 An unaligned clone is created.	as expected
AO-17 Excess sectors are unchanged.	as expected
AO-22 Tool calculates hashes by block.	option not tested
AO-23 Logged information is correct.	as expected
AO-24 Source is unchanged by acquisition.	as expected

Analysis: Expected results achieved

5.2.21   DA-02-OSXCJ

Test Case DA-02-OSXCJ Smart Version 2010/11/03	
Case Summary:	DA-02 Acquire a digital source of type DS to an unaligned clone.
Assertions:	AM-01 The tool uses access interface SRC-AI to access the digital source. AM-02 The tool acquires digital source DS. AM-03 The tool executes in execution environment XE. AM-04 If clone creation is specified, the tool creates a clone of the digital source. AM-06 All visible sectors are acquired from the digital source. AM-08 All sectors acquired from the digital source are acquired accurately. AO-11 If requested, a clone is created during an acquisition of a digital source. AO-13 A clone is created using access interface DST-AI to write to the clone device. AO-14 If an unaligned clone is created, each sector written to the clone is accurately written to the same disk address on the clone that the sector occupied on the digital source. AO-17 If requested, any excess sectors on a clone destination device are not modified. AO-22 If requested, the tool calculates block hashes for a specified block size during an acquisition for each block acquired from the digital source. AO-23 If the tool logs any log significant information, the information is accurately recorded in the log file. AO-24 If the tool executes in a forensically safe execution environment, the digital source is unchanged by the acquisition process.
Tester Name:	brl
Test Host:	WoFat
Test Date:	Fri Feb 25 11:49:12 2011
Drives:	src(4B-SATA) dst (1A-SATA) other (none)
Source Setup:	src hash (SHA1): < 70CC62B43F6A41CA4D6760AA0B9B4C415D3F48E2 > src hash (MD5): < 746B4C06CDD5FBD67C0820DB4325B40C > 156301488 total sectors (80026361856 bytes) Model (ST380815AS) serial # (6QZ5C9V5) N Start LBA Length Start C/H/S End C/H/S boot Partition type 1 P 000000063 020971520 0000/001/01 1023/254/63 AF other 2 P 020971629 010485536 1023/254/63 1023/254/63 AF other 3 P 031457223 006291456 1023/254/63 1023/254/63 A8 other 4 X 037748679 008388694 1023/254/63 1023/254/63 05 extended 5 S 000000039 004194304 1023/254/63 1023/254/63 AF other 6 x 004194343 004194351 1023/254/63 1023/254/63 05 extended 7 S 000000047 004194304 1023/254/63 1023/254/63 AF other 8 S 000000000 000000000 0000/000/00 0000/000/00 00 empty entry 1 020971520 sectors 10737418240 bytes 2 010485536 sectors 5368594432 bytes 3 006291456 sectors 3221225472 bytes 5 004194304 sectors 2147483648 bytes 7 004194304 sectors 2147483648 bytes 4BOSXCJ-sha1 2147483648 29EA089958EF2A695081712FFBA68BA5164C980B
Log Highlights:	====== Destination drive setup ====== 234441648 sectors wiped with 1A ====== Comparison of original to clone drive ====== Sectors compared: 4194304 Sectors match: 4194304 Sectors differ: 0 Bytes differ: 0 Diffs range: run start Fri Feb 25 14:26:55 2011 run finish Fri Feb 25 14:28:27 2011 elapsed time 0:1:32 Normal exit ====== Tool Settings: ====== dst-interface SATA28

```
OS: Linux ubuntu 2.6.32-21-generic #32-Ubuntu SMP Fri Apr 16 08:10:02 UTC
2010 i686 GNU/Linux

======== Excerpt from SMART log ========


SHA1 Span Hashes
 total span hash: 29ea0899 58ef2a69 5081712f fba68ba5 164c980b

IO Summary:(Time: Fri Feb 25 12:00:57 2011)
Bytes Read: 2,147,483,648
2,147,483,648 bytes written to /dev/sdb6
======== End of Excerpt from SMART log ========

====== Source drive rehash ======
Rehash (SHA1) of source: 70CC62B43F6A41CA4D6760AA0B9B4C415D3F48E2
```

Results:

Assertion and Expected Result	Actual Result
AM-01 Source acquired using interface AI.	as expected
AM-02 Source is type DS.	as expected
AM-03 Execution environment is XE.	as expected
AM-04 A clone is created.	as expected
AM-06 All visible sectors acquired.	as expected
AM-08 All sectors accurately acquired.	as expected
AO-11 A clone is created during acquisition.	as expected
AO-13 Clone created using interface AI.	as expected
AO-14 An unaligned clone is created.	as expected
AO-17 Excess sectors are unchanged.	as expected
AO-22 Tool calculates hashes by block.	option not tested
AO-23 Logged information is correct.	as expected
AO-24 Source is unchanged by acquisition.	as expected

Analysis: Expected results achieved

5.2.22   DA-02-OSXJ

Test Case DA-02-OSXJ Smart Version 2010/11/03	
Case Summary:	DA-02 Acquire a digital source of type DS to an unaligned clone.
Assertions:	AM-01 The tool uses access interface SRC-AI to access the digital source. AM-02 The tool acquires digital source DS. AM-03 The tool executes in execution environment XE. AM-04 If clone creation is specified, the tool creates a clone of the digital source. AM-06 All visible sectors are acquired from the digital source. AM-08 All sectors acquired from the digital source are acquired accurately. AO-11 If requested, a clone is created during an acquisition of a digital source. AO-13 A clone is created using access interface DST-AI to write to the clone device. AO-14 If an unaligned clone is created, each sector written to the clone is accurately written to the same disk address on the clone that the sector occupied on the digital source. AO-17 If requested, any excess sectors on a clone destination device are not modified. AO-22 If requested, the tool calculates block hashes for a specified block size during an acquisition for each block acquired from the digital source. AO-23 If the tool logs any log significant information, the information is accurately recorded in the log file. AO-24 If the tool executes in a forensically safe execution environment, the digital source is unchanged by the acquisition process.
Tester Name:	brl
Test Host:	WoFat
Test Date:	Thu Feb 24 13:01:20 2011
Drives:	src(4B-SATA) dst (1A-SATA) other (none)
Source Setup:	src hash (SHA1): < 70CC62B43F6A41CA4D6760AA0B9B4C415D3F48E2 > src hash (MD5): < 746B4C06CDD5FBD67C0820DB4325B40C > 156301488 total sectors (80026361856 bytes) Model (ST380815AS) serial # (6QZ5C9V5) N Start LBA Length Start C/H/S End C/H/S boot Partition type 1 P 000000063 020971520 0000/001/01 1023/254/63 AF other 2 P 020971629 010485536 1023/254/63 1023/254/63 AF other 3 P 031457223 006291456 1023/254/63 1023/254/63 A8 other 4 X 037748679 008388694 1023/254/63 1023/254/63 05 extended 5 S 000000039 004194304 1023/254/63 1023/254/63 AF other 6 x 004194343 004194351 1023/254/63 1023/254/63 05 extended 7 S 000000047 004194304 1023/254/63 1023/254/63 AF other 8 S 000000000 000000000 0000/000/00 0000/000/00 00 empty entry 1 020971520 sectors 10737418240 bytes 2 010485536 sectors 5368594432 bytes 3 006291456 sectors 3221225472 bytes 5 004194304 sectors 2147483648 bytes 7 004194304 sectors 2147483648 bytes 4BOSXJ-sha1 10737418240 37311859444BD914EDAD43D93F2862E76B279A87
Log Highlights:	====== Destination drive setup ====== 234441648 sectors wiped with 1A ====== Comparison of original to clone drive ====== Sectors compared: 20971520 Sectors match: 20971520 Sectors differ: 0 Bytes differ: 0 Diffs range: run start Thu Feb 24 14:07:58 2011 run finish Thu Feb 24 14:15:19 2011 elapsed time 0:7:21 Normal exit ====== Tool Settings: ====== dst-interface SATA28

```
OS: Linux ubuntu 2.6.32-21-generic #32-Ubuntu SMP Fri Apr 16 08:10:02 UTC
2010 i686 GNU/Linux

======== Excerpt from SMART log ========


SHA1 Span Hashes
 total span hash: 37311859 444bd914 edad43d9 3f2862e7 6b279a87

IO Summary:(Time: Thu Feb 24 13:15:07 2011)
Bytes Read: 10,737,418,240
10,737,418,240 bytes written to /dev/sdb1
======== End of Excerpt from SMART log ========

====== Source drive rehash ======
Rehash (SHA1) of source: 70CC62B43F6A41CA4D6760AA0B9B4C415D3F48E2
```

Results:

Assertion and Expected Result	Actual Result
AM-01 Source acquired using interface AI.	as expected
AM-02 Source is type DS.	as expected
AM-03 Execution environment is XE.	as expected
AM-04 A clone is created.	as expected
AM-06 All visible sectors acquired.	as expected
AM-08 All sectors accurately acquired.	as expected
AO-11 A clone is created during acquisition.	as expected
AO-13 Clone created using interface AI.	as expected
AO-14 An unaligned clone is created.	as expected
AO-17 Excess sectors are unchanged.	as expected
AO-22 Tool calculates hashes by block.	option not tested
AO-23 Logged information is correct.	as expected
AO-24 Source is unchanged by acquisition.	as expected

Analysis: Expected results achieved

5.2.23   DA-02-OSXU

Test Case DA-02-OSXU Smart Version 2010/11/03	
Case Summary:	DA-02 Acquire a digital source of type DS to an unaligned clone.
Assertions:	AM-01 The tool uses access interface SRC-AI to access the digital source. AM-02 The tool acquires digital source DS. AM-03 The tool executes in execution environment XE. AM-04 If clone creation is specified, the tool creates a clone of the digital source. AM-06 All visible sectors are acquired from the digital source. AM-08 All sectors acquired from the digital source are acquired accurately. AO-11 If requested, a clone is created during an acquisition of a digital source. AO-13 A clone is created using access interface DST-AI to write to the clone device. AO-14 If an unaligned clone is created, each sector written to the clone is accurately written to the same disk address on the clone that the sector occupied on the digital source. AO-17 If requested, any excess sectors on a clone destination device are not modified. AO-22 If requested, the tool calculates block hashes for a specified block size during an acquisition for each block acquired from the digital source. AO-23 If the tool logs any log significant information, the information is accurately recorded in the log file. AO-24 If the tool executes in a forensically safe execution environment, the digital source is unchanged by the acquisition process.
Tester Name:	brl
Test Host:	WoFat
Test Date:	Fri Feb 25 09:09:41 2011
Drives:	src(4B-SATA) dst (1A-SATA) other (none)
Source Setup:	src hash (SHA1): < 70CC62B43F6A41CA4D6760AA0B9B4C415D3F48E2 > src hash (MD5): < 746B4C06CDD5FBD67C0820DB4325B40C > 156301488 total sectors (80026361856 bytes) Model (ST380815AS) serial # (6QZ5C9V5) N Start LBA Length Start C/H/S End C/H/S boot Partition type 1 P 000000063 020971520 0000/001/01 1023/254/63 AF other 2 P 020971629 010485536 1023/254/63 1023/254/63 AF other 3 P 031457223 006291456 1023/254/63 1023/254/63 A8 other 4 X 037748679 008388694 1023/254/63 1023/254/63 05 extended 5 S 000000039 004194304 1023/254/63 1023/254/63 AF other 6 x 004194343 004194351 1023/254/63 1023/254/63 05 extended 7 S 000000047 004194304 1023/254/63 1023/254/63 AF other 8 S 000000000 000000000 0000/000/00 0000/000/00 00 empty entry 1 020971520 sectors 10737418240 bytes 2 010485536 sectors 5368594432 bytes 3 006291456 sectors 3221225472 bytes 5 004194304 sectors 2147483648 bytes 7 004194304 sectors 2147483648 bytes 4BOSXU-sha1 3221225472 D102A01562C82533C052CE6CFBB1D467EC9B5BC6
Log Highlights:	====== Destination drive setup ====== 234441648 sectors wiped with 1A ====== Comparison of original to clone drive ====== Sectors compared: 6291456 Sectors match: 6291456 Sectors differ: 0 Bytes differ: 0 Diffs range: run start Fri Feb 25 09:35:31 2011 run finish Fri Feb 25 09:37:47 2011 elapsed time 0:2:16 Normal exit ====== Tool Settings: ====== dst-interface SATA28

```
OS: Linux ubuntu 2.6.32-21-generic #32-Ubuntu SMP Fri Apr 16 08:10:02 UTC
2010 i686 GNU/Linux

======== Excerpt from SMART log ========


SHA1 Span Hashes
 total span hash: d102a015 62c82533 c052ce6c fbb1d467 ec9b5bc6

IO Summary:(Time: Fri Feb 25 09:24:45 2011)
Bytes Read: 3,221,225,472
3,221,225,472 bytes written to /dev/sdb3
======== End of Excerpt from SMART log ========

====== Source drive rehash ======
Rehash (SHA1) of source: 70CC62B43F6A41CA4D6760AA0B9B4C415D3F48E2
```

Results:

Assertion and Expected Result	Actual Result
AM-01 Source acquired using interface AI.	as expected
AM-02 Source is type DS.	as expected
AM-03 Execution environment is XE.	as expected
AM-04 A clone is created.	as expected
AM-06 All visible sectors acquired.	as expected
AM-08 All sectors accurately acquired.	as expected
AO-11 A clone is created during acquisition.	as expected
AO-13 Clone created using interface AI.	as expected
AO-14 An unaligned clone is created.	as expected
AO-17 Excess sectors are unchanged.	as expected
AO-22 Tool calculates hashes by block.	option not tested
AO-23 Logged information is correct.	as expected
AO-24 Source is unchanged by acquisition.	as expected

Analysis: Expected results achieved

5.2.24 DA-02-SWAP

Test Case DA-02-SWAP Smart Version 2010/11/03	
Case Summary:	DA-02 Acquire a digital source of type DS to an unaligned clone.
Assertions :	AM-01 The tool uses access interface SRC-AI to access the digital source. AM-02 The tool acquires digital source DS. AM-03 The tool executes in execution environment XE. AM-04 If clone creation is specified, the tool creates a clone of the digital source. AM-06 All visible sectors are acquired from the digital source. AM-08 All sectors acquired from the digital source are acquired accurately. AO-11 If requested, a clone is created during an acquisition of a digital source. AO-13 A clone is created using access interface DST-AI to write to the clone device. AO-14 If an unaligned clone is created, each sector written to the clone is accurately written to the same disk address on the clone that the sector occupied on the digital source. AO-17 If requested, any excess sectors on a clone destination device are not modified. AO-22 If requested, the tool calculates block hashes for a specified block size during an acquisition for each block acquired from the digital source. AO-23 If the tool logs any log significant information, the information is accurately recorded in the log file. AO-24 If the tool executes in a forensically safe execution environment, the digital source is unchanged by the acquisition process.
Tester Name:	brl
Test Host:	WoFat
Test Date:	Mon Feb 7 09:50:10 2011
Drives:	src(43) dst (49-SATA) other (none)
Source Setup:	src hash (SHA1): < 888E2E7F7AD237DC7A732281DD93F325065E5871 > src hash (MD5): < BC39C3F7EE7A50E77B9BA1E65A5AEEF7 > 78125000 total sectors (40000000000 bytes) Model (0BB-75JHC0) serial # (WD-WMAMC46588) N Start LBA Length Start C/H/S End C/H/S boot Partition type 1 P 000000063 020980827 0000/001/01 1023/254/63 0C Fat32X 2 X 020980890 057143205 1023/000/01 1023/254/63 0F extended 3 S 000000063 000032067 1023/001/01 1023/254/63 01 Fat12 4 x 000032130 002104515 1023/000/01 1023/254/63 05 extended 5 S 000000063 002104452 1023/001/01 1023/254/63 06 Fat16 6 x 002136645 004192965 1023/000/01 1023/254/63 05 extended 7 S 000000063 004192902 1023/001/01 1023/254/63 16 other 8 x 006329610 008401995 1023/000/01 1023/254/63 05 extended 9 S 000000063 008401932 1023/001/01 1023/254/63 0B Fat32 10 x 014731605 010490445 1023/000/01 1023/254/63 05 extended 11 S 000000063 010490382 1023/001/01 1023/254/63 83 Linux 12 x 025222050 004209030 1023/000/01 1023/254/63 05 extended 13 S 000000063 004208967 1023/001/01 1023/254/63 82 Linux swap 14 x 029431080 027712125 1023/000/01 1023/254/63 05 extended 15 S 000000063 027712062 1023/001/01 1023/254/63 07 NTFS 16 S 000000000 000000000 0000/000/00 0000/000/00 00 empty entry 17 P 000000000 000000000 0000/000/00 0000/000/00 00 empty entry 18 P 000000000 000000000 0000/000/00 0000/000/00 00 empty entry 1 020980827 sectors 10742183424 bytes 3 000032067 sectors 16418304 bytes 5 002104452 sectors 1077479424 bytes 7 004192902 sectors 2146765824 bytes 9 008401932 sectors 4301789184 bytes 11 010490382 sectors 5371075584 bytes 13 004208967 sectors 2154991104 bytes 15 027712062 sectors 14188575744 bytes 43swap-md5sum 2154991103 4B602964A30FE20D1B22B046A7375A7C 43swap-sha1sum 2154991103 F5B062CC31DA088DF7FAF8F7A47E500BF4244BCF
Log Highlights :	====== Destination drive setup ====== 156301488 sectors wiped with 49

```
====== Comparison of original to clone drive ======
Sectors compared: 4208967
Sectors match: 4208960
Sectors differ: 7
Bytes differ: 3507
Diffs range: 4208960-4208966
run start Mon Feb 7 10:54:46 2011
run finish Mon Feb 7 10:56:13 2011
elapsed time 0:1:27
Normal exit


====== Screen Message: ======
```

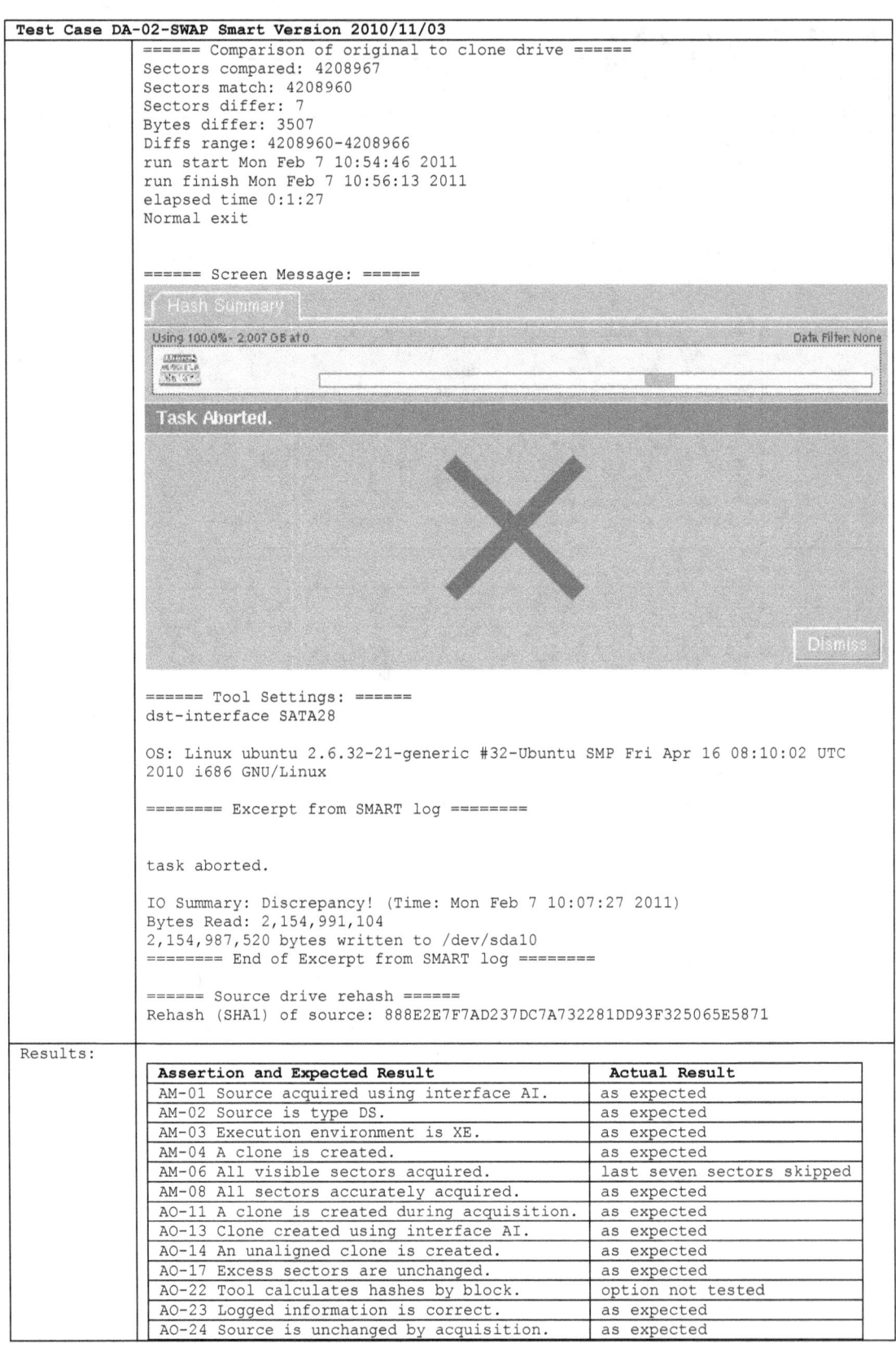

```
====== Tool Settings: ======
dst-interface SATA28

OS: Linux ubuntu 2.6.32-21-generic #32-Ubuntu SMP Fri Apr 16 08:10:02 UTC
2010 i686 GNU/Linux

======== Excerpt from SMART log ========


task aborted.

IO Summary: Discrepancy! (Time: Mon Feb 7 10:07:27 2011)
Bytes Read: 2,154,991,104
2,154,987,520 bytes written to /dev/sda10
======== End of Excerpt from SMART log ========

====== Source drive rehash ======
Rehash (SHA1) of source: 888E2E7F7AD237DC7A732281DD93F325065E5871
```

Results:

Assertion and Expected Result	Actual Result
AM-01 Source acquired using interface AI.	as expected
AM-02 Source is type DS.	as expected
AM-03 Execution environment is XE.	as expected
AM-04 A clone is created.	as expected
AM-06 All visible sectors acquired.	last seven sectors skipped
AM-08 All sectors accurately acquired.	as expected
AO-11 A clone is created during acquisition.	as expected
AO-13 Clone created using interface AI.	as expected
AO-14 An unaligned clone is created.	as expected
AO-17 Excess sectors are unchanged.	as expected
AO-22 Tool calculates hashes by block.	option not tested
AO-23 Logged information is correct.	as expected
AO-24 Source is unchanged by acquisition.	as expected

Test Case DA-02-SWAP Smart Version 2010/11/03	
Analysis:	Expected results not achieved

5.2.25   DA-02-SWAP-ALT

Test Case DA-02-SWAP-ALT Smart Version 2010/11/03	
Case Summary:	DA-02 Acquire a digital source of type DS to an unaligned clone.
Assertions:	AM-01 The tool uses access interface SRC-AI to access the digital source. AM-02 The tool acquires digital source DS. AM-03 The tool executes in execution environment XE. AM-04 If clone creation is specified, the tool creates a clone of the digital source. AM-06 All visible sectors are acquired from the digital source. AM-08 All sectors acquired from the digital source are acquired accurately. AO-11 If requested, a clone is created during an acquisition of a digital source. AO-13 A clone is created using access interface DST-AI to write to the clone device. AO-14 If an unaligned clone is created, each sector written to the clone is accurately written to the same disk address on the clone that the sector occupied on the digital source. AO-17 If requested, any excess sectors on a clone destination device are not modified. AO-22 If requested, the tool calculates block hashes for a specified block size during an acquisition for each block acquired from the digital source. AO-23 If the tool logs any log significant information, the information is accurately recorded in the log file. AO-24 If the tool executes in a forensically safe execution environment, the digital source is unchanged by the acquisition process.
Tester Name:	brl
Test Host:	WoFat
Test Date:	Fri Mar 11 09:45:42 2011
Drives:	src(43) dst (50-SATA) other (none)
Source Setup:	src hash (SHA1): < 888E2E7F7AD237DC7A732281DD93F325065E5871 > src hash (MD5): < BC39C3F7EE7A50E77B9BA1E65A5AEEF7 > 78125000 total sectors (40000000000 bytes) Model (0BB-75JHC0) serial # (WD-WMAMC46588) N Start LBA Length Start C/H/S End C/H/S boot Partition type 1 P 000000063 020980827 0000/001/01 1023/254/63 0C Fat32X 2 X 020980890 057143205 1023/000/01 1023/254/63 0F extended 3 S 000000063 000032067 1023/001/01 1023/254/63 01 Fat12 4 x 000032130 002104515 1023/000/01 1023/254/63 05 extended 5 S 000000063 002104452 1023/001/01 1023/254/63 06 Fat16 6 x 002136645 004192965 1023/000/01 1023/254/63 05 extended 7 S 000000063 004192902 1023/001/01 1023/254/63 16 other 8 x 006329610 008401995 1023/000/01 1023/254/63 05 extended 9 S 000000063 008401932 1023/001/01 1023/254/63 0B Fat32 10 x 014731605 010490445 1023/000/01 1023/254/63 05 extended 11 S 000000063 010490382 1023/001/01 1023/254/63 83 Linux 12 x 025222050 004209030 1023/000/01 1023/254/63 05 extended 13 S 000000063 004208967 1023/001/01 1023/254/63 82 Linux swap 14 x 029431080 027712125 1023/000/01 1023/254/63 05 extended 15 S 000000063 027712062 1023/001/01 1023/254/63 07 NTFS 16 S 000000000 000000000 0000/000/00 0000/000/00 00 empty entry 17 P 000000000 000000000 0000/000/00 0000/000/00 00 empty entry 18 P 000000000 000000000 0000/000/00 0000/000/00 00 empty entry 1 020980827 sectors 10742183424 bytes 3 000032067 sectors 16418304 bytes 5 002104452 sectors 1077479424 bytes 7 004192902 sectors 2146765824 bytes 9 008401932 sectors 4301789184 bytes 11 010490382 sectors 5371075584 bytes 13 004208967 sectors 2154991104 bytes 15 027712062 sectors 14188575744 bytes 43swap-md5sum 2154991103 4B602964A30FE20D1B22B046A7375A7C 43swap-sha1sum 2154991103 F5B062CC31DA088DF7FAF8F7A47E500BF4244BCF
Log Highlights:	====== Destination drive setup ====== 10000001 sectors wiped with 50 ====== Comparison of original to clone drive ======

```
Sectors compared: 4208967
Sectors match: 4208960
Sectors differ: 7
Bytes differ: 3577
Diffs range: 4208960-4208966
Source (4208967) has 1028097 fewer sectors than destination (5237064)
Zero fill: 0
Src Byte fill (43): 0
Dst Byte fill (50): 1028097
Other fill: 0
Other no fill: 0
Zero fill range:
Src fill range:
Dst fill range: 4208967-5237063
Other fill range:
Other not filled range:
run start Fri Mar 11 10:12:51 2011
run finish Fri Mar 11 10:14:53 2011
elapsed time 0:2:2
Normal exit


====== Tool Settings: ======
dst-interface SATA28

OS: Linux ubuntu 2.6.32-21-generic #32-Ubuntu SMP Fri Apr 16 08:10:02 UTC
2010 i686 GNU/Linux

======== Excerpt from SMART log ========


SHA1 Span Hashes
 total span hash: 18b73d89 2d772b88 437ce039 2e1732ca 8fe2a2f4

IO Summary:(Time: Fri Mar 11 10:01:02 2011)
Bytes Read: 2,154,991,104
2,154,991,104 bytes written to /dev/sdb5
======== End of Excerpt from SMART log ========

====== Source drive rehash ======
Rehash (SHA1) of source: 888E2E7F7AD237DC7A732281DD93F325065E5871
```

Results:		
	Assertion and Expected Result	**Actual Result**
	AM-01 Source acquired using interface AI.	as expected
	AM-02 Source is type DS.	as expected
	AM-03 Execution environment is XE.	as expected
	AM-04 A clone is created.	as expected
	AM-06 All visible sectors acquired.	as expected
	AM-08 All sectors accurately acquired.	last seven sectors differ
	AO-11 A clone is created during acquisition.	as expected
	AO-13 Clone created using interface AI.	as expected
	AO-14 An unaligned clone is created.	as expected
	AO-17 Excess sectors are unchanged.	as expected
	AO-22 Tool calculates hashes by block.	option not tested
	AO-23 Logged information is correct.	incorrect hash
	AO-24 Source is unchanged by acquisition.	as expected
Analysis:	Expected results not achieved	

5.2.26   DA-02-THUMB

Test Case DA-02-THUMB Smart Version 2010/11/03	
Case Summary:	DA-02 Acquire a digital source of type DS to an unaligned clone.
Assertions:	AM-01 The tool uses access interface SRC-AI to access the digital source. AM-02 The tool acquires digital source DS. AM-03 The tool executes in execution environment XE. AM-04 If clone creation is specified, the tool creates a clone of the digital source. AM-06 All visible sectors are acquired from the digital source. AM-08 All sectors acquired from the digital source are acquired accurately. AO-11 If requested, a clone is created during an acquisition of a digital source. AO-13 A clone is created using access interface DST-AI to write to the clone device. AO-14 If an unaligned clone is created, each sector written to the clone is accurately written to the same disk address on the clone that the sector occupied on the digital source. AO-17 If requested, any excess sectors on a clone destination device are not modified. AO-22 If requested, the tool calculates block hashes for a specified block size during an acquisition for each block acquired from the digital source. AO-23 If the tool logs any log significant information, the information is accurately recorded in the log file. AO-24 If the tool executes in a forensically safe execution environment, the digital source is unchanged by the acquisition process.
Tester Name:	brl
Test Host:	McGarrett
Test Date:	Wed Feb 2 13:47:00 2011
Drives:	src(D5-THUMB) dst (D6-THUMB) other (none)
Source Setup:	src hash (SHA1): < D68520EF74A336E49DCCF83815B7B08FDC53E38A > src hash (MD5): < C843593624B2B3B878596D8760B19954 > 505856 total sectors (258998272 bytes) Model (usb2.0Flash Disk) serial # ()
Log Highlights:	====== Destination drive setup ====== 4001760 sectors wiped with D6 ====== Comparison of original to clone drive ====== Sectors compared: 505856 Sectors match: 505856 Sectors differ: 0 Bytes differ: 0 Diffs range Source (505856) has 3495904 fewer sectors than destination (4001760) Zero fill: 0 Src Byte fill (D5): 0 Dst Byte fill (D6): 3495904 Other fill: 0 Other no fill: 0 Zero fill range: Src fill range: Dst fill range: 505856-4001759 Other fill range: Other not filled range: 0 source read errors, 0 destination read errors ====== Tool Settings: ====== dst-interface USB OS: Linux ubuntu 2.6.32-21-generic #32-Ubuntu SMP Fri Apr 16 08:10:02 UTC 2010 i686 GNU/Linux ======== Excerpt from SMART log ======== SHA1 Span Hashes

```
total span hash: d68520ef 74a336e4 9dccf838 15b7b08f dc53e38a

IO Summary:(Time: Wed Feb 2 14:57:07 2011)
Bytes Read: 258,998,272
258,998,272 bytes written to /dev/sdb
======== End of Excerpt from SMART log ========

====== Source drive rehash ======
Rehash (SHA1) of source: D68520EF74A336E49DCCF83815B7B08FDC53E38A
```

Results:

Assertion and Expected Result	Actual Result
AM-01 Source acquired using interface AI.	as expected
AM-02 Source is type DS.	as expected
AM-03 Execution environment is XE.	as expected
AM-04 A clone is created.	as expected
AM-06 All visible sectors acquired.	as expected
AM-08 All sectors accurately acquired.	as expected
AO-11 A clone is created during acquisition.	as expected
AO-13 Clone created using interface AI.	as expected
AO-14 An unaligned clone is created.	as expected
AO-17 Excess sectors are unchanged.	as expected
AO-22 Tool calculates hashes by block.	option not tested
AO-23 Logged information is correct.	as expected
AO-24 Source is unchanged by acquisition.	as expected

Analysis: Expected results achieved

5.2.27 DA-04

Test Case DA-04 Smart Version 2010/11/03	
Case Summary:	DA-04 Acquire a physical device to a truncated clone.
Assertions :	AM-01 The tool uses access interface SRC-AI to access the digital source. AM-02 The tool acquires digital source DS. AM-03 The tool executes in execution environment XE. AM-04 If clone creation is specified, the tool creates a clone of the digital source. AM-06 All visible sectors are acquired from the digital source. AM-08 All sectors acquired from the digital source are acquired accurately. AO-11 If requested, a clone is created during an acquisition of a digital source. AO-13 A clone is created using access interface DST-AI to write to the clone device. AO-14 If an unaligned clone is created, each sector written to the clone is accurately written to the same disk address on the clone that the sector occupied on the digital source. AO-19 If there is insufficient space to create a complete clone, a truncated clone is created using all available sectors of the clone device. AO-20 If a truncated clone is created, the tool notifies the user. AO-22 If requested, the tool calculates block hashes for a specified block size during an acquisition for each block acquired from the digital source. AO-23 If the tool logs any log significant information, the information is accurately recorded in the log file. AO-24 If the tool executes in a forensically safe execution environment, the digital source is unchanged by the acquisition process.
Tester Name:	brl
Test Host:	McGarrett
Test Date:	Mon Feb 7 11:14:27 2011
Drives:	src(41) dst (25-IDE) other (none)
Source Setup:	src hash (SHA1): < 15CAA1A307271160D8372668BF8A03FC45A51CC9 > src hash (MD5): < 0A6A8EF78BDC14E2026710D8CCB5607C > 78125000 total sectors (40000000000 bytes) 65534/015/63 (max cyl/hd values) 65535/016/63 (number of cyl/hd) IDE disk: Model (WDC WD400BB-75JHC0) serial # (WD-WMAMC4658355) N Start LBA Length Start C/H/S End C/H/S boot Partition type 1 P 000000063 078107967 0000/001/01 1023/254/63 Boot 07 NTFS 2 P 000000000 000000000 0000/000/00 0000/000/00 00 empty entry 3 P 000000000 000000000 0000/000/00 0000/000/00 00 empty entry 4 P 000000000 000000000 0000/000/00 0000/000/00 00 empty entry 1 078107967 sectors 39991279104 bytes
Log Highlights :	====== Destination drive setup ====== 58633344 sectors wiped with 25 ====== Screen Message: ======

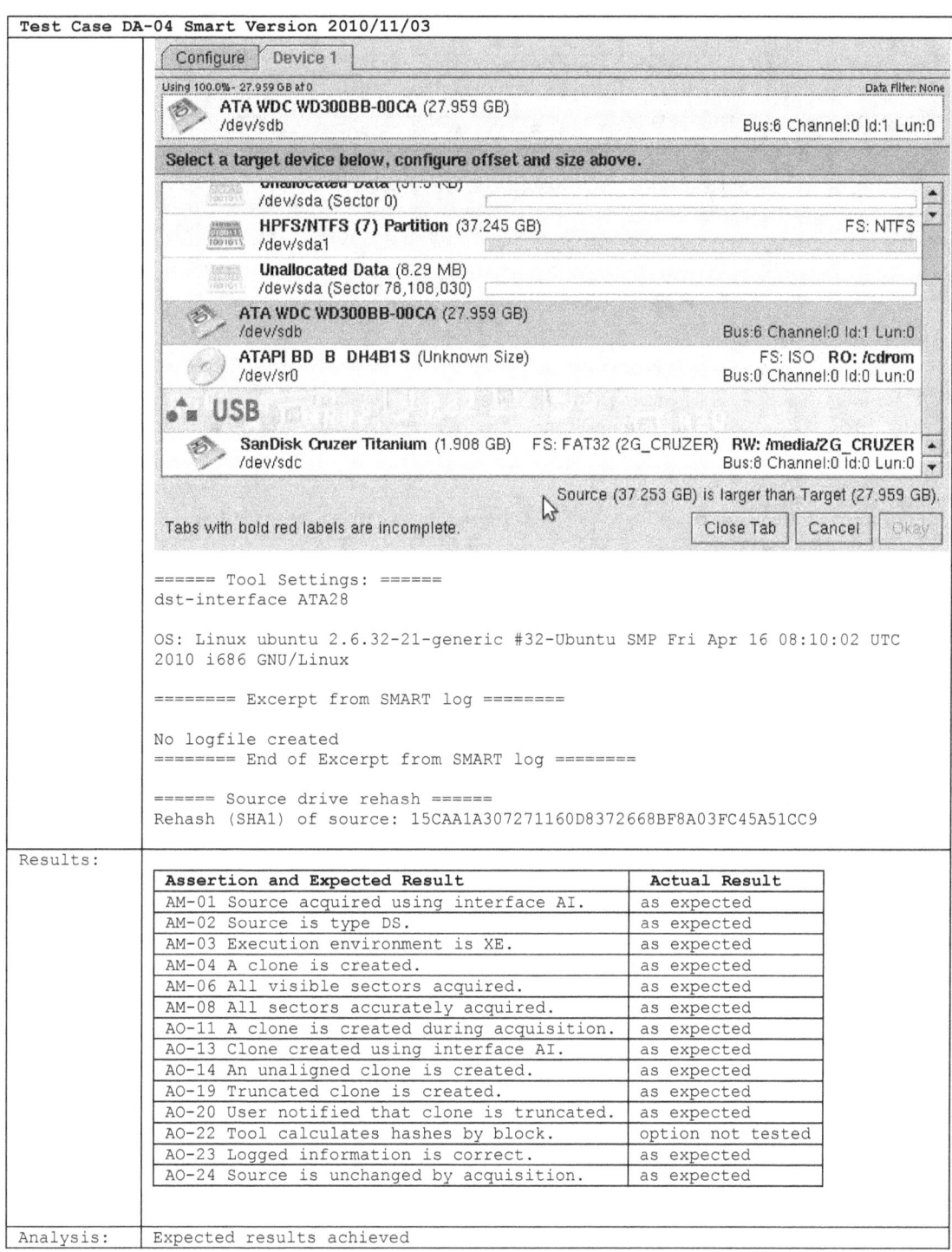

```
====== Tool Settings: ======
dst-interface ATA28

OS: Linux ubuntu 2.6.32-21-generic #32-Ubuntu SMP Fri Apr 16 08:10:02 UTC
2010 i686 GNU/Linux

======== Excerpt from SMART log ========

No logfile created
======== End of Excerpt from SMART log ========

====== Source drive rehash ======
Rehash (SHA1) of source: 15CAA1A307271160D8372668BF8A03FC45A51CC9
```

Results:

Assertion and Expected Result	Actual Result
AM-01 Source acquired using interface AI.	as expected
AM-02 Source is type DS.	as expected
AM-03 Execution environment is XE.	as expected
AM-04 A clone is created.	as expected
AM-06 All visible sectors acquired.	as expected
AM-08 All sectors accurately acquired.	as expected
AO-11 A clone is created during acquisition.	as expected
AO-13 Clone created using interface AI.	as expected
AO-14 An unaligned clone is created.	as expected
AO-19 Truncated clone is created.	as expected
AO-20 User notified that clone is truncated.	as expected
AO-22 Tool calculates hashes by block.	option not tested
AO-23 Logged information is correct.	as expected
AO-24 Source is unchanged by acquisition.	as expected

Analysis: Expected results achieved

5.2.28   DA-06-ATA28

Test Case DA-06-ATA28 Smart Version 2010/11/03	
Case Summary:	DA-06 Acquire a physical device using access interface AI to an image file.
Assertions:	AM-01 The tool uses access interface SRC-AI to access the digital source. AM-02 The tool acquires digital source DS. AM-03 The tool executes in execution environment XE. AM-05 If image file creation is specified, the tool creates an image file on file system type FS. AM-06 All visible sectors are acquired from the digital source. AM-08 All sectors acquired from the digital source are acquired accurately. AO-01 If the tool creates an image file, the data represented by the image file are the same as the data acquired by the tool. AO-05 If the tool creates a multifile image of a requested size then all the individual files shall be no larger than the requested size. AO-22 If requested, the tool calculates block hashes for a specified block size during an acquisition for each block acquired from the digital source. AO-23 If the tool logs any log significant information, the information is accurately recorded in the log file. AO-24 If the tool executes in a forensically safe execution environment, the digital source is unchanged by the acquisition process.
Tester Name:	brl
Test Host:	McGarrett
Test Date:	Wed Feb 9 14:07:47 2011
Drives:	src(01-IDE) dst (none) other (3C-SATA)

Source Setup:	src hash (SHA1): < A48BB5665D6DC57C22DB68E2F723DA9AA8DF82B9 >
	src hash (MD5): < F458F673894753FA6A0EC8B8EC63848E >
	
	Reference SHA1 hashes, Win size: 4193792 (sectors) 2147221504 (bytes)
	  1 0 - 4193791 D0047F1F513422C425D3FBDB615F6140A572249E -
	  2 4193792 - 8387583 8839FBDCF0F7EA3F81C79A491C20F6B684C7DA53 -
	  3 8387584 - 12581375 862AEFA7658E90D5FD4BF4C1A49DBB0AB4D0E8F8 -
	  . . .
	 17 67100672 - 71294463 2DC4CD1666D88C15C8B1DC47F9C2E402769CC83F -
	 18 71294464 - 75488255 3711100F684C4D522847461E28FFD3C89336A007 -
	 19 75488256 - 78165359 B72D506B9F2A20F7F3A045555FC85DF56DAEB7E3 -
	78165360 total sectors (40020664320 bytes)
	Model (0BB-00JHC0) serial # (WD-WMAMC74171)
	 N Start LBA Length Start C/H/S End C/H/S boot Partition type
	 1 P 000000063 020980827 0000/001/01 1023/254/63 0C Fat32X
	 2 X 020980890 057175335 1023/000/01 1023/254/63 0F extended
	 3 S 000000063 000032067 1023/001/01 1023/254/63 01 Fat12
	 4 x 000032130 002104515 1023/000/01 1023/254/63 05 extended
	 5 S 000000063 002104452 1023/001/01 1023/254/63 06 Fat16
	 6 x 002136645 004192965 1023/000/01 1023/254/63 05 extended
	 7 S 000000063 004192902 1023/001/01 1023/254/63 16 other
	 8 x 006329610 008401995 1023/000/01 1023/254/63 05 extended
	 9 S 000000063 008401932 1023/001/01 1023/254/63 0B Fat32
	10 x 014731605 010490445 1023/000/01 1023/254/63 05 extended
	11 S 000000063 010490382 1023/001/01 1023/254/63 83 Linux
	12 x 025222050 004209030 1023/000/01 1023/254/63 05 extended
	13 S 000000063 004208967 1023/001/01 1023/254/63 82 Linux swap
	14 x 029431080 027744255 1023/000/01 1023/254/63 05 extended
	15 S 000000063 027744192 1023/001/01 1023/254/63 07 NTFS
	16 S 000000000 000000000 0000/000/00 0000/000/00 00 empty entry
	17 P 000000000 000000000 0000/000/00 0000/000/00 00 empty entry
	18 P 000000000 000000000 0000/000/00 0000/000/00 00 empty entry
	 1 020980827 sectors 10742183424 bytes
	 3 000032067 sectors 16418304 bytes
	 5 002104452 sectors 1077479424 bytes
	 7 004192902 sectors 2146765824 bytes
	 9 008401932 sectors 4301789184 bytes
	11 010490382 sectors 5371075584 bytes
	13 004208967 sectors 2154991104 bytes
	15 027744192 sectors 14205026304 bytes

Log Highlights:	====== Tool Settings: ======

```
segmentation Standard

OS: Linux ubuntu 2.6.32-21-generic #32-Ubuntu SMP Fri Apr 16 08:10:02 UTC
2010 i686 GNU/Linux


====== Image file segments ======
 1      -rwx------ 1 ubuntu root 8277 2011-02-09 16:08 da-06-ata28
 2      -rwx------ 1 ubuntu root 2147221504 2011-02-09 14:18 da-06-
ata28.image.001
 3      -rwx------ 1 ubuntu root 2147221504 2011-02-09 14:22 da-06-
ata28.image.002
 . . .
 19     -rwx------ 1 ubuntu root 2147221504 2011-02-09 15:33 da-06-
ata28.image.018
 20     -rwx------ 1 ubuntu root 1370677248 2011-02-09 15:36 da-06-
ata28.image.019
 21     -rwx------ 1 ubuntu root 41922 2011-02-09 15:36 da-06-
ata28.image.info
======== Excerpt from SMART log ========

Image Description...
Make and Model: ATA WDC WD400BB-00JH
Serial Number: WD-WMAMC7417100
Device Sectors: 78,165,360

SHA1 Span Hashes
 total span hash: a96a7193 e1d9c270 587b2be7 098638ac 048221d1

SHA1 Segment-Delimited Span Hashes
 1      0 - 2147221503: d0047f1f 513422c4 25d3fbdb 615f6140 a572249e
 2      2147221504 - 4294443007: 8839fbdc f0f7ea3f 81c79a49 1c20f6b6
84c7da53
 3      4294443008 - 6441664511: 862aefa7 658e90d5 fd4bf4c1 a49dbb0a
b4d0e8f8

 17     34355544064 - 36502765567: 2dc4cd16 66d88c15 c8b1dc47 f9c2e402
769cc83f
 18     36502765568 - 38649987071: 3711100f 684c4d52 2847461e 28ffd3c8
9336a007
 19     38649987072 - 40020664319: b72d506b 9f2a20f7 f3a04555 5fc85df5
6daeb7e3

IO Summary:(Time: Wed Feb 9 15:36:50 2011)
Bytes Read: 40,020,664,320
40,020,664,320 bytes written to image "da-06-ata28"
======== End of Excerpt from SMART log ========

====== Source drive rehash ======
Rehash (SHA1) of source: A96A7193E1D9C270587B2BE7098638AC048221D1
```

Results:

Assertion and Expected Result	Actual Result
AM-01 Source acquired using interface AI.	as expected
AM-02 Source is type DS.	as expected
AM-03 Execution environment is XE.	as expected
AM-05 An image is created on file system type FS.	as expected
AM-06 All visible sectors acquired.	as expected
AM-08 All sectors accurately acquired.	88 sectors differ
AO-01 Image file is complete and accurate.	as expected
AO-05 Multifile image created.	as expected
AO-22 Tool calculates hashes by block.	as expected
AO-23 Logged information is correct.	as expected
AO-24 Source is unchanged by acquisition.	source changed

Analysis: Expected results not achieved

5.2.29 DA-06-ATA28-WB

Test Case DA-06-ATA28-WB Smart Version 2010/11/03	
Case Summary:	DA-06 Acquire a physical device using access interface AI to an image file.
Assertions:	AM-01 The tool uses access interface SRC-AI to access the digital source. AM-02 The tool acquires digital source DS. AM-03 The tool executes in execution environment XE. AM-05 If image file creation is specified, the tool creates an image file on file system type FS. AM-06 All visible sectors are acquired from the digital source. AM-08 All sectors acquired from the digital source are acquired accurately. AO-01 If the tool creates an image file, the data represented by the image file is the same as the data acquired by the tool. AO-05 If the tool creates a multifile image of a requested size then all the individual files shall be no larger than the requested size. AO-22 If requested, the tool calculates block hashes for a specified block size during an acquisition for each block acquired from the digital source. AO-23 If the tool logs any log significant information, the information is accurately recorded in the log file. AO-24 If the tool executes in a forensically safe execution environment, the digital source is unchanged by the acquisition process.
Tester Name:	brl
Test Host:	WoFat
Test Date:	Mon Mar 14 13:51:40 2011
Drives:	src (01-IDE) dst (none) other (3C-SATA)

Source Setup:	src hash (SHA1): < A48BB5665D6DC57C22DB68E2F723DA9AA8DF82B9 >
	src hash (MD5): < F458F673894753FA6A0EC8B8EC63848E >
	
	Reference SHA1 hashes, Win size: 4193792 (sectors) 2147221504 (bytes)
	  1 0 - 4193791 D0047F1F513422C425D3FBDB615F6140A572249E -
	  2 4193792 - 8387583 8839FBDCF0F7EA3F81C79A491C20F6B684C7DA53 -
	  3 8387584 - 12581375 862AEFA7658E90D5FD4BF4C1A49DBB0AB4D0E8F8 -
	  . . .
	 17 67100672 - 71294463 2DC4CD1666D88C15C8B1DC47F9C2E402769CC83F -
	 18 71294464 - 75488255 3711100F684C4D522847461E28FFD3C89336A007 -
	 19 75488256 - 78165359 B72D506B9F2A20F7F3A045555FC85DF56DAEB7E3 -
	78165360 total sectors (40020664320 bytes)
	Model (0BB-00JHC0) serial # (WD-WMAMC74171)
	 N Start LBA Length Start C/H/S End C/H/S boot Partition type
	 1 P 000000063 020980827 0000/001/01 1023/254/63 0C Fat32X
	 2 X 020980890 057175335 1023/000/01 1023/254/63 0F extended
	 3 S 000000063 000032067 1023/001/01 1023/254/63 01 Fat12
	 4 x 000032130 002104515 1023/000/01 1023/254/63 05 extended
	 5 S 000000063 002104452 1023/001/01 1023/254/63 06 Fat16
	 6 x 002136645 004192965 1023/000/01 1023/254/63 05 extended
	 7 S 000000063 004192902 1023/001/01 1023/254/63 16 other
	 8 x 006329610 008401995 1023/000/01 1023/254/63 05 extended
	 9 S 000000063 008401932 1023/001/01 1023/254/63 0B Fat32
	10 x 014731605 010490445 1023/000/01 1023/254/63 05 extended
	11 S 000000063 010490382 1023/001/01 1023/254/63 83 Linux
	12 x 025222050 004209030 1023/000/01 1023/254/63 05 extended
	13 S 000000063 004208967 1023/001/01 1023/254/63 82 Linux swap
	14 x 029431080 027744255 1023/000/01 1023/254/63 05 extended
	15 S 000000063 027744192 1023/001/01 1023/254/63 07 NTFS
	16 S 000000000 000000000 0000/000/00 0000/000/00 00 empty entry
	17 P 000000000 000000000 0000/000/00 0000/000/00 00 empty entry
	18 P 000000000 000000000 0000/000/00 0000/000/00 00 empty entry
	1 020980827 sectors 10742183424 bytes
	3 000032067 sectors 16418304 bytes
	5 002104452 sectors 1077479424 bytes
	7 004192902 sectors 2146765824 bytes
	9 008401932 sectors 4301789184 bytes
	11 010490382 sectors 5371075584 bytes
	13 004208967 sectors 2154991104 bytes
	15 027744192 sectors 14205026304 bytes

Log Highlights:	====== Tool Settings: ======

```
segmentation Standard

Write Block: 3 FastBloc IDE

OS: Linux ubuntu 2.6.32-21-generic #32-Ubuntu SMP Fri Apr 16 08:10:02 UTC
2010 i686 GNU/Linux


====== Image file segments ======
  1     -rwxr-xr-x 1 ubuntu ubuntu 8334 2011-03-14 15:52 da-06-ata28-wb
  2     -rwxr-xr-x 1 ubuntu ubuntu 2147221504 2011-03-14 14:11 da-06-ata28-
wb.image.001
  3     -rwxr-xr-x 1 ubuntu ubuntu 2147221504 2011-03-14 14:15 da-06-ata28-
wb.image.002
  . . .
 19     -rwxr-xr-x 1 ubuntu ubuntu 2147221504 2011-03-14 15:27 da-06-ata28-
wb.image.018
 20     -rwxr-xr-x 1 ubuntu ubuntu 1370677248 2011-03-14 15:31 da-06-ata28-
wb.image.019
 21     -rwxr-xr-x 1 ubuntu ubuntu 42183 2011-03-14 15:31 da-06-ata28-
wb.image.info
======== Excerpt from SMART log ========

Image Description...
Make and Model: ATA WDC WD400BB-00JH
Serial Number: WD-WMAMC7417100
Device Sectors: 78,165,360

SHA1 Span Hashes
 total span hash: a48bb566 5d6dc57c 22db68e2 f723da9a a8df82b9

SHA1 Segment-Delimited Span Hashes
  1      0 - 2147221503: d0047f1f 513422c4 25d3fbdb 615f6140 a572249e
  2      2147221504 - 4294443007: 8839fbdc f0f7ea3f 81c79a49 1c20f6b6
84c7da53
  3      4294443008 - 6441664511: 862aefa7 658e90d5 fd4bf4c1 a49dbb0a
b4d0e8f8
                . . .
 17     34355544064 - 36502765567: 2dc4cd16 66d88c15 c8b1dc47 f9c2e402
769cc83f
 18     36502765568 - 38649987071: 3711100f 684c4d52 2847461e 28ffd3c8
9336a007
 19     38649987072 - 40020664319: b72d506b 9f2a20f7 f3a04555 5fc85df5
6daeb7e3

IO Summary:(Time: Mon Mar 14 15:31:03 2011)
Bytes Read: 40,020,664,320
40,020,664,320 bytes written to image "da-06-ata28-wb"
======== End of Excerpt from SMART log ========
```

Results:

Assertion and Expected Result	Actual Result
AM-01 Source acquired using interface AI.	as expected
AM-02 Source is type DS.	as expected
AM-03 Execution environment is XE.	as expected
AM-05 An image is created on file system type FS.	as expected
AM-06 All visible sectors acquired.	as expected
AM-08 All sectors accurately acquired.	as expected
AO-01 Image file is complete and accurate.	as expected
AO-05 Multifile image created.	as expected
AO-22 Tool calculates hashes by block.	as expected
AO-23 Logged information is correct.	as expected
AO-24 Source is unchanged by acquisition.	not checked

Analysis: Expected results achieved

5.2.30 DA-06-ATA48

Test Case DA-06-ATA48 Smart Version 2010/11/03	
Case Summary:	DA-06 Acquire a physical device using access interface AI to an image file.
Assertions:	AM-01 The tool uses access interface SRC-AI to access the digital source. AM-02 The tool acquires digital source DS. AM-03 The tool executes in execution environment XE. AM-05 If image file creation is specified, the tool creates an image file on file system type FS. AM-06 All visible sectors are acquired from the digital source. AM-08 All sectors acquired from the digital source are acquired accurately. AO-01 If the tool creates an image file, the data represented by the image file is the same as the data acquired by the tool. AO-05 If the tool creates a multifile image of a requested size then all the individual files shall be no larger than the requested size. AO-22 If requested, the tool calculates block hashes for a specified block size during an acquisition for each block acquired from the digital source. AO-23 If the tool logs any log significant information, the information is accurately recorded in the log file. AO-24 If the tool executes in a forensically safe execution environment, the digital source is unchanged by the acquisition process.
Tester Name:	brl
Test Host:	WoFat
Test Date:	Tue Feb 8 11:23:19 2011
Drives:	src(4C) dst (none) other (67-SATA)
Source Setup:	src hash (SHA1): < 8FF620D2BEDCCAFE8412EDAAD56C8554F872EFBF > src hash (MD5): < D10F763B56D4CEBA2D1311C61F9FB382 > 390721968 total sectors (200049647616 bytes) 24320/254/63 (max cyl/hd values) 24321/255/63 (number of cyl/hd) IDE disk: Model (WDC WD2000JB-00KFA0) serial # (WD-WMAMR1031111) N Start LBA Length Start C/H/S End C/H/S boot Partition type 1 P 000000063 390700737 0000/001/01 1023/254/63 Boot 07 NTFS 2 P 000000000 000000000 0000/000/00 0000/000/00 00 empty entry 3 P 000000000 000000000 0000/000/00 0000/000/00 00 empty entry 4 P 000000000 000000000 0000/000/00 0000/000/00 00 empty entry 1 390700737 sectors 200038777344 bytes
Log Highlights:	====== Tool Settings: ====== segmentation Standard OS: Linux ubuntu 2.6.32-21-generic #32-Ubuntu SMP Fri Apr 16 08:10:02 UTC 2010 i686 GNU/Linux ====== Image file segments ====== 1 3223 2011-02-09 08:53 da-06-ata48 2 200049647616 2011-02-08 16:47 da-06-ata48.image.001 3 4716 2011-02-08 16:47 da-06-ata48.image.info ======== Excerpt from SMART log ======== Image Description... Make and Model: ATA WDC WD2000JB-00K Serial Number: WD-WMAMR1031111 Device Sectors: 390,721,968 SHA1 Span Hashes total span hash: 8ff620d2 bedccafe 8412edaa d56c8554 f872efbf IO Summary:(Time: Tue Feb 8 16:47:29 2011) Bytes Read: 200,049,647,616 200,049,647,616 bytes written to image "da-06-ata48" ======== End of Excerpt from SMART log ======== ====== Source drive rehash ====== Rehash (SHA1) of source: 8FF620D2BEDCCAFE8412EDAAD56C8554F872EFBF

Test Case DA-06-ATA48 Smart Version 2010/11/03	
Results:	

Assertion and Expected Result	Actual Result
AM-01 Source acquired using interface AI.	as expected
AM-02 Source is type DS.	as expected
AM-03 Execution environment is XE.	as expected
AM-05 An image is created on file system type FS.	as expected
AM-06 All visible sectors acquired.	as expected
AM-08 All sectors accurately acquired.	as expected
AO-01 Image file is complete and accurate.	as expected
AO-05 Multifile image created.	as expected
AO-22 Tool calculates hashes by block.	option not tested
AO-23 Logged information is correct.	as expected
AO-24 Source is unchanged by acquisition.	as expected

Analysis:	Expected results achieved

5.2.31　DA-06-ESATA

Test Case DA-06-ESATA Smart Version 2010/11/03	
Case Summary:	DA-06 Acquire a physical device using access interface AI to an image file.
Assertions:	AM-01 The tool uses access interface SRC-AI to access the digital source. AM-02 The tool acquires digital source DS. AM-03 The tool executes in execution environment XE. AM-05 If image file creation is specified, the tool creates an image file on file system type FS. AM-06 All visible sectors are acquired from the digital source. AM-08 All sectors acquired from the digital source are acquired accurately. AO-01 If the tool creates an image file, the data represented by the image file is the same as the data acquired by the tool. AO-05 If the tool creates a multifile image of a requested size then all the individual files shall be no larger than the requested size. AO-22 If requested, the tool calculates block hashes for a specified block size during an acquisition for each block acquired from the digital source. AO-23 If the tool logs any log significant information, the information is accurately recorded in the log file. AO-24 If the tool executes in a forensically safe execution environment, the digital source is unchanged by the acquisition process.
Tester Name:	brl
Test Host:	McGarrett
Test Date:	Tue Feb 8 13:20:35 2011
Drives:	src (07-SATA) dst (none) other (68-SATA)
Source Setup:	src hash (SHA1): < 655E9BDDB36A3F9C5C4CC8BF32B8C5B41AF9F52E > src hash (MD5): < 2EAF712DAD80F66E30DEA00365B4579B > 156301488 total sectors (80026361856 bytes) Model (WDC WD800JD-32HK) serial # (WD-WMAJ91510044) 　N Start LBA Length Start C/H/S End C/H/S boot Partition type 　1 P 000000063 156280257 0000/001/01 1023/254/63 Boot 07 NTFS 　2 P 000000000 000000000 0000/000/00 0000/000/00 00 empty entry 　3 P 000000000 000000000 0000/000/00 0000/000/00 00 empty entry 　4 P 000000000 000000000 0000/000/00 0000/000/00 00 empty entry 1 156280257 sectors 80015491584 bytes
Log Highlights:	====== Tool Settings: ====== segmentation Transport Media OS: Linux ubuntu 2.6.32-21-generic #32-Ubuntu SMP Fri Apr 16 08:10:02 UTC 2010 i686 GNU/Linux ====== Image file segments ====== 1 　　1036 2011-02-08 10:55 da-06-esata 2 　　80026361856 2011-02-08 10:49 da-06-esata.image.001 3 　　4700 2011-02-08 10:49 da-06-esata.image.info ======== Excerpt from SMART log ======== SHA1 Span Hashes 　total span hash: 655e9bdd b36a3f9c 5c4cc8bf 32b8c5b4 1af9f52e IO Summary:(Time: Tue Feb 8 15:49:46 2011) Bytes Read: 80,026,361,856 80,026,361,856 bytes written to image "da-06-esata" ======== End of Excerpt from SMART log ======== ====== Source drive rehash ====== Rehash (SHA1) of source: 655E9BDDB36A3F9C5C4CC8BF32B8C5B41AF9F52E
Results:	

Assertion and Expected Result	Actual Result
AM-01 Source acquired using interface AI.	as expected
AM-02 Source is type DS.	as expected
AM-03 Execution environment is XE.	as expected

Test Case DA-06-ESATA Smart Version 2010/11/03		
	AM-05 An image is created on file system type FS.	as expected
	AM-06 All visible sectors acquired.	as expected
	AM-08 All sectors accurately acquired.	as expected
	AO-01 Image file is complete and accurate.	as expected
	AO-05 Multifile image created.	as expected
	AO-22 Tool calculates hashes by block.	option not tested
	AO-23 Logged information is correct.	as expected
	AO-24 Source is unchanged by acquisition.	as expected
Analysis:	Expected results achieved	

5.2.32 DA-06-FW

Test Case DA-06-FW Smart Version 2010/11/03	
Case Summary:	DA-06 Acquire a physical device using access interface AI to an image file.
Assertions:	AM-01 The tool uses access interface SRC-AI to access the digital source. AM-02 The tool acquires digital source DS. AM-03 The tool executes in execution environment XE. AM-05 If image file creation is specified, the tool creates an image file on file system type FS. AM-06 All visible sectors are acquired from the digital source. AM-08 All sectors acquired from the digital source are acquired accurately. AO-01 If the tool creates an image file, the data represented by the image file is the same as the data acquired by the tool. AO-05 If the tool creates a multifile image of a requested size then all the individual files shall be no larger than the requested size. AO-22 If requested, the tool calculates block hashes for a specified block size during an acquisition for each block acquired from the digital source. AO-23 If the tool logs any log significant information, the information is accurately recorded in the log file. AO-24 If the tool executes in a forensically safe execution environment, the digital source is unchanged by the acquisition process.
Tester Name:	brl
Test Host:	Max
Test Date:	Wed Feb 9 11:40:50 2011
Drives:	src(63-FU2) dst (none) other (3A-SATA)
Source Setup:	src hash (SHA1): < F7069EDCBEAC863C88DECED82159F22DA96BE99B > src hash (MD5): < EE217BC4FA4F3D1B4021D29B065AA9EC > 117304992 total sectors (60060155904 bytes) Model (SP0612N) serial # () N Start LBA Length Start C/H/S End C/H/S boot Partition type 1 P 000000063 004192902 0000/001/01 0260/254/63 Boot 06 Fat16 2 X 004192965 113097600 0261/000/01 1023/254/63 0F extended 3 S 000000063 113097537 0261/001/01 1023/254/63 0B Fat32 4 S 000000000 000000000 0000/000/00 0000/000/00 00 empty entry 5 P 000000000 000000000 0000/000/00 0000/000/00 00 empty entry 6 P 000000000 000000000 0000/000/00 0000/000/00 00 empty entry 1 004192902 sectors 2146765824 bytes 3 113097537 sectors 57905938944 bytes
Log Highlights:	====== Tool Settings: ====== segmentation Standard OS: Linux ubuntu 2.6.32-21-generic #32-Ubuntu SMP Fri Apr 16 08:10:02 UTC 2010 i686 GNU/Linux ====== Image file segments ====== 1 3407 2011-02-09 16:26 da-06-fw 2 60060155904 2011-02-09 16:17 da-06-fw.image.001 3 7495 2011-02-09 16:17 da-06-fw.image.info ======== Excerpt from SMART log ======== Image Description... Make and Model: DMI SAMSUNG SP0612N Device Sectors: 117,304,992 SHA1 Span Hashes total span hash: f7069edc beac863c 88deced8 2159f22d a96be99b IO Summary:(Time: Wed Feb 9 16:17:48 2011) Bytes Read: 60,060,155,904 60,060,155,904 bytes written to image "da-06-fw" ======== End of Excerpt from SMART log ======== ====== Source drive rehash ====== Rehash (SHA1) of source: F7069EDCBEAC863C88DECED82159F22DA96BE99B

Test Case DA-06-FW Smart Version 2010/11/03	
Results:	

Assertion and Expected Result	Actual Result
AM-01 Source acquired using interface AI.	as expected
AM-02 Source is type DS.	as expected
AM-03 Execution environment is XE.	as expected
AM-05 An image is created on file system type FS.	as expected
AM-06 All visible sectors acquired.	as expected
AM-08 All sectors accurately acquired.	as expected
AO-01 Image file is complete and accurate.	as expected
AO-05 Multifile image created.	as expected
AO-22 Tool calculates hashes by block.	option not tested
AO-23 Logged information is correct.	as expected
AO-24 Source is unchanged by acquisition.	as expected

Analysis:	Expected results achieved

5.2.33   DA-06-SATA28

Test Case DA-06-SATA28 Smart Version 2010/11/03	
Case Summary:	DA-06 Acquire a physical device using access interface AI to an image file.
Assertions:	AM-01 The tool uses access interface SRC-AI to access the digital source. AM-02 The tool acquires digital source DS. AM-03 The tool executes in execution environment XE. AM-05 If image file creation is specified, the tool creates an image file on file system type FS. AM-06 All visible sectors are acquired from the digital source. AM-08 All sectors acquired from the digital source are acquired accurately. AO-01 If the tool creates an image file, the data represented by the image file are the same as the data acquired by the tool. AO-05 If the tool creates a multifile image of a requested size then all the individual files shall be no larger than the requested size. AO-22 If requested, the tool calculates block hashes for a specified block size during an acquisition for each block acquired from the digital source. AO-23 If the tool logs any log significant information, the information is accurately recorded in the log file. AO-24 If the tool executes in a forensically safe execution environment, the digital source is unchanged by the acquisition process.
Tester Name:	brl
Test Host:	McGarrett
Test Date:	Fri Feb 11 09:52:25 2011
Drives:	src(4B-SATA) dst (none) other (68-SATA)
Source Setup:	src hash (SHA1): < 70CC62B43F6A41CA4D6760AA0B9B4C415D3F48E2 > src hash (MD5): < 746B4C06CDD5FBD67C0820DB4325B40C > 156301488 total sectors (80026361856 bytes) Model (ST380815AS) serial # (6QZ5C9V5) N Start LBA Length Start C/H/S End C/H/S boot Partition type 1 P 000000063 020971520 0000/001/01 1023/254/63 AF other 2 P 020971629 010485536 1023/254/63 1023/254/63 AF other 3 P 031457223 006291456 1023/254/63 1023/254/63 A8 other 4 X 037748679 008388694 1023/254/63 1023/254/63 05 extended 5 S 000000039 004194304 1023/254/63 1023/254/63 AF other 6 x 004194343 004194351 1023/254/63 1023/254/63 05 extended 7 S 000000047 004194304 1023/254/63 1023/254/63 AF other 8 S 000000000 000000000 0000/000/00 0000/000/00 00 empty entry 1 020971520 sectors 10737418240 bytes 2 010485536 sectors 5368594432 bytes 3 006291456 sectors 3221225472 bytes 5 004194304 sectors 2147483648 bytes 7 004194304 sectors 2147483648 bytes
Log Highlights:	====== Tool Settings: ====== segmentation Partition Aligned OS: Linux ubuntu 2.6.32-21-generic #32-Ubuntu SMP Fri Apr 16 08:10:02 UTC 2010 i686 GNU/Linux ====== Image file segments ====== 1 3710 2011-02-11 09:39 da-06-sata28 2 32256 2011-02-11 05:01 da-06-sata28.image.001 3 10737418240 2011-02-11 05:30 da-06-sata28.image.002 . . . 11 2147483648 2011-02-11 06:07 da-06-sata28.image.010 12 56404026880 2011-02-11 08:40 da-06-sata28.image.011 13 17544 2011-02-11 08:40 da-06-sata28.image.info ======== Excerpt from SMART log ======== Image Description... Make and Model: ATA ST380815AS Serial Number: 6QZ5C9V5 Device Sectors: 156,301,488 SHA1 Span Hashes

```
            total span hash: 70cc62b4 3f6a41ca 4d6760aa 0b9b4c41 5d3f48e2

            IO Summary:(Time: Fri Feb 11 13:40:49 2011)
            Bytes Read: 80,026,361,856
            80,026,361,856 bytes written to image "da-06-sata28"
            80,026,361,856 bytes written to image "da-06-sata28-image2"
            ======== End of Excerpt from SMART log ========

            ====== Source drive rehash ======
            Rehash (SHA1) of source: 70CC62B43F6A41CA4D6760AA0B9B4C415D3F48E2
```

Results:

Assertion and Expected Result	Actual Result
AM-01 Source acquired using interface AI.	as expected
AM-02 Source is type DS.	as expected
AM-03 Execution environment is XE.	as expected
AM-05 An image is created on file system type FS.	as expected
AM-06 All visible sectors acquired.	as expected
AM-08 All sectors accurately acquired.	as expected
AO-01 Image file is complete and accurate.	as expected
AO-05 Multifile image created.	as expected
AO-22 Tool calculates hashes by block.	option not tested
AO-23 Logged information is correct.	as expected
AO-24 Source is unchanged by acquisition.	as expected

Analysis: Expected results achieved

5.2.34　　DA-06-SATA28-IMAGE2

Test Case DA-06-SATA28-IMAGE2 Smart Version 2010/11/03	
Case Summary:	DA-06 Acquire a physical device using access interface AI to an image file.
Assertions:	AM-01 The tool uses access interface SRC-AI to access the digital source. AM-02 The tool acquires digital source DS. AM-03 The tool executes in execution environment XE. AM-05 If image file creation is specified, the tool creates an image file on file system type FS. AM-06 All visible sectors are acquired from the digital source. AM-08 All sectors acquired from the digital source are acquired accurately. AO-01 If the tool creates an image file, the data represented by the image file are the same as the data acquired by the tool. AO-05 If the tool creates a multifile image of a requested size then all the individual files shall be no larger than the requested size. AO-22 If requested, the tool calculates block hashes for a specified block size during an acquisition for each block acquired from the digital source. AO-23 If the tool logs any log significant information, the information is accurately recorded in the log file. AO-24 If the tool executes in a forensically safe execution environment, the digital source is unchanged by the acquisition process.
Tester Name:	brl
Test Host:	McGarrett
Test Date:	Fri Feb 11 09:50:53 2011
Drives:	src(4B-SATA) dst (none) other (5A-SATA)
Source Setup:	src hash (SHA1): < 70CC62B43F6A41CA4D6760AA0B9B4C415D3F48E2 > src hash (MD5): < 746B4C06CDD5FBD67C0820DB4325B40C > 156301488 total sectors (80026361856 bytes) Model (ST380815AS) serial # (6QZ5C9V5) N Start LBA Length Start C/H/S End C/H/S boot Partition type 1 P 000000063 020971520 0000/001/01 1023/254/63 AF other 2 P 020971629 010485536 1023/254/63 1023/254/63 AF other 3 P 031457223 006291456 1023/254/63 1023/254/63 A8 other 4 X 037748679 008388694 1023/254/63 1023/254/63 05 extended 5 S 000000039 004194304 1023/254/63 1023/254/63 AF other 6 x 004194343 004194351 1023/254/63 1023/254/63 05 extended 7 S 000000047 004194304 1023/254/63 1023/254/63 AF other 8 S 000000000 000000000 0000/000/00 0000/000/00 00 empty entry 1 020971520 sectors 10737418240 bytes 2 010485536 sectors 5368594432 bytes 3 006291456 sectors 3221225472 bytes 5 004194304 sectors 2147483648 bytes 7 004194304 sectors 2147483648 bytes
Log Highlights:	====== Tool Settings: ====== segmentation Partition Aligned OS: Linux ubuntu 2.6.32-21-generic #32-Ubuntu SMP Fri Apr 16 08:10:02 UTC 2010 i686 GNU/Linux ====== Image file segments ====== 1 6985 2011-02-11 09:39 da-06-sata28-image2 2 32256 2011-02-11 05:01 da-06-sata28-image2.image.001 3 10737418240 2011-02-11 05:30 da-06-sata28-image2.image.002 . . . 11 2147483648 2011-02-11 06:07 da-06-sata28-image2.image.010 12 56404026880 2011-02-11 08:40 da-06-sata28-image2.image.011 13 25627 2011-02-11 08:40 da-06-sata28-image2.image.info ======== Excerpt from SMART log ======== Image Description... Make and Model: ATA ST380815AS Serial Number: 6QZ5C9V5 Device Sectors: 156,301,488 SHA1 Span Hashes

```
        total span hash: 70cc62b4 3f6a41ca 4d6760aa 0b9b4c41 5d3f48e2

        IO Summary:(Time: Fri Feb 11 13:40:49 2011)
        Bytes Read: 80,026,361,856
        80,026,361,856 bytes written to image "da-06-sata28"
        80,026,361,856 bytes written to image "da-06-sata28-image2"
        ======== End of Excerpt from SMART log ========

        ====== Source drive rehash ======
        Rehash (SHA1) of source: 70CC62B43F6A41CA4D6760AA0B9B4C415D3F48E2
```

Results:	

Assertion and Expected Result	Actual Result
AM-01 Source acquired using interface AI.	as expected
AM-02 Source is type DS.	as expected
AM-03 Execution environment is XE.	as expected
AM-05 An image is created on file system type FS.	as expected
AM-06 All visible sectors acquired.	as expected
AM-08 All sectors accurately acquired.	as expected
AO-01 Image file is complete and accurate.	as expected
AO-05 Multifile image created.	as expected
AO-22 Tool calculates hashes by block.	option not tested
AO-23 Logged information is correct.	as expected
AO-24 Source is unchanged by acquisition.	as expected

Analysis:	Expected results achieved

5.2.35 DA-06-SATA48

Test Case DA-06-SATA48 Smart Version 2010/11/03	
Case Summary:	DA-06 Acquire a physical device using access interface AI to an image file.
Assertions:	AM-01 The tool uses access interface SRC-AI to access the digital source. AM-02 The tool acquires digital source DS. AM-03 The tool executes in execution environment XE. AM-05 If image file creation is specified, the tool creates an image file on file system type FS. AM-06 All visible sectors are acquired from the digital source. AM-08 All sectors acquired from the digital source are acquired accurately. AO-01 If the tool creates an image file, the data represented by the image file are the same as the data acquired by the tool. AO-05 If the tool creates a multifile image of a requested size then all the individual files shall be no larger than the requested size. AO-22 If requested, the tool calculates block hashes for a specified block size during an acquisition for each block acquired from the digital source. AO-23 If the tool logs any log significant information, the information is accurately recorded in the log file. AO-24 If the tool executes in a forensically safe execution environment, the digital source is unchanged by the acquisition process.
Tester Name:	brl
Test Host:	WoFat
Test Date:	Thu Feb 10 09:33:49 2011
Drives:	src(0D-SATA) dst (none) other (67-SATA)
Source Setup:	src hash (SHA1): < BAAD80E8781E55F2E3EF528CA73BD41D228C1377 > src hash (MD5): < 1FA7C3CBE60EB9E89863DED2411E40C9 > 488397168 total sectors (250059350016 bytes) 30400/254/63 (max cyl/hd values) 30401/255/63 (number of cyl/hd) Model (WDC WD2500JD-22F) serial # (WD-WMAEH2678216) N Start LBA Length Start C/H/S End C/H/S boot Partition type 1 P 000000063 488375937 0000/001/01 1023/254/63 Boot 07 NTFS 2 P 000000000 000000000 0000/000/00 0000/000/00 00 empty entry 3 P 000000000 000000000 0000/000/00 0000/000/00 00 empty entry 4 P 000000000 000000000 0000/000/00 0000/000/00 00 empty entry 1 488375937 sectors 250048479744 bytes
Log Highlights:	====== Tool Settings: ====== segmentation Standard OS: Linux ubuntu 2.6.32-21-generic #32-Ubuntu SMP Fri Apr 16 08:10:02 UTC 2010 i686 GNU/Linux ====== Image file segments ====== 1 3225 2011-02-10 15:00 da-06-sata48 2 250059350016 2011-02-10 14:46 da-06-sata48.image.001 3 4720 2011-02-10 14:46 da-06-sata48.image.info ======== Excerpt from SMART log ======== Image Description... Make and Model: ATA WDC WD2500JD-22F Serial Number: WD-WMAEH2678216 Device Sectors: 488,397,168 SHA1 Span Hashes total span hash: baad80e8 781e55f2 e3ef528c a73bd41d 228c1377 IO Summary:(Time: Thu Feb 10 14:46:21 2011) Bytes Read: 250,059,350,016 250,059,350,016 bytes written to image "da-06-sata48" ======== End of Excerpt from SMART log ======== ====== Source drive rehash ====== Rehash (SHA1) of source: BAAD80E8781E55F2E3EF528CA73BD41D228C1377

Results:

Assertion and Expected Result	Actual Result
AM-01 Source acquired using interface AI.	as expected
AM-02 Source is type DS.	as expected
AM-03 Execution environment is XE.	as expected
AM-05 An image is created on file system type FS.	as expected
AM-06 All visible sectors acquired.	as expected
AM-08 All sectors accurately acquired.	as expected
AO-01 Image file is complete and accurate.	as expected
AO-05 Multifile image created.	as expected
AO-22 Tool calculates hashes by block.	option not tested
AO-23 Logged information is correct.	as expected
AO-24 Source is unchanged by acquisition.	as expected

Analysis: Expected results achieved

5.2.36   DA-06-SCSI

Test Case DA-06-SCSI Smart Version 2010/11/03	
Case Summary:	DA-06 Acquire a physical device using access interface AI to an image file.
Assertions:	AM-01 The tool uses access interface SRC-AI to access the digital source. AM-02 The tool acquires digital source DS. AM-03 The tool executes in execution environment XE. AM-05 If image file creation is specified, the tool creates an image file on file system type FS. AM-06 All visible sectors are acquired from the digital source. AM-08 All sectors acquired from the digital source are acquired accurately. AO-01 If the tool creates an image file, the data represented by the image file are the same as the data acquired by the tool. AO-05 If the tool creates a multifile image of a requested size then all the individual files shall be no larger than the requested size. AO-22 If requested, the tool calculates block hashes for a specified block size during an acquisition for each block acquired from the digital source. AO-23 If the tool logs any log significant information, the information is accurately recorded in the log file. AO-24 If the tool executes in a forensically safe execution environment, the digital source is unchanged by the acquisition process.
Tester Name:	brl
Test Host:	Max
Test Date:	Tue Feb 8 15:03:13 2011
Drives:	src(E0) dst (none) other (3A-SATA)
Source Setup:	src hash (SHA1): < 4A6941F1337A8A22B10FC844B4D7FA6158BECB82 > src hash (MD5): < A97C8F36B7AC9D5233B90AC09284F938 > Reference SHA1 hashes, Win size: 4193792 (sectors) 1 0 - 4193791 E6589BB7F40DF7B5C62C7F81737E9D3554BE158D - 2 4193792 - 8387583 E5FF0E3954874B5A69BB54151670A76DDA493D9F - 3 8387584 - 12581375 674B40188B6E23456CB3A1EFCFB4CF5A6425FBC3 - 4 12581376 - 16775167 96D57D71F13BF2F6DB1DDEAA1772654930CF758A - 5 16775168 - 20968959 F0A0F715C3E177264AB36BDE9580CD40B58DC89A - 17938985 total sectors (9184760320 bytes) Model (ATLAS10K2-TY092J) serial # (169028142436)
Log Highlights:	====== Tool Settings: ====== segmentation Fixed Size(2GB) OS: Linux ubuntu 2.6.32-21-generic #32-Ubuntu SMP Fri Apr 16 08:10:02 UTC 2010 i686 GNU/Linux ====== Image file segments ====== 1 3897 2011-02-08 10:38 da-06-scsi 2 2147221504 2011-02-08 10:13 da-06-scsi.image.001 3 2147221504 2011-02-08 10:19 da-06-scsi.image.002 . . . 5 2147221504 2011-02-08 10:30 da-06-scsi.image.004 6 595874304 2011-02-08 10:31 da-06-scsi.image.005 7 5605 2011-02-08 10:32 da-06-scsi.image.info ======== Excerpt from SMART log ======== Image Description... Make and Model: QUANTUM ATLAS10K2-TY092J Serial Number: 169028142436 Device Sectors: 17,938,985 SHA1 Span Hashes total span hash: 4a6941f1 337a8a22 b10fc844 b4d7fa61 58becb82 SHA1 Segment-Delimited Span Hashes 1 0 - 2147221503: e6589bb7 f40df7b5 c62c7f81 737e9d35 54be158d 2 2147221504 - 4294443007: e5ff0e39 54874b5a 69bb5415 1670a76d da493d9f 3 4294443008 - 6441664511: 674b4018 8b6e2345 6cb3a1ef cfb4cf5a

```
                    6425fbc3
                     4      6441664512 - 8588886015: 96d57d71 f13bf2f6 db1ddeaa 17726549
                    30cf758a
                     5      8588886016 - 9184760319: f0a0f715 c3e17726 4ab36bde 9580cd40
                    b58dc89a

                    IO Summary:(Time: Tue Feb 8 15:32:02 2011)
                    Bytes Read: 9,184,760,320
                    9,184,760,320 bytes written to image "da-06-scsi"
                    ======== End of Excerpt from SMART log ========

                    ====== Source drive rehash ======
                    Rehash (SHA1) of source: 4A6941F1337A8A22B10FC844B4D7FA6158BECB82
```

	Assertion and Expected Result	Actual Result
Results:	AM-01 Source acquired using interface AI.	as expected
	AM-02 Source is type DS.	as expected
	AM-03 Execution environment is XE.	as expected
	AM-05 An image is created on file system type FS.	as expected
	AM-06 All visible sectors acquired.	as expected
	AM-08 All sectors accurately acquired.	as expected
	AO-01 Image file is complete and accurate.	as expected
	AO-05 Multifile image created.	as expected
	AO-22 Tool calculates hashes by block.	as expected
	AO-23 Logged information is correct.	as expected
	AO-24 Source is unchanged by acquisition.	as expected

Analysis:	Expected results achieved

5.2.37   DA-06-USB

Test Case DA-06-USB Smart Version 2010/11/03	
Case Summary:	DA-06 Acquire a physical device using access interface AI to an image file.
Assertions:	AM-01 The tool uses access interface SRC-AI to access the digital source. AM-02 The tool acquires digital source DS. AM-03 The tool executes in execution environment XE. AM-05 If image file creation is specified, the tool creates an image file on file system type FS. AM-06 All visible sectors are acquired from the digital source. AM-08 All sectors acquired from the digital source are acquired accurately. AO-01 If the tool creates an image file, the data represented by the image file are the same as the data acquired by the tool. AO-05 If the tool creates a multifile image of a requested size then all the individual files shall be no larger than the requested size. AO-22 If requested, the tool calculates block hashes for a specified block size during an acquisition for each block acquired from the digital source. AO-23 If the tool logs any log significant information, the information is accurately recorded in the log file. AO-24 If the tool executes in a forensically safe execution environment, the digital source is unchanged by the acquisition process.
Tester Name:	brl
Test Host:	Max
Test Date:	Fri Feb 11 08:49:44 2011
Drives:	src(63-FU2) dst (none) other (3A-SATA)
Source Setup:	src hash (SHA1): < F7069EDCBEAC863C88DECED82159F22DA96BE99B > src hash (MD5): < EE217BC4FA4F3D1B4021D29B065AA9EC > 117304992 total sectors (60060155904 bytes) Model (SP0612N) serial # () <pre>N Start LBA Length Start C/H/S End C/H/S boot Partition type 1 P 000000063 004192902 0000/001/01 0260/254/63 Boot 06 Fat16 2 X 004192965 113097600 0261/000/01 1023/254/63 0F extended 3 S 000000063 113097537 0261/000/01 1023/254/63 0B Fat32 4 S 000000000 000000000 0000/000/00 0000/000/00 00 empty entry 5 P 000000000 000000000 0000/000/00 0000/000/00 00 empty entry 6 P 000000000 000000000 0000/000/00 0000/000/00 00 empty entry 1 004192902 sectors 2146765824 bytes 3 113097537 sectors 57905938944 bytes</pre>
Log Highlights:	====== Tool Settings: ====== segmentation Standard OS: Linux ubuntu 2.6.32-21-generic #32-Ubuntu SMP Fri Apr 16 08:10:02 UTC 2010 i686 GNU/Linux ====== Image file segments ====== <pre>1 3410 2011-02-11 12:31 da-06-usb 2 60060155904 2011-02-11 11:35 da-06-usb.image.001 3 7492 2011-02-11 11:35 da-06-usb.image.info</pre> ======== Excerpt from SMART log ======== Image Description... Make and Model: SAMSUNG SP0612N Device Sectors: 117,304,992 SHA1 Span Hashes total span hash: f7069edc beac863c 88deced8 2159f22d a96be99b IO Summary:(Time: Fri Feb 11 11:35:42 2011) Bytes Read: 60,060,155,904 60,060,155,904 bytes written to image "da-06-usb" ======== End of Excerpt from SMART log ======== ====== Source drive rehash ====== Rehash (SHA1) of source: F7069EDCBEAC863C88DECED82159F22DA96BE99B

Test Case DA-06-USB Smart Version 2010/11/03

Results:

Assertion and Expected Result	Actual Result
AM-01 Source acquired using interface AI.	as expected
AM-02 Source is type DS.	as expected
AM-03 Execution environment is XE.	as expected
AM-05 An image is created on file system type FS.	as expected
AM-06 All visible sectors acquired.	as expected
AM-08 All sectors accurately acquired.	as expected
AO-01 Image file is complete and accurate.	as expected
AO-05 Multifile image created.	as expected
AO-22 Tool calculates hashes by block.	option not tested
AO-23 Logged information is correct.	as expected
AO-24 Source is unchanged by acquisition.	as expected

Analysis: Expected results achieved

5.2.38 DA-07-CF

Test Case DA-07-CF Smart Version 2010/11/03	
Case Summary:	DA-07 Acquire a digital source of type DS to an image file.
Assertions:	AM-01 The tool uses access interface SRC-AI to access the digital source. AM-02 The tool acquires digital source DS. AM-03 The tool executes in execution environment XE. AM-05 If image file creation is specified, the tool creates an image file on file system type FS. AM-06 All visible sectors are acquired from the digital source. AM-08 All sectors acquired from the digital source are acquired accurately. AO-01 If the tool creates an image file, the data represented by the image file is the same as the data acquired by the tool. AO-05 If the tool creates a multifile image of a requested size then all the individual files shall be no larger than the requested size. AO-22 If requested, the tool calculates block hashes for a specified block size during an acquisition for each block acquired from the digital source. AO-23 If the tool logs any log significant information, the information is accurately recorded in the log file. AO-24 If the tool executes in a forensically safe execution environment, the digital source is unchanged by the acquisition process.
Tester Name:	brl
Test Host:	Max
Test Date:	Tue Feb 15 09:43:07 2011
Drives:	src(C1-CF) dst (none) other (3A-SATA)

Source Setup:	src hash (SHA1): < 5B8235178DF99FA307430C088F81746606638A0B >
	src hash (MD5): < 776DF8B4D2589E21DEBCF589EDC16D78 >
	
	Reference MD5 hashes, Win size: 245248 (sectors)
	  1 0 - 245247 DFB67FA9539278F2B167407E05C88458 -
	  2 245248 - 490495 71E39B26895582AE06DA7CF2CC113865 -
	  3 490496 - 735743 6F545BC113A824B0E57B7E699C23DA06 -
	503808 total sectors (257949696 bytes)
	Model (CF) serial # ()
	N Start LBA Length Start C/H/S End C/H/S boot Partition type
	1 P 778135908 1141509631 0357/116/40 0357/032/45 Boot 72 other
	2 P 168689522 1936028240 0288/115/43 0367/114/50 Boot 65 other
	3 P 1869881465 1936028192 0366/032/33 0357/032/43 Boot 79 other
	4 P 2885681152 000055499 0372/097/50 0000/010/00 Boot 0D other
	1 1141509631 sectors 584452931072 bytes
	2 1936028240 sectors 991246458880 bytes
	3 1936028192 sectors 991246434304 bytes
	4 000055499 sectors 28415488 bytes

Log Highlights:	====== Tool Settings: ======
	segmentation Fixed Size (120 MB)
	
	OS: Linux ubuntu 2.6.32-21-generic #32-Ubuntu SMP Fri Apr 16 08:10:02 UTC 2010 i686 GNU/Linux
	
	====== Image file segments ======
	  1 3464 2011-02-15 05:10 da-07-cf
	  2 125566976 2011-02-15 04:55 da-07-cf.image.001
	  3 125566976 2011-02-15 04:57 da-07-cf.image.002
	  4 6815744 2011-02-15 04:58 da-07-cf.image.003
	  5 4161 2011-02-15 04:58 da-07-cf.image.info
	======== Excerpt from SMART log ========
	
	Image Description...
	Make and Model: USB2.0 HS-CF
	Device Sectors: 503,808
	FS Type: FAT32
	OS FS Type: vfat
	Volume Name: NO NAME
	Max. Filesize: 2.000 GB

```
MD5 Span Hashes
 total span hash: 776df8b4d2589e21debcf589edc16d78

MD5 Segment-Delimited Span Hashes
 1      0 - 125566975: dfb67fa9539278f2b167407e05c88458
 2      125566976 - 251133951: 71e39b26895582ae06da7cf2cc113865
 3      251133952 - 257949695: 6f545bc113a824b0e57b7e699c23da06

IO Summary:(Time: Tue Feb 15 09:58:04 2011)
Bytes Read: 257,949,696
257,949,696 bytes written to image "da-07-cf"
======== End of Excerpt from SMART log ========

====== Source drive rehash ======
Rehash (SHA1) of source: 5B8235178DF99FA307430C088F81746606638A0B
```

Results:

Assertion and Expected Result	Actual Result
AM-01 Source acquired using interface AI.	as expected
AM-02 Source is type DS.	as expected
AM-03 Execution environment is XE.	as expected
AM-05 An image is created on file system type FS.	as expected
AM-06 All visible sectors acquired.	as expected
AM-08 All sectors accurately acquired.	as expected
AO-01 Image file is complete and accurate.	as expected
AO-05 Multifile image created.	as expected
AO-22 Tool calculates hashes by block.	as expected
AO-23 Logged information is correct.	as expected
AO-24 Source is unchanged by acquisition.	as expected

Analysis: Expected results achieved

5.2.39 DA-07-EXT2

Test Case DA-07-EXT2 Smart Version 2010/11/03	
Case Summary:	DA-07 Acquire a digital source of type DS to an image file.
Assertions:	AM-01 The tool uses access interface SRC-AI to access the digital source. AM-02 The tool acquires digital source DS. AM-03 The tool executes in execution environment XE. AM-05 If image file creation is specified, the tool creates an image file on file system type FS. AM-06 All visible sectors are acquired from the digital source. AM-08 All sectors acquired from the digital source are acquired accurately. AO-01 If the tool creates an image file, the data represented by the image file is the same as the data acquired by the tool. AO-05 If the tool creates a multifile image of a requested size then all the individual files shall be no larger than the requested size. AO-22 If requested, the tool calculates block hashes for a specified block size during an acquisition for each block acquired from the digital source. AO-23 If the tool logs any log significant information, the information is accurately recorded in the log file. AO-24 If the tool executes in a forensically safe execution environment, the digital source is unchanged by the acquisition process.
Tester Name:	brl
Test Host:	McGarrett
Test Date:	Mon Feb 28 13:52:20 2011
Drives:	src(43) dst (none) other (3A-SATA)

Source Setup:	src hash (SHA1): < 888E2E7F7AD237DC7A732281DD93F325065E5871 >
	src hash (MD5): < BC39C3F7EE7A50E77B9BA1E65A5AEEF7 >
	
	Reference SHA1 hashes, Win size: 4193792 (sectors) 2147221504 (bytes)
	  1 0 - 4193791 3E62C6B5B7F62262E670857BEAD459ED1A968214 -
	  2 4193792 - 8387583 A804E0B2935D9E457E26359ED0CDFA8AD4B53496 -
	  3 8387584 - 10490381 D9406898C56FB4B179014175A05CC694416EA626 -
	78125000 total sectors (40000000000 bytes)
	Model (0BB-75JHC0) serial # (WD-WMAMC46588)
	N Start LBA Length Start C/H/S End C/H/S boot Partition type
	 1 P 000000063 020980827 0000/001/01 1023/254/63 0C Fat32X
	 2 X 020980890 057143205 1023/000/01 1023/254/63 0F extended
	 3 S 000000063 000032067 1023/001/01 1023/254/63 01 Fat12
	 4 x 000032130 002104515 1023/000/01 1023/254/63 05 extended
	 5 S 000000063 002104452 1023/001/01 1023/254/63 06 Fat16
	 6 x 002136645 004192965 1023/000/01 1023/254/63 05 extended
	 7 S 000000063 004192902 1023/001/01 1023/254/63 16 other
	 8 x 006329610 008401995 1023/000/01 1023/254/63 05 extended
	 9 S 000000063 008401932 1023/001/01 1023/254/63 0B Fat32
	10 x 014731605 010490445 1023/000/01 1023/254/63 05 extended
	11 S 000000063 010490382 1023/001/01 1023/254/63 83 Linux
	12 x 025222050 004209030 1023/000/01 1023/254/63 05 extended
	13 S 000000063 004208967 1023/001/01 1023/254/63 82 Linux swap
	14 x 029431080 027712125 1023/000/01 1023/254/63 05 extended
	15 S 000000063 027712062 1023/001/01 1023/254/63 07 NTFS
	16 S 000000000 000000000 0000/000/00 0000/000/00 00 empty entry
	17 P 000000000 000000000 0000/000/00 0000/000/00 00 empty entry
	18 P 000000000 000000000 0000/000/00 0000/000/00 00 empty entry
	1 020980827 sectors 10742183424 bytes
	3 000032067 sectors 16418304 bytes
	5 002104452 sectors 1077479424 bytes
	7 004192902 sectors 2146765824 bytes
	9 008401932 sectors 4301789184 bytes
	11 010490382 sectors 5371075584 bytes
	13 004208967 sectors 2154991104 bytes
	15 027712062 sectors 14188575744 bytes
	43ext2-md5sum 5371075583 C7A84DE9ACBCB05463604CE8823D0874
	43ext2-sha1sum 5371075583 283BCC32DE892C12C37698AF7E38703619E57F57

Log Highlights:	====== Tool Settings: ====== segmentation Transport Media (2GB)

```
OS: Linux ubuntu 2.6.32-21-generic #32-Ubuntu SMP Fri Apr 16 08:10:02 UTC
2010 i686 GNU/Linux


====== Image file segments ======
1       1034 2011-02-28 14:43 da-07-ext2
2       2147221504 2011-02-28 14:03 da-07-ext2.image.001
3       2147221504 2011-02-28 14:11 da-07-ext2.image.002
4       1076632576 2011-02-28 14:14 da-07-ext2.image.003
5       4410 2011-02-28 14:14 da-07-ext2.image.info
======== Excerpt from SMART log ========


SHA1 Span Hashes
 total span hash: 283bcc32 de892c12 c37698af 7e387036 19e57f57

SHA1 Segment-Delimited Span Hashes
1       0 - 2147221503: 3e62c6b5 b7f62262 e670857b ead459ed 1a968214
2       2147221504 - 4294443007: a804e0b2 935d9e45 7e26359e d0cdfa8a
d4b53496
3       4294443008 - 5371075583: d9406898 c56fb4b1 79014175 a05cc694
416ea626

IO Summary:(Time: Mon Feb 28 14:14:58 2011)
Bytes Read: 5,371,075,584
5,371,075,584 bytes written to image "da-07-ext2"
======== End of Excerpt from SMART log ========

====== Source drive rehash ======
Rehash (SHA1) of source: 888E2E7F7AD237DC7A732281DD93F325065E5871
```

	Assertion and Expected Result	Actual Result
Results:		
	AM-01 Source acquired using interface AI.	as expected
	AM-02 Source is type DS.	as expected
	AM-03 Execution environment is XE.	as expected
	AM-05 An image is created on file system type FS.	as expected
	AM-06 All visible sectors acquired.	as expected
	AM-08 All sectors accurately acquired.	as expected
	AO-01 Image file is complete and accurate.	as expected
	AO-05 Multifile image created.	as expected
	AO-22 Tool calculates hashes by block.	as expected
	AO-23 Logged information is correct.	as expected
	AO-24 Source is unchanged by acquisition.	as expected

Analysis:	Expected results achieved

5.2.40   DA-07-F12

Test Case DA-07-F12 Smart Version 2010/11/03	
Case Summary:	DA-07 Acquire a digital source of type DS to an image file.
Assertions:	AM-01 The tool uses access interface SRC-AI to access the digital source. AM-02 The tool acquires digital source DS. AM-03 The tool executes in execution environment XE. AM-05 If image file creation is specified, the tool creates an image file on file system type FS. AM-06 All visible sectors are acquired from the digital source. AM-08 All sectors acquired from the digital source are acquired accurately. AO-01 If the tool creates an image file, the data represented by the image file are the same as the data acquired by the tool. AO-05 If the tool creates a multifile image of a requested size then all the individual files shall be no larger than the requested size. AO-22 If requested, the tool calculates block hashes for a specified block size during an acquisition for each block acquired from the digital source. AO-23 If the tool logs any log significant information, the information is accurately recorded in the log file. AO-24 If the tool executes in a forensically safe execution environment, the digital source is unchanged by the acquisition process.
Tester Name:	brl
Test Host:	McGarrett
Test Date:	Tue Mar 1 13:41:22 2011
Drives:	src(43) dst (none) other (3A-SATA)
Source Setup:	src hash (SHA1): < 888E2E7F7AD237DC7A732281DD93F325065E5871 > src hash (MD5): < BC39C3F7EE7A50E77B9BA1E65A5AEEF7 > 78125000 total sectors (40000000000 bytes) Model (0BB-75JHC0) serial # (WD-WMAMC46588) N Start LBA Length Start C/H/S End C/H/S boot Partition type 1 P 000000063 020980827 0000/001/01 1023/254/63 0C Fat32X 2 X 020980890 057143205 1023/000/01 1023/254/63 0F extended 3 S 000000063 000032067 1023/001/01 1023/254/63 01 Fat12 4 x 000032130 002104515 1023/000/01 1023/254/63 05 extended 5 S 000000063 002104452 1023/001/01 1023/254/63 06 Fat16 6 x 002136645 004192965 1023/000/01 1023/254/63 05 extended 7 S 000000063 004192902 1023/001/01 1023/254/63 16 other 8 x 006329610 008401995 1023/000/01 1023/254/63 05 extended 9 S 000000063 008401932 1023/001/01 1023/254/63 0B Fat32 10 x 014731605 010490445 1023/000/01 1023/254/63 05 extended 11 S 000000063 010490382 1023/001/01 1023/254/63 83 Linux 12 x 025222050 004209030 1023/000/01 1023/254/63 05 extended 13 S 000000063 004208967 1023/001/01 1023/254/63 82 Linux swap 14 x 029431080 027712125 1023/000/01 1023/254/63 05 extended 15 S 000000063 027712062 1023/001/01 1023/254/63 07 NTFS 16 S 000000000 000000000 0000/000/00 0000/000/00 00 empty entry 17 P 000000000 000000000 0000/000/00 0000/000/00 00 empty entry 18 P 000000000 000000000 0000/000/00 0000/000/00 00 empty entry 1 020980827 sectors 10742183424 bytes 3 000032067 sectors 16418304 bytes 5 002104452 sectors 1077479424 bytes 7 004192902 sectors 2146765824 bytes 9 008401932 sectors 4301789184 bytes 11 010490382 sectors 5371075584 bytes 13 004208967 sectors 2154991104 bytes 15 027712062 sectors 14188575744 bytes 43F12-md5sum 16418303 CBA0C9984F51778E89DEF0C6BED06864 43F12-sha1sum 16418303 6853B517F50BF3CCADED3DB5FEAE08C18C62FCA0
Log Highlights:	====== Tool Settings: ====== segmentation Standard OS: Linux ubuntu 2.6.32-21-generic #32-Ubuntu SMP Fri Apr 16 08:10:02 UTC 2010 i686 GNU/Linux ====== Image file segments ======

```
Test Case DA-07-F12 Smart Version 2010/11/03
        1      2897 2011-03-01 13:57 da-07-f12
        2   16418304 2011-03-01 13:52 da-07-f12.image.001
        3      2384 2011-03-01 13:52 da-07-f12.image.info
        ======== Excerpt from SMART log ========

        FS Type: FAT12
        OS FS Type: vfat
        Volume Name: F12
        Max. Filesize: 2.000 GB

        SHA1 Span Hashes
         total span hash: 6853b517 f50bf3cc aded3db5 feae08c1 8c62fca0

        IO Summary:(Time: Tue Mar 1 13:52:14 2011)
        Bytes Read: 16,418,304
        16,418,304 bytes written to image "da-07-f12"
        ======== End of Excerpt from SMART log ========

        ====== Source drive rehash ======
        Rehash (SHA1) of source: 888E2E7F7AD237DC7A732281DD93F325065E5871
```

Results:	Assertion and Expected Result	Actual Result
	AM-01 Source acquired using interface AI.	as expected
	AM-02 Source is type DS.	as expected
	AM-03 Execution environment is XE.	as expected
	AM-05 An image is created on file system type FS.	as expected
	AM-06 All visible sectors acquired.	as expected
	AM-08 All sectors accurately acquired.	as expected
	AO-01 Image file is complete and accurate.	as expected
	AO-05 Multifile image created.	as expected
	AO-22 Tool calculates hashes by block.	option not tested
	AO-23 Logged information is correct.	as expected
	AO-24 Source is unchanged by acquisition.	as expected

Analysis:	Expected results achieved

5.2.41   DA-07-F16

Test Case DA-07-F16 Smart Version 2010/11/03	
Case Summary:	DA-07 Acquire a digital source of type DS to an image file.
Assertions:	AM-01 The tool uses access interface SRC-AI to access the digital source. AM-02 The tool acquires digital source DS. AM-03 The tool executes in execution environment XE. AM-05 If image file creation is specified, the tool creates an image file on file system type FS. AM-06 All visible sectors are acquired from the digital source. AM-08 All sectors acquired from the digital source are acquired accurately. AO-01 If the tool creates an image file, the data represented by the image file are the same as the data acquired by the tool. AO-05 If the tool creates a multifile image of a requested size then all the individual files shall be no larger than the requested size. AO-22 If requested, the tool calculates block hashes for a specified block size during an acquisition for each block acquired from the digital source. AO-23 If the tool logs any log significant information, the information is accurately recorded in the log file. AO-24 If the tool executes in a forensically safe execution environment, the digital source is unchanged by the acquisition process.
Tester Name:	brl
Test Host:	McGarrett
Test Date:	Tue Mar 1 15:30:22 2011
Drives:	src(01-IDE) dst (none) other (3A-SATA)

Source Setup:	src hash (SHA1): < A48BB5665D6DC57C22DB68E2F723DA9AA8DF82B9 >
	src hash (MD5): < F458F673894753FA6A0EC8B8EC63848E >
	
	Reference MD5 hashes, Win size: 1330688 (sectors)
	  1 0 - 1330687 B5B8419FE6F5C18E13A0F7220A209659 -
	  2 1330688 - 2661375 8E3880213F96D4B4EF9D6D460B831B1B -
	
	Reference SHA1 hashes, Win size: 1330688 (sectors)
	  1 0 - 1330687 66436779F2547289EB42CA2A724316410F7BE5AF -
	  2 1330688 - 2661375 5E6ACAD3878A057FC6AC00A5D526151789259D4D -
	78165360 total sectors (40020664320 bytes)
	Model (0BB-00JHC0) serial # (WD-WMAMC74171)
	 N Start LBA Length Start C/H/S End C/H/S boot Partition type
	 1 P 000000063 020980827 0000/001/01 1023/254/63 0C Fat32X
	 2 X 020980890 057175335 1023/000/01 1023/254/63 0F extended
	 3 S 000000063 000032067 1023/001/01 1023/254/63 01 Fat12
	 4 x 000032130 002104515 1023/000/01 1023/254/63 05 extended
	 5 S 000000063 002104452 1023/001/01 1023/254/63 06 Fat16
	 6 x 002136645 004192965 1023/000/01 1023/254/63 05 extended
	 7 S 000000063 004192902 1023/001/01 1023/254/63 16 other
	 8 x 006329610 008401995 1023/000/01 1023/254/63 05 extended
	 9 S 000000063 008401932 1023/001/01 1023/254/63 0B Fat32
	10 x 014731605 010490445 1023/000/01 1023/254/63 05 extended
	11 S 000000063 010490382 1023/001/01 1023/254/63 83 Linux
	12 x 025222050 004209030 1023/000/01 1023/254/63 05 extended
	13 S 000000063 004208967 1023/001/01 1023/254/63 82 Linux swap
	14 x 029431080 027744255 1023/000/01 1023/254/63 05 extended
	15 S 000000063 027744192 1023/001/01 1023/254/63 07 NTFS
	16 S 000000000 000000000 0000/000/00 0000/000/00 00 empty entry
	17 P 000000000 000000000 0000/000/00 0000/000/00 00 empty entry
	18 P 000000000 000000000 0000/000/00 0000/000/00 00 empty entry
	1 020980827 sectors 10742183424 bytes
	3 000032067 sectors 16418304 bytes
	5 002104452 sectors 1077479424 bytes
	7 004192902 sectors 2146765824 bytes
	9 008401932 sectors 4301789184 bytes
	11 010490382 sectors 5371075584 bytes
	13 004208967 sectors 2154991104 bytes
	15 027744192 sectors 14205026304 bytes
	01F16-md5 1077479423 8B24F3D793188AF2473F69B267AFDA42
	01F16-sha1 1077479423 074BA831B10132F4BF9F86AFAB37CB7FEF482C7D

Log	

```
Test Case DA-07-F16 Smart Version 2010/11/03
```

| Highlights: | ```
====== Tool Settings: ======
segmentation Fixed Size (650 MB)

OS: Linux ubuntu 2.6.32-21-generic #32-Ubuntu SMP Fri Apr 16 08:10:02 UTC
2010 i686 GNU/Linux


====== Image file segments ======
1       4095 2011-03-01 16:00 da-07-f16
2   681312256 2011-03-01 15:50 da-07-fat16.image.001
3   396167168 2011-03-01 15:51 da-07-fat16.image.002
4       5730 2011-03-01 15:51 da-07-fat16.image.info
======== Excerpt from SMART log ========

FS Type: FAT16
OS FS Type: vfat
Volume Name: F16
Max. Filesize: 2.000 GB

SHA1 Span Hashes
 total span hash: 074ba831 b10132f4 bf9f86af ab37cb7f ef482c7d
MD5 Span Hashes
 total span hash: 8b24f3d793188af2473f69b267afda42

MD5 Segment-Delimited Span Hashes
1       0 - 681312255: b5b8419fe6f5c18e13a0f7220a209659
2       681312256 - 1077479423: 8e3880213f96d4b4ef9d6d460b831b1b

SHA1 Segment-Delimited Span Hashes
1       0 - 681312255: 66436779 f2547289 eb42ca2a 72431641 0f7be5af
2       681312256 - 1077479423: 5e6acad3 878a057f c6ac00a5 d5261517
89259d4d

IO Summary:(Time: Tue Mar 1 15:51:28 2011)
Bytes Read: 1,077,479,424
1,077,479,424 bytes written to image "da-07-fat16"
======== End of Excerpt from SMART log ========


====== Source drive rehash ======
Rehash (SHA1) of source: A48BB5665D6DC57C22DB68E2F723DA9AA8DF82B9
``` |
| Results: | |

Assertion and Expected Result	Actual Result
AM-01 Source acquired using interface AI.	as expected
AM-02 Source is type DS.	as expected
AM-03 Execution environment is XE.	as expected
AM-05 An image is created on file system type FS.	as expected
AM-06 All visible sectors acquired.	as expected
AM-08 All sectors accurately acquired.	as expected
AO-01 Image file is complete and accurate.	as expected
AO-05 Multifile image created.	as expected
AO-22 Tool calculates hashes by block.	as expected
AO-23 Logged information is correct.	as expected
AO-24 Source is unchanged by acquisition.	as expected

Analysis:	Expected results achieved
```

5.2.42   DA-07-F32

Test Case DA-07-F32 Smart Version 2010/11/03	
Case Summary:	DA-07 Acquire a digital source of type DS to an image file.
Assertions:	AM-01 The tool uses access interface SRC-AI to access the digital source. AM-02 The tool acquires digital source DS. AM-03 The tool executes in execution environment XE. AM-05 If image file creation is specified, the tool creates an image file on file system type FS. AM-06 All visible sectors are acquired from the digital source. AM-08 All sectors acquired from the digital source are acquired accurately. AO-01 If the tool creates an image file, the data represented by the image file are the same as the data acquired by the tool. AO-05 If the tool creates a multifile image of a requested size then all the individual files shall be no larger than the requested size. AO-22 If requested, the tool calculates block hashes for a specified block size during an acquisition for each block acquired from the digital source. AO-23 If the tool logs any log significant information, the information is accurately recorded in the log file. AO-24 If the tool executes in a forensically safe execution environment, the digital source is unchanged by the acquisition process.
Tester Name:	brl
Test Host:	McGarrett
Test Date:	Wed Mar 2 09:30:56 2011
Drives:	src(43) dst (none) other (3A-SATA)
Source Setup:	src hash (SHA1): < 888E2E7F7AD237DC7A732281DD93F325065E5871 > src hash (MD5): < BC39C3F7EE7A50E77B9BA1E65A5AEEF7 > 78125000 total sectors (40000000000 bytes) Model (0BB-75JHC0) serial # (WD-WMAMC46588) N Start LBA Length Start C/H/S End C/H/S boot Partition type 1 P 000000063 020980827 0000/001/01 1023/254/63 0C Fat32X 2 X 020980890 057143205 1023/000/01 1023/254/63 0F extended 3 S 000000063 000032067 1023/001/01 1023/254/63 01 Fat12 4 x 000032130 002104515 1023/000/01 1023/254/63 05 extended 5 S 000000063 002104452 1023/001/01 1023/254/63 06 Fat16 6 x 002136645 004192965 1023/000/01 1023/254/63 05 extended 7 S 000000063 004192902 1023/001/01 1023/254/63 16 other 8 x 006329610 008401995 1023/000/01 1023/254/63 05 extended 9 S 000000063 008401932 1023/001/01 1023/254/63 0B Fat32 10 x 014731605 010490445 1023/000/01 1023/254/63 05 extended 11 S 000000063 010490382 1023/001/01 1023/254/63 83 Linux 12 x 025222050 004209030 1023/000/01 1023/254/63 05 extended 13 S 000000063 004208967 1023/001/01 1023/254/63 82 Linux swap 14 x 029431080 027712125 1023/000/01 1023/254/63 05 extended 15 S 000000063 027712062 1023/001/01 1023/254/63 07 NTFS 16 S 000000000 000000000 0000/000/00 0000/000/00 00 empty entry 17 P 000000000 000000000 0000/000/00 0000/000/00 00 empty entry 18 P 000000000 000000000 0000/000/00 0000/000/00 00 empty entry 1 020980827 sectors 10742183424 bytes 3 000032067 sectors 16418304 bytes 5 002104452 sectors 1077479424 bytes 7 004192902 sectors 2146765824 bytes 9 008401932 sectors 4301789184 bytes 11 010490382 sectors 5371075584 bytes 13 004208967 sectors 2154991104 bytes 15 027712062 sectors 14188575744 bytes 43F32-md5sum 4301789183 2C4D8D450E5AD28329F616D87114CCFE 43F32-sha1sum 4301789183 72462489BCF79A98B59B6A8CD938FEB46FA2A781
Log Highlights:	====== Tool Settings: ====== segmentation Standard OS: Linux ubuntu 2.6.32-21-generic #32-Ubuntu SMP Fri Apr 16 08:10:02 UTC 2010 i686 GNU/Linux ====== Image file segments ======

```
Test Case DA-07-F32 Smart Version 2010/11/03
           1     2903 2011-03-02 10:11 da-07-f32
           2     4301789184 2011-03-02 09:42 da-07-f32.image.001
           3     2393 2011-03-02 09:42 da-07-f32.image.info
        ======== Excerpt from SMART log ========

        FS Type: FAT32
        OS FS Type: vfat
        Volume Name: F32
        Max. Filesize: 2.000 GB

        SHA1 Span Hashes
         total span hash: 72462489 bcf79a98 b59b6a8c d938feb4 6fa2a781

        IO Summary:(Time: Wed Mar 2 09:42:39 2011)
        Bytes Read: 4,301,789,184
        4,301,789,184 bytes written to image "da-07-f32"
        ======== End of Excerpt from SMART log ========

        ====== Source drive rehash ======
        Rehash (SHA1) of source: 888E2E7F7AD237DC7A732281DD93F325065E5871
```

Results:

Assertion and Expected Result	Actual Result
AM-01 Source acquired using interface AI.	as expected
AM-02 Source is type DS.	as expected
AM-03 Execution environment is XE.	as expected
AM-05 An image is created on file system type FS.	as expected
AM-06 All visible sectors acquired.	as expected
AM-08 All sectors accurately acquired.	as expected
AO-01 Image file is complete and accurate.	as expected
AO-05 Multifile image created.	as expected
AO-22 Tool calculates hashes by block.	option not tested
AO-23 Logged information is correct.	as expected
AO-24 Source is unchanged by acquisition.	as expected

Analysis: Expected results achieved

5.2.43   DA-07-F32X

Test Case DA-07-F32X Smart Version 2010/11/03	
Case Summary:	DA-07 Acquire a digital source of type DS to an image file.
Assertions:	AM-01 The tool uses access interface SRC-AI to access the digital source. AM-02 The tool acquires digital source DS. AM-03 The tool executes in execution environment XE. AM-05 If image file creation is specified, the tool creates an image file on file system type FS. AM-06 All visible sectors are acquired from the digital source. AM-08 All sectors acquired from the digital source are acquired accurately. AO-01 If the tool creates an image file, the data represented by the image file are the same as the data acquired by the tool. AO-05 If the tool creates a multifile image of a requested size then all the individual files shall be no larger than the requested size. AO-22 If requested, the tool calculates block hashes for a specified block size during an acquisition for each block acquired from the digital source. AO-23 If the tool logs any log significant information, the information is accurately recorded in the log file. AO-24 If the tool executes in a forensically safe execution environment, the digital source is unchanged by the acquisition process.
Tester Name:	brl
Test Host:	McGarrett
Test Date:	Wed Mar 2 11:40:54 2011
Drives:	src(01-IDE) dst (none) other (3A-SATA)

Source Setup:	src hash (SHA1): < A48BB5665D6DC57C22DB68E2F723DA9AA8DF82B9 >
	src hash (MD5): < F458F673894753FA6A0EC8B8EC63848E >
	
	Reference SHA1 hashes, Win size: 8388096 (sectors)
	  1 0 - 8388095 00C863AB485A389BA57D5CD73E0E0D7F6B2909D4 -
	  2 8388096 - 16776191 AD945E125ADB0C69FC7C0BD77E94111983CB718F -
	  3 16776192 - 25164287 C4FCFBA0B7403B529C494BD71936C2499617839A -
	78165360 total sectors (40020664320 bytes)
	Model (0BB-00JHC0) serial # (WD-WMAMC74171)
	N Start LBA Length Start C/H/S End C/H/S boot Partition type
	 1 P 000000063 020980827 0000/001/01 1023/254/63 0C Fat32X
	 2 X 020980890 057175335 1023/000/01 1023/254/63 0F extended
	 3 S 000000063 000032067 1023/001/01 1023/254/63 01 Fat12
	 4 x 000032130 002104515 1023/000/01 1023/254/63 05 extended
	 5 S 000000063 002104452 1023/001/01 1023/254/63 06 Fat16
	 6 x 002136645 004192965 1023/000/01 1023/254/63 05 extended
	 7 S 000000063 004192902 1023/001/01 1023/254/63 16 other
	 8 x 006329610 008401995 1023/000/01 1023/254/63 05 extended
	 9 S 000000063 008401932 1023/001/01 1023/254/63 0B Fat32
	10 x 014731605 010490445 1023/000/01 1023/254/63 05 extended
	11 S 000000063 010490382 1023/001/01 1023/254/63 83 Linux
	12 x 025222050 004209030 1023/000/01 1023/254/63 05 extended
	13 S 000000063 004208967 1023/001/01 1023/254/63 82 Linux swap
	14 x 029431080 027744255 1023/000/01 1023/254/63 05 extended
	15 S 000000063 027744192 1023/001/01 1023/254/63 07 NTFS
	16 S 000000000 000000000 0000/000/00 0000/000/00 00 empty entry
	17 P 000000000 000000000 0000/000/00 0000/000/00 00 empty entry
	18 P 000000000 000000000 0000/000/00 0000/000/00 00 empty entry
	1 020980827 sectors 10742183424 bytes
	3 000032067 sectors 16418304 bytes
	5 002104452 sectors 1077479424 bytes
	7 004192902 sectors 2146765824 bytes
	9 008401932 sectors 4301789184 bytes
	11 010490382 sectors 5371075584 bytes
	13 004208967 sectors 2154991104 bytes
	15 027744192 sectors 14205026304 bytes
	01F32X-md5 10742183423 B5BFD9CE3990C577EF89C5AFB925F947
	01F32X-sha1 10742183423 30BA6CF583A176C5DB533E3A2F57BFD5A4A870C1

Log Highlights:	====== Tool Settings: ====== segmentation Fixed Size (4 GB)

```
OS: Linux ubuntu 2.6.32-21-generic #32-Ubuntu SMP Fri Apr 16 08:10:02 UTC
2010 i686 GNU/Linux


====== Image file segments ======
1       3506 2011-03-02 14:59 da-07-f32x
2       4294705152 2011-03-02 14:43 da-07-f32x.image.001
3       4294705152 2011-03-02 14:49 da-07-f32x.image.002
4       2152773120 2011-03-02 14:52 da-07-f32x.image.003
5       4307 2011-03-02 14:52 da-07-f32x.image.info
======== Excerpt from SMART log ========

FS Type: FAT32
OS FS Type: vfat
Volume Name: F32X
Max. Filesize: 2.000 GB

SHA1 Span Hashes
 total span hash: 30ba6cf5 83a176c5 db533e3a 2f57bfd5 a4a870c1

SHA1 Segment-Delimited Span Hashes
1     0 - 4294705151: 00c863ab 485a389b a57d5cd7 3e0e0d7f 6b2909d4
2       4294705152 - 8589410303: ad945e12 5adb0c69 fc7c0bd7 7e941119
83cb718f
3       8589410304 - 10742183423: c4fcfba0 b7403b52 9c494bd7 1936c249
9617839a

IO Summary:(Time: Wed Mar 2 14:52:41 2011)
Bytes Read: 10,742,183,424
10,742,183,424 bytes written to image "da-07-f32x"
======== End of Excerpt from SMART log ========


====== Source drive rehash ======
Rehash (SHA1) of source: A48BB5665D6DC57C22DB68E2F723DA9AA8DF82B9
```

Results:

Assertion and Expected Result	Actual Result
AM-01 Source acquired using interface AI.	as expected
AM-02 Source is type DS.	as expected
AM-03 Execution environment is XE.	as expected
AM-05 An image is created on file system type FS.	as expected
AM-06 All visible sectors acquired.	as expected
AM-08 All sectors accurately acquired.	as expected
AO-01 Image file is complete and accurate.	as expected
AO-05 Multifile image created.	as expected
AO-22 Tool calculates hashes by block.	as expected
AO-23 Logged information is correct.	as expected
AO-24 Source is unchanged by acquisition.	as expected

Analysis: Expected results achieved

5.2.44　　DA-07-NTFS

Test Case DA-07-NTFS Smart Version 2010/11/03	
Case Summary:	DA-07 Acquire a digital source of type DS to an image file.
Assertions:	AM-01 The tool uses access interface SRC-AI to access the digital source. AM-02 The tool acquires digital source DS. AM-03 The tool executes in execution environment XE. AM-05 If image file creation is specified, the tool creates an image file on file system type FS. AM-06 All visible sectors are acquired from the digital source. AM-08 All sectors acquired from the digital source are acquired accurately. AO-01 If the tool creates an image file, the data represented by the image file are the same as the data acquired by the tool. AO-05 If the tool creates a multifile image of a requested size then all the individual files shall be no larger than the requested size. AO-22 If requested, the tool calculates block hashes for a specified block size during an acquisition for each block acquired from the digital source. AO-23 If the tool logs any log significant information, the information is accurately recorded in the log file. AO-24 If the tool executes in a forensically safe execution environment, the digital source is unchanged by the acquisition process.
Tester Name:	brl
Test Host:	McGarrett
Test Date:	Thu Mar 3 10:03:28 2011
Drives:	src(43) dst (none) other (3A-SATA)
Source Setup:	src hash (SHA1): < 888E2E7F7AD237DC7A732281DD93F325065E5871 > src hash (MD5): < BC39C3F7EE7A50E77B9BA1E65A5AEEF7 > 78125000 total sectors (40000000000 bytes) Model (0BB-75JHC0) serial # (WD-WMAMC46588) N Start LBA Length Start C/H/S End C/H/S boot Partition type 1 P 000000063 020980827 0000/001/01 1023/254/63 0C Fat32X 2 X 020980890 057143205 1023/000/01 1023/254/63 0F extended 3 S 000000063 000032067 1023/001/01 1023/254/63 01 Fat12 4 x 000032130 002104515 1023/000/01 1023/254/63 05 extended 5 S 000000063 002104452 1023/001/01 1023/254/63 06 Fat16 6 x 002136645 004192965 1023/000/01 1023/254/63 05 extended 7 S 000000063 004192902 1023/001/01 1023/254/63 16 other 8 x 006329610 008401995 1023/000/01 1023/254/63 05 extended 9 S 000000063 008401932 1023/001/01 1023/254/63 0B Fat32 10 x 014731605 010490445 1023/000/01 1023/254/63 05 extended 11 S 000000063 010490382 1023/001/01 1023/254/63 83 Linux 12 x 025222050 004209030 1023/000/01 1023/254/63 05 extended 13 S 000000063 004208967 1023/001/01 1023/254/63 82 Linux swap 14 x 029431080 027712125 1023/000/01 1023/254/63 05 extended 15 S 000000063 027712062 1023/001/01 1023/254/63 07 NTFS 16 S 000000000 000000000 0000/000/00 0000/000/00 00 empty entry 17 P 000000000 000000000 0000/000/00 0000/000/00 00 empty entry 18 P 000000000 000000000 0000/000/00 0000/000/00 00 empty entry 1 020980827 sectors 10742183424 bytes 3 000032067 sectors 16418304 bytes 5 002104452 sectors 1077479424 bytes 7 004192902 sectors 2146765824 bytes 9 008401932 sectors 4301789184 bytes 11 010490382 sectors 5371075584 bytes 13 004208967 sectors 2154991104 bytes 15 027712062 sectors 14188575744 bytes 43ntfs-md5sum 14188575744 5D42FA317C802ACFEF2D313092D7411E 43ntfs-sha1sum 14188575744 73eb2d27564b060db796efb78694a10e6b43d23f
Log Highlights:	====== Tool Settings: ====== segmentation Fixed Size (15 GB) OS: Linux ubuntu 2.6.32-21-generic #32-Ubuntu SMP Fri Apr 16 08:10:02 UTC 2010 i686 GNU/Linux

```
====== Image file segments ======
1      2915 2011-03-03 10:35 da-07-ntfs
2      14188575744 2011-03-03 10:25 da-07-ntfs.image.001
3      2401 2011-03-03 10:25 da-07-ntfs.image.info
======= Excerpt from SMART log ========

FS Type: NTFS
OS FS Type: ntfs
Volume Name: NT
Max. Filesize: 17592.000 GB

SHA1 Span Hashes
 total span hash: 73eb2d27 564b060d b796efb7 8694a10e 6b43d23f

IO Summary:(Time: Thu Mar 3 10:25:53 2011)
Bytes Read: 14,188,575,744
14,188,575,744 bytes written to image "da-07-ntfs"
======== End of Excerpt from SMART log ========

====== Source drive rehash ======
Rehash (SHA1) of source: 888E2E7F7AD237DC7A732281DD93F325065E5871
```

Results:

Assertion and Expected Result	Actual Result
AM-01 Source acquired using interface AI.	as expected
AM-02 Source is type DS.	as expected
AM-03 Execution environment is XE.	as expected
AM-05 An image is created on file system type FS.	as expected
AM-06 All visible sectors acquired.	as expected
AM-08 All sectors accurately acquired.	as expected
AO-01 Image file is complete and accurate.	as expected
AO-05 Multifile image created.	as expected
AO-22 Tool calculates hashes by block.	option not tested
AO-23 Logged information is correct.	as expected
AO-24 Source is unchanged by acquisition.	as expected

Analysis: Expected results achieved

5.2.45   DA-07-OSX

Test Case DA-07-OSX Smart Version 2010/11/03	
Case Summary:	DA-07 Acquire a digital source of type DS to an image file.
Assertions:	AM-01 The tool uses access interface SRC-AI to access the digital source. AM-02 The tool acquires digital source DS. AM-03 The tool executes in execution environment XE. AM-05 If image file creation is specified, the tool creates an image file on file system type FS. AM-06 All visible sectors are acquired from the digital source. AM-08 All sectors acquired from the digital source are acquired accurately. AO-01 If the tool creates an image file, the data represented by the image file are the same as the data acquired by the tool. AO-05 If the tool creates a multifile image of a requested size then all the individual files shall be no larger than the requested size. AO-22 If requested, the tool calculates block hashes for a specified block size during an acquisition for each block acquired from the digital source. AO-23 If the tool logs any log significant information, the information is accurately recorded in the log file. AO-24 If the tool executes in a forensically safe execution environment, the digital source is unchanged by the acquisition process.
Tester Name:	brl
Test Host:	WoFat
Test Date:	Mon Feb 28 11:21:22 2011
Drives:	src(4B-SATA) dst (none) other (67-SATA)
Source Setup:	src hash (SHA1): < 70CC62B43F6A41CA4D6760AA0B9B4C415D3F48E2 > src hash (MD5): < 746B4C06CDD5FBD67C0820DB4325B40C > 156301488 total sectors (80026361856 bytes) Model (ST380815AS) serial # (6QZ5C9V5) N Start LBA Length Start C/H/S End C/H/S boot Partition type 1 P 000000063 020971520 0000/001/01 1023/254/63 AF other 2 P 020971629 010485536 1023/254/63 1023/254/63 AF other 3 P 031457223 006291456 1023/254/63 1023/254/63 A8 other 4 X 037748679 008388694 1023/254/63 1023/254/63 05 extended 5 S 000000039 004194304 1023/254/63 1023/254/63 AF other 6 x 004194343 004194351 1023/254/63 1023/254/63 05 extended 7 S 000000047 004194304 1023/254/63 1023/254/63 AF other 8 S 000000000 000000000 0000/000/00 0000/000/00 00 empty entry 1 020971520 sectors 10737418240 bytes 2 010485536 sectors 5368594432 bytes 3 006291456 sectors 3221225472 bytes 5 004194304 sectors 2147483648 bytes 7 004194304 sectors 2147483648 bytes 4BOSX-sha1 5368594432 3DE70998AD136E66CD09B9B4F2F5164E77B3B705
Log Highlights:	====== Tool Settings: ====== segmentation Standard OS: Linux ubuntu 2.6.32-21-generic #32-Ubuntu SMP Fri Apr 16 08:10:02 UTC 2010 i686 GNU/Linux ====== Image file segments ====== 1 2884 2011-02-28 13:19 da-07-osx 2 5368594432 2011-02-28 11:43 da-07-osx.image.001 3 2367 2011-02-28 11:43 da-07-osx.image.info ======== Excerpt from SMART log ======== FS Type: HFS+ OS FS Type: hfsplus Max. Filesize: 2.000 GB SHA1 Span Hashes total span hash: 3de70998 ad136e66 cd09b9b4 f2f5164e 77b3b705

Test Case DA-07-OSX Smart Version 2010/11/03	
	IO Summary:(Time: Mon Feb 28 11:43:28 2011) Bytes Read: 5,368,594,432 5,368,594,432 bytes written to image "da-07-osx" ======== End of Excerpt from SMART log ======== ====== Source drive rehash ====== Rehash (SHA1) of source: 70CC62B43F6A41CA4D6760AA0B9B4C415D3F48E2
Results:	

Assertion and Expected Result	Actual Result
AM-01 Source acquired using interface AI.	as expected
AM-02 Source is type DS.	as expected
AM-03 Execution environment is XE.	as expected
AM-05 An image is created on file system type FS.	as expected
AM-06 All visible sectors acquired.	as expected
AM-08 All sectors accurately acquired.	as expected
AO-01 Image file is complete and accurate.	as expected
AO-05 Multifile image created.	as expected
AO-22 Tool calculates hashes by block.	option not tested
AO-23 Logged information is correct.	as expected
AO-24 Source is unchanged by acquisition.	as expected

Analysis:	Expected results achieved

5.2.46   DA-07-OSXC

Test Case DA-07-OSXC Smart Version 2010/11/03	
Case Summary:	DA-07 Acquire a digital source of type DS to an image file.
Assertions:	AM-01 The tool uses access interface SRC-AI to access the digital source. AM-02 The tool acquires digital source DS. AM-03 The tool executes in execution environment XE. AM-05 If image file creation is specified, the tool creates an image file on file system type FS. AM-06 All visible sectors are acquired from the digital source. AM-08 All sectors acquired from the digital source are acquired accurately. AO-01 If the tool creates an image file, the data represented by the image file are the same as the data acquired by the tool. AO-05 If the tool creates a multifile image of a requested size then all the individual files shall be no larger than the requested size. AO-22 If requested, the tool calculates block hashes for a specified block size during an acquisition for each block acquired from the digital source. AO-23 If the tool logs any log significant information, the information is accurately recorded in the log file. AO-24 If the tool executes in a forensically safe execution environment, the digital source is unchanged by the acquisition process.
Tester Name:	brl
Test Host:	WoFat
Test Date:	Tue Mar 1 14:13:50 2011
Drives:	src(4B-SATA) dst (none) other (67-SATA)
Source Setup:	src hash (SHA1): < 70CC62B43F6A41CA4D6760AA0B9B4C415D3F48E2 > src hash (MD5): < 746B4C06CDD5FBD67C0820DB4325B40C > 156301488 total sectors (80026361856 bytes) Model (ST380815AS) serial # (6QZ5C9V5) N Start LBA Length Start C/H/S End C/H/S boot Partition type 1 P 000000063 020971520 0000/001/01 1023/254/63 AF other 2 P 020971629 010485536 1023/254/63 1023/254/63 AF other 3 P 031457223 006291456 1023/254/63 1023/254/63 A8 other 4 X 037748679 008388694 1023/254/63 1023/254/63 05 extended 5 S 000000039 004194304 1023/254/63 1023/254/63 AF other 6 x 004194343 004194351 1023/254/63 1023/254/63 05 extended 7 S 000000047 004194304 1023/254/63 1023/254/63 AF other 8 S 000000000 000000000 0000/000/00 0000/000/00 00 empty entry 1 020971520 sectors 10737418240 bytes 2 010485536 sectors 5368594432 bytes 3 006291456 sectors 3221225472 bytes 5 004194304 sectors 2147483648 bytes 7 004194304 sectors 2147483648 bytes 4BOSXC-sha1 2147483648 2D6303D74F9EDE617639643DCCF41EC2091D5F37
Log Highlights:	====== Tool Settings: ====== segmentation Standard OS: Linux ubuntu 2.6.32-21-generic #32-Ubuntu SMP Fri Apr 16 08:10:02 UTC 2010 i686 GNU/Linux ====== Image file segments ====== 1 2911 2011-03-01 14:27 da-07-osxc 2 2147483648 2011-03-01 14:23 da-07-osxc.image.001 3 2397 2011-03-01 14:23 da-07-osxc.image.info ======== Excerpt from SMART log ======== FS Type: FAT32 OS FS Type: vfat Volume Name: FAT3 Max. Filesize: 2.000 GB SHA1 Span Hashes total span hash: 2d6303d7 4f9ede61 7639643d ccf41ec2 091d5f37

```
Test Case DA-07-OSXC Smart Version 2010/11/03

              IO Summary:(Time: Tue Mar 1 14:23:07 2011)
              Bytes Read: 2,147,483,648
              2,147,483,648 bytes written to image "da-07-osxc"
              ======== End of Excerpt from SMART log ========

              ====== Source drive rehash ======
              Rehash (SHA1) of source: 70CC62B43F6A41CA4D6760AA0B9B4C415D3F48E2

Results:
```

Assertion and Expected Result	Actual Result
AM-01 Source acquired using interface AI.	as expected
AM-02 Source is type DS.	as expected
AM-03 Execution environment is XE.	as expected
AM-05 An image is created on file system type FS.	as expected
AM-06 All visible sectors acquired.	as expected
AM-08 All sectors accurately acquired.	as expected
AO-01 Image file is complete and accurate.	as expected
AO-05 Multifile image created.	as expected
AO-22 Tool calculates hashes by block.	option not tested
AO-23 Logged information is correct.	as expected
AO-24 Source is unchanged by acquisition.	as expected

```
Analysis:      Expected results achieved
```

5.2.47 DA-07-OSXCJ

Test Case DA-07-OSXCJ Smart Version 2010/11/03	
Case Summary:	DA-07 Acquire a digital source of type DS to an image file.
Assertions:	AM-01 The tool uses access interface SRC-AI to access the digital source. AM-02 The tool acquires digital source DS. AM-03 The tool executes in execution environment XE. AM-05 If image file creation is specified, the tool creates an image file on file system type FS. AM-06 All visible sectors are acquired from the digital source. AM-08 All sectors acquired from the digital source are acquired accurately. AO-01 If the tool creates an image file, the data represented by the image file are the same as the data acquired by the tool. AO-05 If the tool creates a multifile image of a requested size then all the individual files shall be no larger than the requested size. AO-22 If requested, the tool calculates block hashes for a specified block size during an acquisition for each block acquired from the digital source. AO-23 If the tool logs any log significant information, the information is accurately recorded in the log file. AO-24 If the tool executes in a forensically safe execution environment, the digital source is unchanged by the acquisition process.
Tester Name:	brl
Test Host:	WoFat
Test Date:	Tue Mar 1 16:08:22 2011
Drives:	src(4B-SATA) dst (none) other (67-SATA)
Source Setup:	src hash (SHA1): < 70CC62B43F6A41CA4D6760AA0B9B4C415D3F48E2 > src hash (MD5): < 746B4C06CDD5FBD67C0820DB4325B40C > 156301488 total sectors (80026361856 bytes) Model (ST380815AS) serial # (6QZ5C9V5) N Start LBA Length Start C/H/S End C/H/S boot Partition type 1 P 000000063 020971520 0000/001/01 1023/254/63 AF other 2 P 020971629 010485536 1023/254/63 1023/254/63 AF other 3 P 031457223 006291456 1023/254/63 1023/254/63 A8 other 4 X 037748679 008388694 1023/254/63 1023/254/63 05 extended 5 S 000000039 004194304 1023/254/63 1023/254/63 AF other 6 x 004194343 004194351 1023/254/63 1023/254/63 05 extended 7 S 000000047 004194304 1023/254/63 1023/254/63 AF other 8 S 000000000 000000000 0000/000/00 0000/000/00 00 empty entry 1 020971520 sectors 10737418240 bytes 2 010485536 sectors 5368594432 bytes 3 006291456 sectors 3221225472 bytes 5 004194304 sectors 2147483648 bytes 7 004194304 sectors 2147483648 bytes 4BOSXCJ-sha1 2147483648 29EA089958EF2A695081712FFBA68BA5164C980B
Log Highlights:	====== Tool Settings: ====== segmentation Standard OS: Linux ubuntu 2.6.32-21-generic #32-Ubuntu SMP Fri Apr 16 08:10:02 UTC 2010 i686 GNU/Linux ====== Image file segments ====== 1 2918 2011-03-01 16:29 da-07-osxcj 2 2147483648 2011-03-01 16:24 da-07-osxcj.image.001 3 2400 2011-03-01 16:24 da-07-osxcj.image.info ======== Excerpt from SMART log ======== FS Type: FAT32 OS FS Type: vfat Volume Name: FAT2 Max. Filesize: 2.000 GB SHA1 Span Hashes total span hash: 29ea0899 58ef2a69 5081712f fba68ba5 164c980b

	IO Summary:(Time: Tue Mar 1 16:24:01 2011) Bytes Read: 2,147,483,648 2,147,483,648 bytes written to image "da-07-osxcj" ======== End of Excerpt from SMART log ======== ====== Source drive rehash ====== Rehash (SHA1) of source: 70CC62B43F6A41CA4D6760AA0B9B4C415D3F48E2
Results:	

Assertion and Expected Result	Actual Result
AM-01 Source acquired using interface AI.	as expected
AM-02 Source is type DS.	as expected
AM-03 Execution environment is XE.	as expected
AM-05 An image is created on file system type FS.	as expected
AM-06 All visible sectors acquired.	as expected
AM-08 All sectors accurately acquired.	as expected
AO-01 Image file is complete and accurate.	as expected
AO-05 Multifile image created.	as expected
AO-22 Tool calculates hashes by block.	option not tested
AO-23 Logged information is correct.	as expected
AO-24 Source is unchanged by acquisition.	as expected

Analysis:	Expected results achieved

5.2.48   DA-07-OSXJ

Test Case DA-07-OSXJ Smart Version 2010/11/03	
Case Summary:	DA-07 Acquire a digital source of type DS to an image file.
Assertions:	AM-01 The tool uses access interface SRC-AI to access the digital source. AM-02 The tool acquires digital source DS. AM-03 The tool executes in execution environment XE. AM-05 If image file creation is specified, the tool creates an image file on file system type FS. AM-06 All visible sectors are acquired from the digital source. AM-08 All sectors acquired from the digital source are acquired accurately. AO-01 If the tool creates an image file, the data represented by the image file are the same as the data acquired by the tool. AO-05 If the tool creates a multifile image of a requested size then all the individual files shall be no larger than the requested size. AO-22 If requested, the tool calculates block hashes for a specified block size during an acquisition for each block acquired from the digital source. AO-23 If the tool logs any log significant information, the information is accurately recorded in the log file. AO-24 If the tool executes in a forensically safe execution environment, the digital source is unchanged by the acquisition process.
Tester Name:	brl
Test Host:	WoFat
Test Date:	Mon Feb 28 08:58:19 2011
Drives:	src(4B-SATA) dst (none) other (67-SATA)
Source Setup:	src hash (SHA1): < 70CC62B43F6A41CA4D6760AA0B9B4C415D3F48E2 > src hash (MD5): < 746B4C06CDD5FBD67C0820DB4325B40C > 156301488 total sectors (80026361856 bytes) Model (ST380815AS) serial # (6QZ5C9V5) N Start LBA Length Start C/H/S End C/H/S boot Partition type 1 P 000000063 020971520 0000/001/01 1023/254/63 AF other 2 P 020971629 010485536 1023/254/63 1023/254/63 AF other 3 P 031457223 006291456 1023/254/63 1023/254/63 A8 other 4 X 037748679 008388694 1023/254/63 1023/254/63 05 extended 5 S 000000039 004194304 1023/254/63 1023/254/63 AF other 6 x 004194343 004194351 1023/254/63 1023/254/63 05 extended 7 S 000000047 004194304 1023/254/63 1023/254/63 AF other 8 S 000000000 000000000 0000/000/00 0000/000/00 00 empty entry 1 020971520 sectors 10737418240 bytes 2 010485536 sectors 5368594432 bytes 3 006291456 sectors 3221225472 bytes 5 004194304 sectors 2147483648 bytes 7 004194304 sectors 2147483648 bytes 4BOSXJ-sha1 10737418240 37311859444BD914EDAD43D93F2862E76B279A87
Log Highlights:	====== Tool Settings: ====== segmentation Standard OS: Linux ubuntu 2.6.32-21-generic #32-Ubuntu SMP Fri Apr 16 08:10:02 UTC 2010 i686 GNU/Linux ====== Image file segments ====== 1 2893 2011-02-28 09:18 da-07-osxj 2 10737418240 2011-02-28 09:18 da-07-osxj.image.001 3 2372 2011-02-28 09:18 da-07-osxj.image.info ======== Excerpt from SMART log ======== FS Type: HFS+ OS FS Type: hfsplus Max. Filesize: 2.000 GB SHA1 Span Hashes total span hash: 37311859 444bd914 edad43d9 3f2862e7 6b279a87

	IO Summary:(Time: Mon Feb 28 09:18:07 2011) Bytes Read: 10,737,418,240 10,737,418,240 bytes written to image "da-07-osxj" ======== End of Excerpt from SMART log ======== ====== Source drive rehash ====== Rehash (SHA1) of source: 70CC62B43F6A41CA4D6760AA0B9B4C415D3F48E2

Results:	

Assertion and Expected Result	Actual Result
AM-01 Source acquired using interface AI.	as expected
AM-02 Source is type DS.	as expected
AM-03 Execution environment is XE.	as expected
AM-05 An image is created on file system type FS.	as expected
AM-06 All visible sectors acquired.	as expected
AM-08 All sectors accurately acquired.	as expected
AO-01 Image file is complete and accurate.	as expected
AO-05 Multifile image created.	as expected
AO-22 Tool calculates hashes by block.	option not tested
AO-23 Logged information is correct.	as expected
AO-24 Source is unchanged by acquisition.	as expected

Analysis:	Expected results achieved

5.2.49   DA-07-OSXU

Test Case DA-07-OSXU Smart Version 2010/11/03	
Case Summary:	DA-07 Acquire a digital source of type DS to an image file.
Assertions:	AM-01 The tool uses access interface SRC-AI to access the digital source. AM-02 The tool acquires digital source DS. AM-03 The tool executes in execution environment XE. AM-05 If image file creation is specified, the tool creates an image file on file system type FS. AM-06 All visible sectors are acquired from the digital source. AM-08 All sectors acquired from the digital source are acquired accurately. AO-01 If the tool creates an image file, the data represented by the image file are the same as the data acquired by the tool. AO-05 If the tool creates a multifile image of a requested size then all the individual files shall be no larger than the requested size. AO-22 If requested, the tool calculates block hashes for a specified block size during an acquisition for each block acquired from the digital source. AO-23 If the tool logs any log significant information, the information is accurately recorded in the log file. AO-24 If the tool executes in a forensically safe execution environment, the digital source is unchanged by the acquisition process.
Tester Name:	brl
Test Host:	WoFat
Test Date:	Tue Mar 1 09:49:48 2011
Drives:	src(4B-SATA) dst (none) other (67-SATA)
Source Setup:	src hash (SHA1): < 70CC62B43F6A41CA4D6760AA0B9B4C415D3F48E2 > src hash (MD5): < 746B4C06CDD5FBD67C0820DB4325B40C > 156301488 total sectors (80026361856 bytes) Model (ST380815AS) serial # (6QZ5C9V5) N Start LBA Length Start C/H/S End C/H/S boot Partition type 1 P 000000063 020971520 0000/001/01 1023/254/63 AF other 2 P 020971629 010485536 1023/254/63 1023/254/63 AF other 3 P 031457223 006291456 1023/254/63 1023/254/63 A8 other 4 X 037748679 008388694 1023/254/63 1023/254/63 05 extended 5 S 000000039 004194304 1023/254/63 1023/254/63 AF other 6 x 004194343 004194351 1023/254/63 1023/254/63 05 extended 7 S 000000047 004194304 1023/254/63 1023/254/63 AF other 8 S 000000000 000000000 0000/000/00 0000/000/00 00 empty entry 1 020971520 sectors 10737418240 bytes 2 010485536 sectors 5368594432 bytes 3 006291456 sectors 3221225472 bytes 5 004194304 sectors 2147483648 bytes 7 004194304 sectors 2147483648 bytes 4BOSXU-sha1 3221225472 D102A01562C82533C052CE6CFBB1D467EC9B5BC6
Log Highlights:	====== Tool Settings: ====== segmentation Standard OS: Linux ubuntu 2.6.32-21-generic #32-Ubuntu SMP Fri Apr 16 08:10:02 UTC 2010 i686 GNU/Linux ====== Image file segments ====== 1 2908 2011-03-01 10:13 da-07-osxu 2 3221225472 2011-03-01 10:00 da-07-osxu.image.001 3 2392 2011-03-01 10:00 da-07-osxu.image.info ======== Excerpt from SMART log ======== FS Type: UFS OS FS Type: ufs Volume Name: OSXU Max. Filesize: 2.000 GB SHA1 Span Hashes total span hash: d102a015 62c82533 c052ce6c fbb1d467 ec9b5bc6

```
                    IO Summary:(Time: Tue Mar 1 10:00:41 2011)
                    Bytes Read: 3,221,225,472
                    3,221,225,472 bytes written to image "da-07-osxu"
                    ======== End of Excerpt from SMART log ========

                    ====== Source drive rehash ======
                    Rehash (SHA1) of source: 70CC62B43F6A41CA4D6760AA0B9B4C415D3F48E2
```

Results:

Assertion and Expected Result	Actual Result
AM-01 Source acquired using interface AI.	as expected
AM-02 Source is type DS.	as expected
AM-03 Execution environment is XE.	as expected
AM-05 An image is created on file system type FS.	as expected
AM-06 All visible sectors acquired.	as expected
AM-08 All sectors accurately acquired.	as expected
AO-01 Image file is complete and accurate.	as expected
AO-05 Multifile image created.	as expected
AO-22 Tool calculates hashes by block.	option not tested
AO-23 Logged information is correct.	as expected
AO-24 Source is unchanged by acquisition.	as expected

Analysis: | Expected results achieved

5.2.50 DA-07-PART

Test Case DA-07-PART Smart Version 2010/11/03	
Case Summary:	DA-07 Acquire a digital source of type DS to an image file.
Assertions:	AM-01 The tool uses access interface SRC-AI to access the digital source. AM-02 The tool acquires digital source DS. AM-03 The tool executes in execution environment XE. AM-05 If image file creation is specified, the tool creates an image file on file system type FS. AM-06 All visible sectors are acquired from the digital source. AM-08 All sectors acquired from the digital source are acquired accurately. AO-01 If the tool creates an image file, the data represented by the image file are the same as the data acquired by the tool. AO-05 If the tool creates a multifile image of a requested size then all the individual files shall be no larger than the requested size. AO-22 If requested, the tool calculates block hashes for a specified block size during an acquisition for each block acquired from the digital source. AO-23 If the tool logs any log significant information, the information is accurately recorded in the log file. AO-24 If the tool executes in a forensically safe execution environment, the digital source is unchanged by the acquisition process.
Tester Name:	brl
Test Host:	Max
Test Date:	Thu Mar 3 11:18:10 2011
Drives:	src(D5-THUMB) dst (none) other (5A-SATA)

Source Setup:	src hash (SHA1): < D68520EF74A336E49DCCF83815B7B08FDC53E38A >
	src hash (MD5): < C843593624B2B3B878596D8760B19954 >
	
	Reference SHA1 hashes, Win size: 81408 (sectors)
	  1 0 - 81407 D5C035F4AD3BDDC18255F402C52B7B722ED23B70 -
	  2 81408 - 162815 06A786B45A8995D2CA5E377B08073080F5E12EEE -
	  3 162816 - 244223 3061D34425F177504444D711731A5FBD73FE55FB -
	  4 244224 - 325631 62AA71381E93B0D6EA026A048F23ABD232ECE3ED -
	  5 325632 - 407039 DB8A599ECD7666EB4B33AA67D928F27F9BF34233 -
	  6 407040 - 488447 392664CE2CDDFA62C687A430A4628D3C9ACCCE09 -
	  7 488448 - 569855 4EC26AADA68187FA625F355FE58F55D0129841DE -
	505856 total sectors (258998272 bytes)
	Model (usb2.0Flash Disk) serial # ()

Log Highlights:	====== Tool Settings: ======
	segmentation Standard
	
	OS: Linux ubuntu 2.6.32-21-generic #32-Ubuntu SMP Fri Apr 16 08:10:02 UTC 2010 i686 GNU/Linux
	
	====== Image file segments ======
	  1 2911 2011-03-03 11:34 da-07-part
	  2 41680896 2011-03-03 11:26 da-07-part.image.001
	  3 2102 2011-03-03 11:26 da-07-part.image.info
	======== Excerpt from SMART log ========
	
	Image Description...
	Make and Model: CRUCIAL usb2.0Flash Disk
	Device Sectors: 505,856
	
	SHA1 Span Hashes
	 total span hash: 06a786b4 5a8995d2 ca5e377b 08073080 f5e12eee
	
	IO Summary:(Time: Thu Mar 3 11:26:56 2011)
	Bytes Read: 41,680,896
	41,680,896 bytes written to image "da-07-part"
	======== End of Excerpt from SMART log ========
	
	====== Source drive rehash ======

Test Case DA-07-PART Smart Version 2010/11/03	
	Rehash (SHA1) of source: D68520EF74A336E49DCCF83815B7B08FDC53E38A
Results:	

Assertion and Expected Result	Actual Result
AM-01 Source acquired using interface AI.	as expected
AM-02 Source is type DS.	as expected
AM-03 Execution environment is XE.	as expected
AM-05 An image is created on file system type FS.	as expected
AM-06 All visible sectors acquired.	as expected
AM-08 All sectors accurately acquired.	as expected
AO-01 Image file is complete and accurate.	as expected
AO-05 Multifile image created.	as expected
AO-22 Tool calculates hashes by block.	as expected
AO-23 Logged information is correct.	as expected
AO-24 Source is unchanged by acquisition.	as expected

Analysis:	Expected results achieved

5.2.51   DA-07-SWAP

Test Case DA-07-SWAP Smart Version 2010/11/03	
Case Summary:	DA-07 Acquire a digital source of type DS to an image file.
Assertions:	AM-01 The tool uses access interface SRC-AI to access the digital source. AM-02 The tool acquires digital source DS. AM-03 The tool executes in execution environment XE. AM-05 If image file creation is specified, the tool creates an image file on file system type FS. AM-06 All visible sectors are acquired from the digital source. AM-08 All sectors acquired from the digital source are acquired accurately. AO-01 If the tool creates an image file, the data represented by the image file are the same as the data acquired by the tool. AO-05 If the tool creates a multifile image of a requested size then all the individual files shall be no larger than the requested size. AO-22 If requested, the tool calculates block hashes for a specified block size during an acquisition for each block acquired from the digital source. AO-23 If the tool logs any log significant information, the information is accurately recorded in the log file. AO-24 If the tool executes in a forensically safe execution environment, the digital source is unchanged by the acquisition process.
Tester Name:	brl
Test Host:	McGarrett
Test Date:	Wed Mar 2 15:48:38 2011
Drives:	src(43) dst (none) other (3A-SATA)

Source Setup:	src hash (SHA1): < 888E2E7F7AD237DC7A732281DD93F325065E5871 >
	 src hash (MD5): < BC39C3F7EE7A50E77B9BA1E65A5AEEF7 >
	 78125000 total sectors (40000000000 bytes)
	 Model (0BB-75JHC0) serial # (WD-WMAMC46588)
	 N Start LBA Length Start C/H/S End C/H/S boot Partition type
	  1 P 000000063 020980827 0000/001/01 1023/254/63 0C Fat32X
	  2 X 020980890 057143205 1023/000/01 1023/254/63 0F extended
	  3 S 000000063 000032067 1023/001/01 1023/254/63 01 Fat12
	  4 x 000032130 002104515 1023/000/01 1023/254/63 05 extended
	  5 S 000000063 002104452 1023/001/01 1023/254/63 06 Fat16
	  6 x 002136645 004192965 1023/000/01 1023/254/63 05 extended
	  7 S 000000063 004192902 1023/001/01 1023/254/63 16 other
	  8 x 006329610 008401995 1023/000/01 1023/254/63 05 extended
	  9 S 000000063 008401932 1023/001/01 1023/254/63 0B Fat32
	 10 x 014731605 010490445 1023/000/01 1023/254/63 05 extended
	 11 S 000000063 010490382 1023/001/01 1023/254/63 83 Linux
	 12 x 025222050 004209030 1023/000/01 1023/254/63 05 extended
	 13 S 000000063 004208967 1023/001/01 1023/254/63 82 Linux swap
	 14 x 029431080 027712125 1023/000/01 1023/254/63 05 extended
	 15 S 000000063 027712062 1023/001/01 1023/254/63 07 NTFS
	 16 S 000000000 000000000 0000/000/00 0000/000/00 00 empty entry
	 17 P 000000000 000000000 0000/000/00 0000/000/00 00 empty entry
	 18 P 000000000 000000000 0000/000/00 0000/000/00 00 empty entry
	 1 020980827 sectors 10742183424 bytes
	 3 000032067 sectors 16418304 bytes
	 5 002104452 sectors 1077479424 bytes
	 7 004192902 sectors 2146765824 bytes
	 9 008401932 sectors 4301789184 bytes
	 11 010490382 sectors 5371075584 bytes
	 13 004208967 sectors 2154991104 bytes
	 15 027712062 sectors 14188575744 bytes
	 43swap-md5sum 2154991103 4B602964A30FE20D1B22B046A7375A7C
	 43swap-sha1sum 2154991103 F5B062CC31DA088DF7FAF8F7A47E500BF4244BCF

Log Highlights:	====== Tool Settings: ====== segmentation Standard OS: Linux ubuntu 2.6.32-21-generic #32-Ubuntu SMP Fri Apr 16 08:10:02 UTC 2010 i686 GNU/Linux

Test Case DA-07-SWAP Smart Version 2010/11/03

```
====== Image file segments ======
1       2817 2011-03-02 16:03 da-07-swap
2       2154991104 2011-03-02 15:58 da-07-swap.image.001
3       2122 2011-03-02 15:58 da-07-swap.image.info
======== Excerpt from SMART log ========


SHA1 Span Hashes
 total span hash: 18b73d89 2d772b88 437ce039 2e1732ca 8fe2a2f4

IO Summary:(Time: Wed Mar 2 15:58:31 2011)
Bytes Read: 2,154,991,104
2,154,991,104 bytes written to image "da-07-swap"
======== End of Excerpt from SMART log ========

====== Source drive rehash ======
Rehash (SHA1) of source: 888E2E7F7AD237DC7A732281DD93F325065E5871
```

Results:

Assertion and Expected Result	Actual Result
AM-01 Source acquired using interface AI.	as expected
AM-02 Source is type DS.	as expected
AM-03 Execution environment is XE.	as expected
AM-05 An image is created on file system type FS.	as expected
AM-06 All visible sectors acquired.	as expected
AM-08 All sectors accurately acquired.	last seven sectors differ
AO-01 Image file is complete and accurate.	as expected
AO-05 Multifile image created.	as expected
AO-22 Tool calculates hashes by block.	option not tested
AO-23 Logged information is correct.	as expected
AO-24 Source is unchanged by acquisition.	as expected

Analysis: Expected results not achieved

5.2.52   DA-07-THUMB

Test Case DA-07-THUMB Smart Version 2010/11/03	
Case Summary:	DA-07 Acquire a digital source of type DS to an image file.
Assertions:	AM-01 The tool uses access interface SRC-AI to access the digital source. AM-02 The tool acquires digital source DS. AM-03 The tool executes in execution environment XE. AM-05 If image file creation is specified, the tool creates an image file on file system type FS. AM-06 All visible sectors are acquired from the digital source. AM-08 All sectors acquired from the digital source are acquired accurately. AO-01 If the tool creates an image file, the data represented by the image file is the same as the data acquired by the tool. AO-05 If the tool creates a multifile image of a requested size then all the individual files shall be no larger than the requested size. AO-22 If requested, the tool calculates block hashes for a specified block size during an acquisition for each block acquired from the digital source. AO-23 If the tool logs any log significant information, the information is accurately recorded in the log file. AO-24 If the tool executes in a forensically safe execution environment, the digital source is unchanged by the acquisition process.
Tester Name:	brl
Test Host:	Max
Test Date:	Tue Feb 15 13:44:22 2011
Drives:	src(D5-THUMB) dst (none) other (3A-SATA)

Source Setup:	src hash (SHA1): < D68520EF74A336E49DCCF83815B7B08FDC53E38A >
	src hash (MD5): < C843593624B2B3B878596D8760B19954 >
	
	Reference SHA1 hashes, Win size: 81408 (sectors)
	  1 0 - 81407 D5C035F4AD3BDDC18255F402C52B7B722ED23B70 -
	  2 81408 - 162815 06A786B45A8995D2CA5E377B08073080F5E12EEE -
	  3 162816 - 244223 3061D34425F177504444D711731A5FBD73FE55FB -
	  4 244224 - 325631 62AA71381E93B0D6EA026A048F23ABD232ECE3ED -
	  5 325632 - 407039 DB8A599ECD7666EB4B33AA67D928F27F9BF34233 -
	  6 407040 - 488447 392664CE2CDDFA62C687A430A4628D3C9ACCCE09 -
	  7 488448 - 569855 4EC26AADA68187FA625F355FE58F55D0129841DE -
	505856 total sectors (258998272 bytes)
	Model (usb2.0Flash Disk) serial # ()

Log Highlights:	====== Tool Settings: ======
	segmentation Fixed Size (40 MB)
	
	OS: Linux ubuntu 2.6.32-21-generic #32-Ubuntu SMP Fri Apr 16 08:10:02 UTC 2010 i686 GNU/Linux
	
	====== Image file segments ======
	  1 4257 2011-02-15 14:17 da-07-thumb
	  2 41680896 2011-02-15 14:06 da-07-thumb.image.001
	  3 41680896 2011-02-15 14:07 da-07-thumb.image.002
	  . . .
	  7 41680896 2011-02-15 14:10 da-07-thumb.image.006
	  8 8912896 2011-02-15 14:11 da-07-thumb.image.007
	  9 7330 2011-02-15 14:11 da-07-thumb.image.info
	======== Excerpt from SMART log ========
	
	Image Description...
	Make and Model: CRUCIAL usb2.0Flash Disk
	Device Sectors: 505,856
	FS Type: FAT32
	OS FS Type: vfat
	Volume Name: NO NAME
	Max. Filesize: 2.000 GB
	
	SHA1 Span Hashes

```
total span hash: d68520ef 74a336e4 9dccf838 15b7b08f dc53e38a

SHA1 Segment-Delimited Span Hashes
1     0 - 41680895: d5c035f4 ad3bddc1 8255f402 c52b7b72 2ed23b70
2     41680896 - 83361791: 06a786b4 5a8995d2 ca5e377b 08073080 f5e12eee
3     83361792 - 125042687: 3061d344 25f17750 4444d711 731a5fbd 73fe55fb
              . . .
6     166723584 - 208404479: db8a599e cd7666eb 4b33aa67 d928f27f 9bf34233
7     208404480 - 250085375: 392664ce 2cddfa62 c687a430 a4628d3c 9accce09
8     250085376 - 258998271: 4ec26aad a68187fa 625f355f e58f55d0 129841de

========= End of Excerpt from SMART log =========


====== Source drive rehash ======
Rehash (SHA1) of source: D68520EF74A336E49DCCF83815B7B08FDC53E38A
```

	Assertion and Expected Result	Actual Result
Results:	AM-01 Source acquired using interface AI.	as expected
	AM-02 Source is type DS.	as expected
	AM-03 Execution environment is XE.	as expected
	AM-05 An image is created on file system type FS.	as expected
	AM-06 All visible sectors acquired.	as expected
	AM-08 All sectors accurately acquired.	as expected
	AO-01 Image file is complete and accurate.	as expected
	AO-05 Multifile image created.	as expected
	AO-22 Tool calculates hashes by block.	as expected
	AO-23 Logged information is correct.	as expected
	AO-24 Source is unchanged by acquisition.	as expected

Analysis:	Expected results achieved

5.2.53   DA-08-ATA28

Test Case DA-08-ATA28 Smart Version 2010/11/03	
Case Summary:	DA-08 Acquire a physical drive with hidden sectors to an image file.
Assertions:	AM-01 The tool uses access interface SRC-AI to access the digital source. AM-02 The tool acquires digital source DS. AM-03 The tool executes in execution environment XE. AM-05 If image file creation is specified, the tool creates an image file on file system type FS. AM-06 All visible sectors are acquired from the digital source. AM-07 All hidden sectors are acquired from the digital source. AM-08 All sectors acquired from the digital source are acquired accurately. AO-01 If the tool creates an image file, the data represented by the image file are the same as the data acquired by the tool. AO-05 If the tool creates a multifile image of a requested size then all the individual files shall be no larger than the requested size. AO-22 If requested, the tool calculates block hashes for a specified block size during an acquisition for each block acquired from the digital source. AO-23 If the tool logs any log significant information, the information is accurately recorded in the log file. AO-24 If the tool executes in a forensically safe execution environment, the digital source is unchanged by the acquisition process.
Tester Name:	brl
Test Host:	WoFat
Test Date:	Wed Feb 16 09:45:34 2011
Drives:	src(42) dst (none) other (67-SATA)
Source Setup:	src hash (SHA1): < 5A75399023056E0EB905082B35F8FAA1DB049229 > src hash (MD5): < F4B9AAB24554EEEB2A962BDA554A9252 > 78165360 total sectors (40020664320 bytes) 65534/015/63 (max cyl/hd values) 65535/016/63 (number of cyl/hd) IDE disk: Model (WDC WD400JB-00JJC0) serial # (WD-WCAMA3958512) N Start LBA Length Start C/H/S End C/H/S boot Partition type 1 P 000000063 070348572 0000/001/01 1023/254/63 Boot 07 NTFS 2 P 000000000 000000000 0000/000/00 0000/000/00 00 empty entry 3 P 000000000 000000000 0000/000/00 0000/000/00 00 empty entry 4 P 000000000 000000000 0000/000/00 0000/000/00 00 empty entry 1 070348572 sectors 36018468864 bytes HPA created BIOS, XBIOS and Direct disk geometry Reporter (BXDR) BXDR 128 /S70000000 /P /fbxdrlog.txt Setting Maximum Addressable Sector to 70000000 MAS now set to 70000000 Hashes with HPA in place md5:9BF3C3DEADE47056A1DDC073C5F6B2E2 sha1:D76F909482B00767B62C295CADE202F92E61CD2E
Log Highlights:	====== Tool Settings: ====== segmentation Standard OS: Linux ubuntu 2.6.32-21-generic #32-Ubuntu SMP Fri Apr 16 08:10:02 UTC 2010 i686 GNU/Linux ====== Image file segments ====== 1 3219 2011-02-16 11:03 da-08-ata28 2 40020664320 2011-02-16 10:48 da-08-ata28.image.001 3 4712 2011-02-16 10:48 da-08-ata28.image.info ======== Excerpt from SMART log ======== Image Description... Make and Model: ATA WDC WD400JB-00JJ Serial Number: WD-WCAMA3958512

Test Case DA-08-ATA28 Smart Version 2010/11/03

	Device Sectors: 78,165,360 SHA1 Span Hashes total span hash: 5a753990 23056e0e b905082b 35f8faa1 db049229 IO Summary:(Time: Wed Feb 16 10:48:46 2011) Bytes Read: 40,020,664,320 40,020,664,320 bytes written to image "da-08-ata28" ======== End of Excerpt from SMART log ======== ====== Source drive rehash ====== Rehash (SHA1) of source: 5A75399023056E0EB905082B35F8FAA1DB049229
Results:	

Assertion and Expected Result	Actual Result
AM-01 Source acquired using interface AI.	as expected
AM-02 Source is type DS.	as expected
AM-03 Execution environment is XE.	as expected
AM-05 An image is created on file system type FS.	as expected
AM-06 All visible sectors acquired.	as expected
AM-07 All hidden sectors acquired.	as expected
AM-08 All sectors accurately acquired.	as expected
AO-01 Image file is complete and accurate.	as expected
AO-05 Multifile image created.	as expected
AO-22 Tool calculates hashes by block.	option not tested
AO-23 Logged information is correct.	as expected
AO-24 Source is unchanged by acquisition.	as expected

Analysis:	Expected results achieved

5.2.54   DA-08-DCO

Test Case DA-08-DCO Smart Version 2010/11/03	
Case Summary:	DA-08 Acquire a physical drive with hidden sectors to an image file.
Assertions:	AM-01 The tool uses access interface SRC-AI to access the digital source.
	AM-02 The tool acquires digital source DS.
	AM-03 The tool executes in execution environment XE.
	AM-05 If image file creation is specified, the tool creates an image file on file system type FS.
	AM-06 All visible sectors are acquired from the digital source.
	AM-07 All hidden sectors are acquired from the digital source.
	AM-08 All sectors acquired from the digital source are acquired accurately.
	AO-01 If the tool creates an image file, the data represented by the image file are the same as the data acquired by the tool.
	AO-05 If the tool creates a multifile image of a requested size then all the individual files shall be no larger than the requested size.
	AO-22 If requested, the tool calculates block hashes for a specified block size during an acquisition for each block acquired from the digital source.
	AO-23 If the tool logs any log significant information, the information is accurately recorded in the log file.
	AO-24 If the tool executes in a forensically safe execution environment, the digital source is unchanged by the acquisition process.
Tester Name:	brl
Test Host:	WoFat
Test Date:	Wed Feb 16 13:28:35 2011
Drives:	src(15-SATA) dst (none) other (67-SATA)
Source Setup:	src hash (SHA1): < 76B22DDE84CE61F090791DDBB79057529AAF00E1 >
	src hash (MD5): < 9B4A9D124107819A9CE6F253FE7DC675 >
	156301488 total sectors (80026361856 bytes)
	Model (0JD-00HKA0) serial # (WD-WMAJ91513490)
	DCO Created with Maximum LBA Sectors = 140,000,000
	Hashes with DCO in place:
	md5: E5F8B277A39ED0F49794E9916CD62DD9
	sha1: AC64CF1B3736BB2FE40C14D871E6F207BC432C2F
Log Highlights:	====== Tool Settings: ======
	segmentation Standard
	OS: Linux ubuntu 2.6.32-21-generic #32-Ubuntu SMP Fri Apr 16 08:10:02 UTC 2010 i686 GNU/Linux
	====== Image file segments ======
	1 2967 2011-02-16 15:45 da-08-dco
	2 71680000512 2011-02-16 14:53 da-08-dco.image.001
	3 2236 2011-02-16 14:53 da-08-dco.image.info
	======== Excerpt from SMART log ========
	Image Description...
	Make and Model: ATA WDC WD800JD-00HK
	Serial Number: WD-WMAJ91513490
	Device Sectors: 140,000,001
	SHA1 Span Hashes
	total span hash: ac64cf1b 3736bb2f e40c14d8 71e6f207 bc432c2f
	IO Summary:(Time: Wed Feb 16 14:53:24 2011)
	Bytes Read: 71,680,000,512
	71,680,000,512 bytes written to image "da-08-dco"
	======== End of Excerpt from SMART log ========
	====== Source drive rehash ======
	Rehash (SHA1) of source: AC64CF1B3736BB2FE40C14D871E6F207BC432C2F

Results:		
	Assertion and Expected Result	**Actual Result**
	AM-01 Source acquired using interface AI.	as expected
	AM-02 Source is type DS.	as expected
	AM-03 Execution environment is XE.	as expected
	AM-05 An image is created on file system type FS.	as expected
	AM-06 All visible sectors acquired.	as expected
	AM-07 All hidden sectors acquired.	DCO not acquired
	AM-08 All sectors accurately acquired.	as expected
	AO-01 Image file is complete and accurate.	as expected
	AO-05 Multifile image created.	as expected
	AO-22 Tool calculates hashes by block.	option not tested
	AO-23 Logged information is correct.	as expected
	AO-24 Source is unchanged by acquisition.	as expected
Analysis:	Expected results not achieved	

5.2.55   DA-08-SATA48

Test Case DA-08-SATA48 Smart Version 2010/11/03	
Case Summary:	DA-08 Acquire a physical drive with hidden sectors to an image file.
Assertions:	AM-01 The tool uses access interface SRC-AI to access the digital source. AM-02 The tool acquires digital source DS. AM-03 The tool executes in execution environment XE. AM-05 If image file creation is specified, the tool creates an image file on file system type FS. AM-06 All visible sectors are acquired from the digital source. AM-07 All hidden sectors are acquired from the digital source. AM-08 All sectors acquired from the digital source are acquired accurately. AO-01 If the tool creates an image file, the data represented by the image file are the same as the data acquired by the tool. AO-05 If the tool creates a multifile image of a requested size then all the individual files shall be no larger than the requested size. AO-22 If requested, the tool calculates block hashes for a specified block size during an acquisition for each block acquired from the digital source. AO-23 If the tool logs any log significant information, the information is accurately recorded in the log file. AO-24 If the tool executes in a forensically safe execution environment, the digital source is unchanged by the acquisition process.
Tester Name:	brl
Test Host:	McGarrett
Test Date:	Wed Feb 16 10:22:32 2011
Drives:	src(1E-SATA) dst (none) other (68-SATA)
Source Setup:	src hash (SHA1): < 3E7439D9E99ACD030B969C1BE5B1430BF7183573 > src hash (MD5): < 8E1CF5E20E86362E0EACF12EDDEF42A6 > 625142448 total sectors (320072933376 bytes) 38912/254/63 (max cyl/hd values) 38913/255/63 (number of cyl/hd) Model (ST3320620AS) serial # (5QF3X4F6) HPA created HPA Created with Maximum LBA Sectors = 560,000,000 Hashes with HPA in place md5: 3655FA5086B6864154898533DFAE2442 sha1: EB1045B57DE7CDA28FE9504E3FA238D0B5DBC587
Log Highlights:	====== Tool Settings: ====== segmentation Standard OS: Linux ubuntu 2.6.32-21-generic #32-Ubuntu SMP Fri Apr 16 08:10:02 UTC 2010 i686 GNU/Linux ====== Image file segments ====== 1 2990 2011-02-16 16:00 da-08-sata48 2 320072933376 2011-02-16 15:52 da-08-sata48.image.001 3 2247 2011-02-16 15:52 da-08-sata48.image.info ======== Excerpt from SMART log ======== Image Description... Make and Model: ATA ST3320620AS Serial Number: 5QF3X4F6 Device Sectors: 625,142,448 SHA1 Span Hashes total span hash: 3e7439d9 e99acd03 0b969c1b e5b1430b f7183573 IO Summary:(Time: Wed Feb 16 15:52:56 2011) Bytes Read: 320,072,933,376 320,072,933,376 bytes written to image "da-08-sata48" ======== End of Excerpt from SMART log ========

```
Test Case DA-08-SATA48 Smart Version 2010/11/03
```

	`====== Source drive rehash ======` `Rehash (SHA1) of source: 3E7439D9E99ACD030B969C1BE5B1430BF7183573`
Results:	

Assertion and Expected Result	Actual Result
AM-01 Source acquired using interface AI.	as expected
AM-02 Source is type DS.	as expected
AM-03 Execution environment is XE.	as expected
AM-05 An image is created on file system type FS.	as expected
AM-06 All visible sectors acquired.	as expected
AM-07 All hidden sectors acquired.	as expected
AM-08 All sectors accurately acquired.	as expected
AO-01 Image file is complete and accurate.	as expected
AO-05 Multifile image created.	as expected
AO-22 Tool calculates hashes by block.	option not tested
AO-23 Logged information is correct.	as expected
AO-24 Source is unchanged by acquisition.	as expected

Analysis:	Expected results achieved

5.2.56   DA-09

Test Case DA-09 Smart Version 2010/11/03	
Case Summary:	DA-09 Acquire a digital source that has at least one faulty data sector.
Assertions:	AM-01 The tool uses access interface SRC-AI to access the digital source. AM-02 The tool acquires digital source DS. AM-03 The tool executes in execution environment XE. AM-05 If image file creation is specified, the tool creates an image file on file system type FS. AM-06 All visible sectors are acquired from the digital source. AM-08 All sectors acquired from the digital source are acquired accurately. AM-09 If unresolved errors occur while reading from the selected digital source, the tool notifies the user of the error type and location within the digital source. AM-10 If unresolved errors occur while reading from the selected digital source, the tool uses a benign fill in the destination object in place of the inaccessible data. AO-01 If the tool creates an image file, the data represented by the image file are the same as the data acquired by the tool. AO-05 If the tool creates a multifile image of a requested size then all the individual files shall be no larger than the requested size. AO-22 If requested, the tool calculates block hashes for a specified block size during an acquisition for each block acquired from the digital source. AO-23 If the tool logs any log significant information, the information is accurately recorded in the log file. AO-24 If the tool executes in a forensically safe execution environment, the digital source is unchanged by the acquisition process.
Tester Name:	brl
Test Host:	Max
Test Date:	Wed Feb 16 15:35:10 2011
Drives:	src(ED-BAD-CPR4) dst (24-SATA) other (none)
Source Setup:	No before hash for ED-BAD-CPR4 Known Bad Sector List for ED-BAD-CPR4 Manufacturer: Maxtor Model: DiamondMax Plus 9 Serial Number: Y23EGSJE Capacity: 60GB Interface: SATA 35 faulty sectors 6160328, 6160362, 10041157, 10041995, 10118634, 10209448, 11256569, 14115689, 14778391, 14778392, 14778449, 14778479, 14778517, 14778518, 14778519, 14778520, 14778521, 14778551, 14778607, 14778626, 14778627, 14778650, 14778668, 14778669, 14778709, 14778727, 14778747, 14778772, 14778781, 14778870, 14778949, 14778953, 14779038, 14779113, 14779321
Log Highlights:	====== Destination drive setup ====== 156301488 sectors wiped with 24 ====== Comparison of original to clone drive ====== Sectors compared: 120103200 Sectors match: 120102768 Sectors differ: 432 Bytes differ: 220752 Diffs range 6160328-6160535, 10041152-10041159, 10041992-10041999, 10118632-10118639, 10209448-10209455, 11256568-11256575, 14115688-14115695, 14778384-14778399, 14778448-14778455, 14778472-14778479, 14778512-14778527, 14778544-14778551, 14778600-14778607, 14778624-14778631, 14778648-14778655, 14778664-14778671, 14778704-14778711, 14778720-14778727, 14778744-14778751, 14778768-14778783, 14778864-14778871, 14778944-14778959, 14779032-14779039, 14779112-14779119,

```
14779320-14779327
Source (120103200) has 36198288 fewer sectors than destination (156301488)
Zero fill: 0
Src Byte fill (ED): 0
Dst Byte fill (24): 36198288
Other fill: 0
Other no fill: 0
Zero fill range:
Src fill range:
Dst fill range: 120103200-156301487
Other fill range:
Other not filled range:
0 source read errors, 0 destination read errors

OS: Linux ubuntu 2.6.32-21-generic #32-Ubuntu SMP Fri Apr 16 08:10:02 UTC
2010 i686 GNU/Linux

======== Excerpt from SMART log ========


SHA1 Span Hashes
 total span hash: d9c6f034 cd8d6867 9f64f0df c4988002 f613c452

         Logged Error Runs
 Run Start Run End Run Length
byte sector byte sector sector
3154087936 6160328 3154194431 6160535 208
5141069824 10041152 5141073919 10041159 8
5141499904 10041992 5141503999 10041999 8
5180739584 10118632 5180743679 10118639 8
5227237376 10209448 5227241471 10209455 8
5763362816 11256568 5763366911 11256575 8
7227232256 14115688 7227236351 14115695 8
7566532608 14778384 7566540799 14778399 16
7566565376 14778448 7566569471 14778455 8
7566577664 14778472 7566581759 14778479 8
7566598144 14778512 7566606335 14778527 16
7566614528 14778544 7566618623 14778551 8
7566643200 14778600 7566647295 14778607 8
7566655488 14778624 7566659583 14778631 8
7566667776 14778648 7566671871 14778655 8
7566675968 14778664 7566680063 14778671 8
7566696448 14778704 7566700543 14778711 8
7566704640 14778720 7566708735 14778727 8
7566716928 14778744 7566721023 14778751 8
7566729216 14778768 7566737407 14778783 16
7566778368 14778864 7566782463 14778871 8
7566819328 14778944 7566827519 14778959 16
7566864384 14779032 7566868479 14779039 8
7566905344 14779112 7566909439 14779119 8
7567011840 14779320 7567015935 14779327 8

IO Summary:(Time: Thu Feb 17 11:33:38 2011)
Bytes Read: 61,492,838,400
61,492,838,400 bytes written to /dev/sda
======== End of Excerpt from SMART log ========
```

Results:

Assertion and Expected Result	Actual Result
AM-01 Source acquired using interface AI.	as expected
AM-02 Source is type DS.	as expected
AM-03 Execution environment is XE.	as expected
AM-05 An image is created on file system type FS.	as expected
AM-06 All visible sectors acquired.	some sectors skipped
AM-08 All sectors accurately acquired.	as expected
AM-09 Error logged.	as expected
AM-10 Benign fill replaces inaccessible sectors.	as expected

Test Case DA-09 Smart Version 2010/11/03		
	AO-01 Image file is complete and accurate.	as expected
	AO-05 Multifile image created.	as expected
	AO-22 Tool calculates hashes by block.	option not tested
	AO-23 Logged information is correct.	as expected
	AO-24 Source is unchanged by acquisition.	not checked
Analysis:	Expected results not achieved	

5.2.57 DA-10-GZIP

Test Case DA-10-GZIP Smart Version 2010/11/03	
Case Summary:	DA-10 Acquire a digital source to an image file in an alternate format.
Assertions:	AM-01 The tool uses access interface SRC-AI to access the digital source. AM-02 The tool acquires digital source DS. AM-03 The tool executes in execution environment XE. AM-05 If image file creation is specified, the tool creates an image file on file system type FS. AM-06 All visible sectors are acquired from the digital source. AM-08 All sectors acquired from the digital source are acquired accurately. AO-01 If the tool creates an image file, the data represented by the image file are the same as the data acquired by the tool. AO-02 If an image file format is specified, the tool creates an image file in the specified format. AO-05 If the tool creates a multifile image of a requested size then all the individual files shall be no larger than the requested size. AO-22 If requested, the tool calculates block hashes for a specified block size during an acquisition for each block acquired from the digital source. AO-23 If the tool logs any log significant information, the information is accurately recorded in the log file. AO-24 If the tool executes in a forensically safe execution environment, the digital source is unchanged by the acquisition process.
Tester Name:	brl
Test Host:	McGarrett
Test Date:	Thu Feb 17 15:32:43 2011
Drives:	src(41) dst (none) other (68-SATA)
Source Setup:	src hash (SHA1): < 15CAA1A307271160D8372668BF8A03FC45A51CC9 > src hash (MD5): < 0A6A8EF78BDC14E2026710D8CCB5607C > 78125000 total sectors (40000000000 bytes) 65534/015/63 (max cyl/hd values) 65535/016/63 (number of cyl/hd) IDE disk: Model (WDC WD400BB-75JHC0) serial # (WD-WMAMC4658355) N Start LBA Length Start C/H/S End C/H/S boot Partition type 1 P 000000063 078107967 0000/001/01 1023/254/63 Boot 07 NTFS 2 P 000000000 000000000 0000/000/00 0000/000/00 00 empty entry 3 P 000000000 000000000 0000/000/00 0000/000/00 00 empty entry 4 P 000000000 000000000 0000/000/00 0000/000/00 00 empty entry 1 078107967 sectors 39991279104 bytes
Log Highlights:	====== Tool Settings: ====== segmentation Standard OS: Linux ubuntu 2.6.32-21-generic #32-Ubuntu SMP Fri Apr 16 08:10:02 UTC 2010 i686 GNU/Linux ====== Image file segments ====== 1 3209 2011-02-18 08:32 da-10-gzip 2 913568945 2011-02-17 16:38 da-10-gzip.image.001.gz 3 4940 2011-02-17 16:38 da-10-gzip.image.info ======= Excerpt from SMART log ======== Image Description... Make and Model: ATA WDC WD400BB-75JH Serial Number: WD-WMAMC4658355 Device Sectors: 78,125,000 SHA1 Span Hashes total span hash: 15caa1a3 07271160 d8372668 bf8a03fc 45a51cc9 IO Summary:(Time: Thu Feb 17 16:38:47 2011) Bytes Read: 40,000,000,000 40,000,000,000 bytes written to image "da-10-gzip" ======== End of Excerpt from SMART log ========

Test Case DA-10-GZIP Smart Version 2010/11/03	
	====== Source drive rehash ====== Rehash (SHA1) of source: 15CAA1A307271160D8372668BF8A03FC45A51CC9
Results:	

Assertion and Expected Result	Actual Result
AM-01 Source acquired using interface AI.	as expected
AM-02 Source is type DS.	as expected
AM-03 Execution environment is XE.	as expected
AM-05 An image is created on file system type FS.	as expected
AM-06 All visible sectors acquired.	as expected
AM-08 All sectors accurately acquired.	as expected
AO-01 Image file is complete and accurate.	as expected
AO-02 Image file in specified format.	as expected
AO-05 Multifile image created.	as expected
AO-22 Tool calculates hashes by block.	option not tested
AO-23 Logged information is correct.	as expected
AO-24 Source is unchanged by acquisition.	as expected

Analysis:	Expected results achieved

5.2.58   DA-10-BZIP2

Test Case DA-10-BZIP2 Smart Version 2010/11/03	
Case Summary:	DA-10 Acquire a digital source to an image file in an alternate format.
Assertions:	AM-01 The tool uses access interface SRC-AI to access the digital source. AM-02 The tool acquires digital source DS. AM-03 The tool executes in execution environment XE. AM-05 If image file creation is specified, the tool creates an image file on file system type FS. AM-06 All visible sectors are acquired from the digital source. AM-08 All sectors acquired from the digital source are acquired accurately. AO-01 If the tool creates an image file, the data represented by the image file are the same as the data acquired by the tool. AO-02 If an image file format is specified, the tool creates an image file in the specified format. AO-05 If the tool creates a multifile image of a requested size then all the individual files shall be no larger than the requested size. AO-22 If requested, the tool calculates block hashes for a specified block size during an acquisition for each block acquired from the digital source. AO-23 If the tool logs any log significant information, the information is accurately recorded in the log file. AO-24 If the tool executes in a forensically safe execution environment, the digital source is unchanged by the acquisition process.
Tester Name:	brl
Test Host:	McGarrett
Test Date:	Thu Feb 17 09:29:34 2011
Drives:	src(41) dst (none) other (68-SATA)
Source Setup:	src hash (SHA1): < 15CAA1A307271160D8372668BF8A03FC45A51CC9 > src hash (MD5): < 0A6A8EF78BDC14E2026710D8CCB5607C > 78125000 total sectors (40000000000 bytes) 65534/015/63 (max cyl/hd values) 65535/016/63 (number of cyl/hd) IDE disk: Model (WDC WD400BB-75JHC0) serial # (WD-WMAMC4658355) N Start LBA Length Start C/H/S End C/H/S boot Partition type 1 P 000000063 078107967 0000/001/01 1023/254/63 Boot 07 NTFS 2 P 000000000 000000000 0000/000/00 0000/000/00 00 empty entry 3 P 000000000 000000000 0000/000/00 0000/000/00 00 empty entry 4 P 000000000 000000000 0000/000/00 0000/000/00 00 empty entry 1 078107967 sectors 39991279104 bytes
Log Highlights:	====== Tool Settings: ====== segmentation Standard OS: Linux ubuntu 2.6.32-21-generic #32-Ubuntu SMP Fri Apr 16 08:10:02 UTC 2010 i686 GNU/Linux ====== Image file segments ====== 1 3216 2011-02-17 10:36 da-10-bzip2 2 517502063 2011-02-17 10:29 da-10-bzip2.image.001.bz2 3 4951 2011-02-17 10:29 da-10-bzip2.image.info ======== Excerpt from SMART log ======== Image Description... Make and Model: ATA WDC WD400BB-75JH Serial Number: WD-WMAMC4658355 Device Sectors: 78,125,000 SHA1 Span Hashes total span hash: 15caa1a3 07271160 d8372668 bf8a03fc 45a51cc9 IO Summary:(Time: Thu Feb 17 10:29:35 2011) Bytes Read: 40,000,000,000 40,000,000,000 bytes written to image "da-10-bzip2" ======== End of Excerpt from SMART log ========

Test Case DA-10-BZIP2 Smart Version 2010/11/03		
	====== Source drive rehash ====== Rehash (SHA1) of source: 15CAA1A307271160D8372668BF8A03FC45A51CC9	
Results:		
	Assertion and Expected Result	**Actual Result**
	AM-01 Source acquired using interface AI.	as expected
	AM-02 Source is type DS.	as expected
	AM-03 Execution environment is XE.	as expected
	AM-05 An image is created on file system type FS.	as expected
	AM-06 All visible sectors acquired.	as expected
	AM-08 All sectors accurately acquired.	as expected
	AO-01 Image file is complete and accurate.	as expected
	AO-02 Image file in specified format.	as expected
	AO-05 Multifile image created.	as expected
	AO-22 Tool calculates hashes by block.	option not tested
	AO-23 Logged information is correct.	as expected
	AO-24 Source is unchanged by acquisition.	as expected
Analysis:	Expected results achieved	

5.2.59   DA-10-EWCOMPRESS

Test Case DA-10-EWCOMPRESS Smart Version 2010/11/03	
Case Summary:	DA-10 Acquire a digital source to an image file in an alternate format.
Assertions:	AM-01 The tool uses access interface SRC-AI to access the digital source. AM-02 The tool acquires digital source DS. AM-03 The tool executes in execution environment XE. AM-05 If image file creation is specified, the tool creates an image file on file system type FS. AM-06 All visible sectors are acquired from the digital source. AM-08 All sectors acquired from the digital source are acquired accurately. AO-01 If the tool creates an image file, the data represented by the image file are the same as the data acquired by the tool. AO-02 If an image file format is specified, the tool creates an image file in the specified format. AO-05 If the tool creates a multifile image of a requested size then all the individual files shall be no larger than the requested size. AO-22 If requested, the tool calculates block hashes for a specified block size during an acquisition for each block acquired from the digital source. AO-23 If the tool logs any log significant information, the information is accurately recorded in the log file. AO-24 If the tool executes in a forensically safe execution environment, the digital source is unchanged by the acquisition process.
Tester Name:	brl
Test Host:	WoFat
Test Date:	Thu Feb 17 09:47:19 2011
Drives:	src(43) dst (none) other (67-SATA)
Source Setup:	src hash (SHA1): < 888E2E7F7AD237DC7A732281DD93F325065E5871 > src hash (MD5): < BC39C3F7EE7A50E77B9BA1E65A5AEEF7 > 78125000 total sectors (40000000000 bytes) Model (0BB-75JHC0) serial # (WD-WMAMC46588) N Start LBA Length Start C/H/S End C/H/S boot Partition type 1 P 000000063 020980827 0000/001/01 1023/254/63 0C Fat32X 2 X 020980890 057143205 1023/000/01 1023/254/63 0F extended 3 S 000000063 000032067 1023/001/01 1023/254/63 01 Fat12 4 x 000032130 002104515 1023/000/01 1023/254/63 05 extended 5 S 000000063 002104452 1023/001/01 1023/254/63 06 Fat16 6 x 002136645 004192965 1023/000/01 1023/254/63 05 extended 7 S 000000063 004192902 1023/001/01 1023/254/63 16 other 8 x 006329610 008401995 1023/000/01 1023/254/63 05 extended 9 S 000000063 008401932 1023/001/01 1023/254/63 0B Fat32 10 x 014731605 010490445 1023/000/01 1023/254/63 05 extended 11 S 000000063 010490382 1023/001/01 1023/254/63 83 Linux 12 x 025222050 004209030 1023/000/01 1023/254/63 05 extended 13 S 000000063 004208967 1023/001/01 1023/254/63 82 Linux swap 14 x 029431080 027712125 1023/000/01 1023/254/63 05 extended 15 S 000000063 027712062 1023/001/01 1023/254/63 07 NTFS 16 S 000000000 000000000 0000/000/00 0000/000/00 00 empty entry 17 P 000000000 000000000 0000/000/00 0000/000/00 00 empty entry 18 P 000000000 000000000 0000/000/00 0000/000/00 00 empty entry 1 020980827 sectors 10742183424 bytes 3 000032067 sectors 16418304 bytes 5 002104452 sectors 1077479424 bytes 7 004192902 sectors 2146765824 bytes 9 008401932 sectors 4301789184 bytes 11 010490382 sectors 5371075584 bytes 13 004208967 sectors 2154991104 bytes 15 027712062 sectors 14188575744 bytes
Log Highlights:	====== Tool Settings: ====== segmentation Standard OS: Linux ubuntu 2.6.32-21-generic #32-Ubuntu SMP Fri Apr 16 08:10:02 UTC 2010 i686 GNU/Linux

```
====== Image file segments ======
1      5037 2011-02-17 11:46 da-10-ewcompress
2     29091 2011-02-17 11:12 da-10-ewcompress.image.info
3 632749100 2011-02-17 11:12 da-10-ewcompress.image.s01
======== Excerpt from SMART log ========


Image Description...
Make and Model: ATA WDC WD400BB-75JH
Serial Number: WD-WMAMC4658888
Device Sectors: 78,125,000


SHA1 Span Hashes
 total span hash: 888e2e7f 7ad237dc 7a732281 dd93f325 065e5871


IO Summary:(Time: Thu Feb 17 11:12:27 2011)
Bytes Read: 40,000,000,000
40,000,000,000 bytes written to image "da-10-ewcompress"
======== End of Excerpt from SMART log ========


====== Source drive rehash ======
Rehash (SHA1) of source: 888E2E7F7AD237DC7A732281DD93F325065E5871
```

Results:

Assertion and Expected Result	Actual Result
AM-01 Source acquired using interface AI.	as expected
AM-02 Source is type DS.	as expected
AM-03 Execution environment is XE.	as expected
AM-05 An image is created on file system type FS.	as expected
AM-06 All visible sectors acquired.	as expected
AM-08 All sectors accurately acquired.	as expected
AO-01 Image file is complete and accurate.	as expected
AO-02 Image file in specified format.	as expected
AO-05 Multifile image created.	as expected
AO-22 Tool calculates hashes by block.	option not tested
AO-23 Logged information is correct.	as expected
AO-24 Source is unchanged by acquisition.	as expected

Analysis: Expected results achieved

5.2.60 DA-12

Test Case DA-12 Smart Version 2010/11/03	
Case Summary:	DA-12 Attempt to create an image file where there is insufficient space.
Assertions:	AM-01 The tool uses access interface SRC-AI to access the digital source. AM-02 The tool acquires digital source DS. AM-03 The tool executes in execution environment XE. AM-05 If image file creation is specified, the tool creates an image file on file system type FS. AO-04 If the tool is creating an image file and there is insufficient space on the image destination device to contain the image file, the tool shall notify the user. AO-23 If the tool logs any log significant information, the information is accurately recorded in the log file. AO-24 If the tool executes in a forensically safe execution environment, the digital source is unchanged by the acquisition process.
Tester Name:	brl
Test Host:	Max
Test Date:	Fri Feb 18 14:59:10 2011
Drives:	src(E0) dst (none) other (74-SATA-SSD)
Source Setup:	src hash (SHA1): < 4A6941F1337A8A22B10FC844B4D7FA6158BECB82 > src hash (MD5): < A97C8F36B7AC9D5233B90AC09284F938 > 17938985 total sectors (9184760320 bytes) Model (ATLAS10K2-TY092J) serial # (169028142436)
Log Highlights:	====== Screen Message: ====== 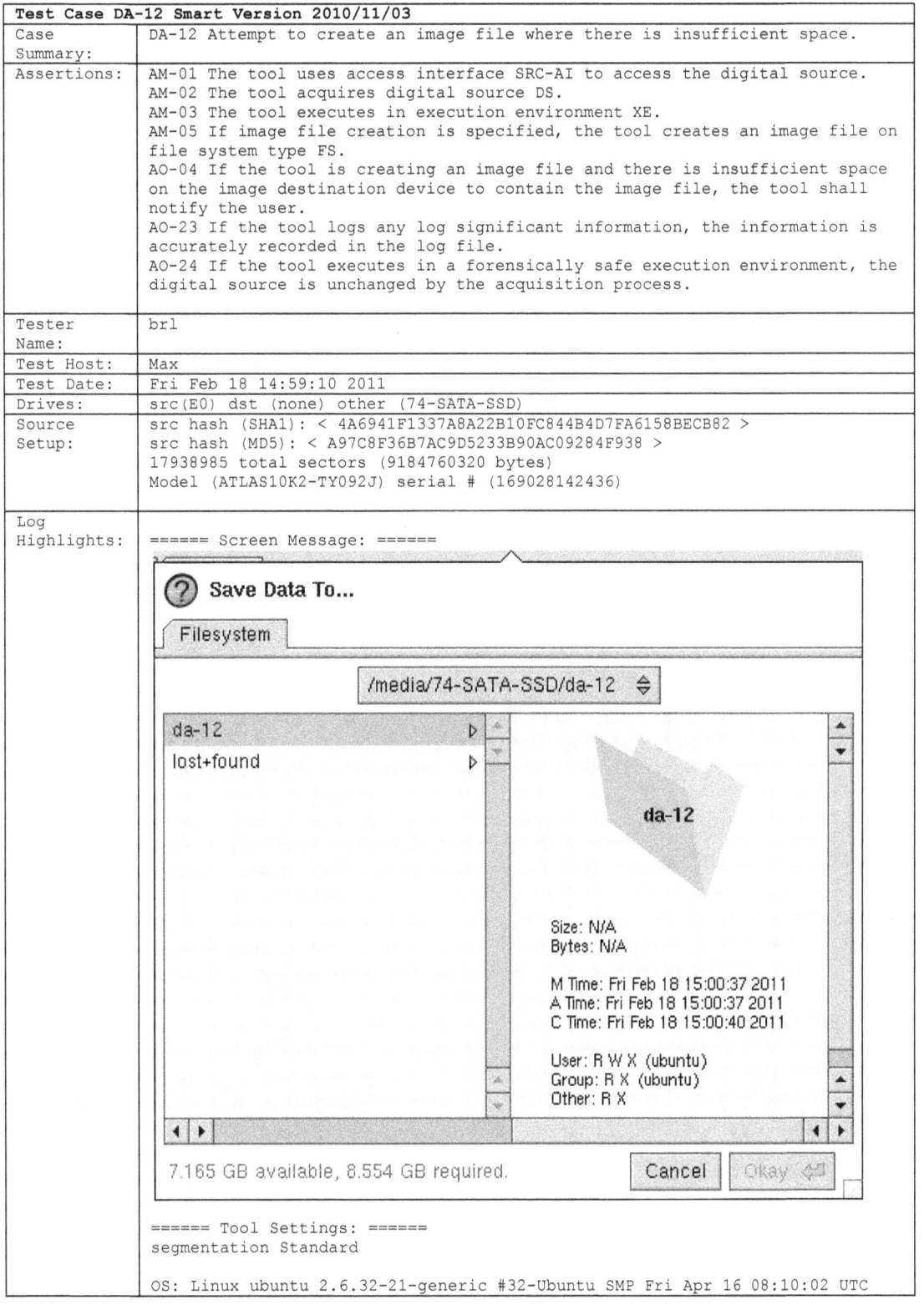 ====== Tool Settings: ====== segmentation Standard OS: Linux ubuntu 2.6.32-21-generic #32-Ubuntu SMP Fri Apr 16 08:10:02 UTC

```
2010 i686 GNU/Linux

======== Excerpt from SMART log ========

No logfile created
======== End of Excerpt from SMART log ========
```

Results:

Assertion and Expected Result	Actual Result
AM-01 Source acquired using interface AI.	as expected
AM-02 Source is type DS.	as expected
AM-03 Execution environment is XE.	as expected
AM-05 An image is created on file system type FS.	as expected
AO-04 User notified if space exhausted.	as expected
AO-23 Logged information is correct.	as expected
AO-24 Source is unchanged by acquisition.	not checked

Analysis: Expected results achieved

5.2.61   DA-12-FIXED

Test Case DA-12-FIXED Smart Version 2010/11/03	
Case Summary:	DA-12 Attempt to create an image file where there is insufficient space.
Assertions:	AM-01 The tool uses access interface SRC-AI to access the digital source. AM-02 The tool acquires digital source DS. AM-03 The tool executes in execution environment XE. AM-05 If image file creation is specified, the tool creates an image file on file system type FS. AO-04 If the tool is creating an image file and there is insufficient space on the image destination device to contain the image file, the tool shall notify the user. AO-23 If the tool logs any log significant information, the information is accurately recorded in the log file. AO-24 If the tool executes in a forensically safe execution environment, the digital source is unchanged by the acquisition process.
Tester Name:	brl
Test Host:	Max
Test Date:	Fri Feb 18 15:15:58 2011
Drives:	src(E0) dst (none) other (74-SATA-SSD)
Source Setup:	src hash (SHA1): < 4A6941F1337A8A22B10FC844B4D7FA6158BECB82 > src hash (MD5): < A97C8F36B7AC9D5233B90AC09284F938 > 17938985 total sectors (9184760320 bytes) Model (ATLAS10K2-TY092J) serial # (169028142436)
Log Highlights:	====== Screen Message: ====== 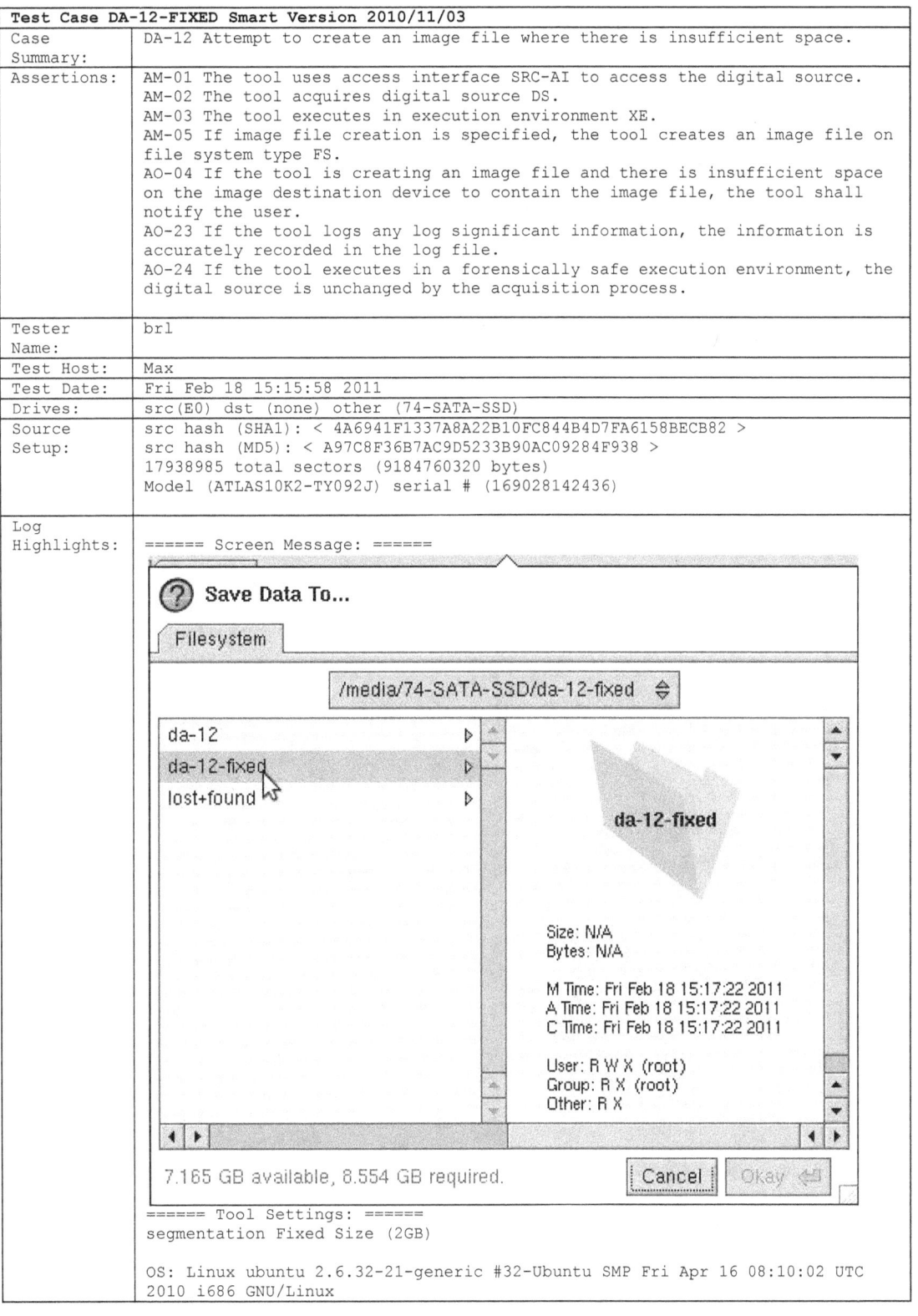 ====== Tool Settings: ====== segmentation Fixed Size (2GB) OS: Linux ubuntu 2.6.32-21-generic #32-Ubuntu SMP Fri Apr 16 08:10:02 UTC 2010 i686 GNU/Linux

Test Case DA-12-FIXED Smart Version 2010/11/03	
	======== Excerpt from SMART log ======== No logfile created ======== End of Excerpt from SMART log ========
Results:	

Assertion and Expected Result	Actual Result
AM-01 Source acquired using interface AI.	as expected
AM-02 Source is type DS.	as expected
AM-03 Execution environment is XE.	as expected
AM-05 An image is created on file system type FS.	as expected
AO-04 User notified if space exhausted.	as expected
AO-23 Logged information is correct.	as expected
AO-24 Source is unchanged by acquisition.	not checked

Analysis:	Expected results achieved

5.2.62 DA-12-PARTALIGNED

Case Summary:	DA-12 Attempt to create an image file where there is insufficient space.
Assertions:	AM-01 The tool uses access interface SRC-AI to access the digital source. AM-02 The tool acquires digital source DS. AM-03 The tool executes in execution environment XE. AM-05 If image file creation is specified, the tool creates an image file on file system type FS. AO-04 If the tool is creating an image file and there is insufficient space on the image destination device to contain the image file, the tool shall notify the user. AO-23 If the tool logs any log significant information, the information is accurately recorded in the log file. AO-24 If the tool executes in a forensically safe execution environment, the digital source is unchanged by the acquisition process.
Tester Name:	brl
Test Host:	Max
Test Date:	Fri Feb 18 15:14:39 2011
Drives:	src(43) dst (none) other (74-SATA-SSD)
Source Setup:	src hash (SHA1): < 888E2E7F7AD237DC7A732281DD93F325065E5871 > src hash (MD5): < BC39C3F7EE7A50E77B9BA1E65A5AEEF7 > 78125000 total sectors (40000000000 bytes) Model (0BB-75JHC0) serial # (WD-WMAMC46588) N Start LBA Length Start C/H/S End C/H/S boot Partition type 1 P 000000063 020980827 0000/001/01 1023/254/63 0C Fat32X 2 X 020980890 057143205 1023/000/01 1023/254/63 0F extended 3 S 000000063 000032067 1023/001/01 1023/254/63 01 Fat12 4 x 000032130 002104515 1023/000/01 1023/254/63 05 extended 5 S 000000063 002104452 1023/001/01 1023/254/63 06 Fat16 6 x 002136645 004192965 1023/000/01 1023/254/63 05 extended 7 S 000000063 004192902 1023/001/01 1023/254/63 16 other 8 x 006329610 008401995 1023/000/01 1023/254/63 05 extended 9 S 000000063 008401932 1023/001/01 1023/254/63 0B Fat32 10 x 014731605 010490445 1023/000/01 1023/254/63 05 extended 11 S 000000063 010490382 1023/001/01 1023/254/63 83 Linux 12 x 025222050 004209030 1023/000/01 1023/254/63 05 extended 13 S 000000063 004208967 1023/001/01 1023/254/63 82 Linux swap 14 x 029431080 027712125 1023/000/01 1023/254/63 05 extended 15 S 000000063 027712062 1023/001/01 1023/254/63 07 NTFS 16 S 000000000 000000000 0000/000/00 0000/000/00 00 empty entry 17 P 000000000 000000000 0000/000/00 0000/000/00 00 empty entry 18 P 000000000 000000000 0000/000/00 0000/000/00 00 empty entry 1 020980827 sectors 10742183424 bytes 3 000032067 sectors 16418304 bytes 5 002104452 sectors 1077479424 bytes 7 004192902 sectors 2146765824 bytes 9 008401932 sectors 4301789184 bytes 11 010490382 sectors 5371075584 bytes 13 004208967 sectors 2154991104 bytes 15 027712062 sectors 14188575744 bytes
Log Highlights:	====== Screen Message: ======

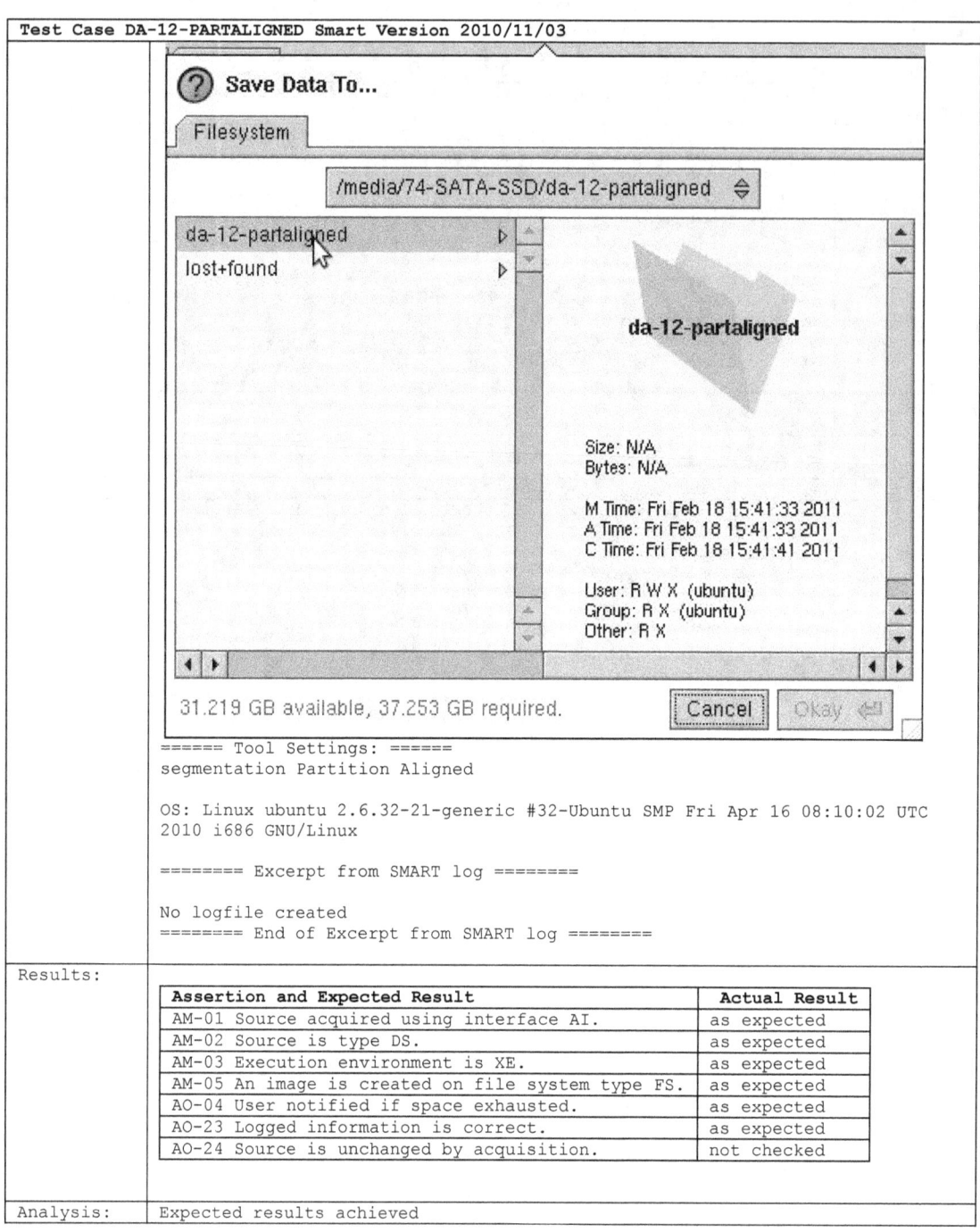

```
====== Tool Settings: ======
segmentation Partition Aligned

OS: Linux ubuntu 2.6.32-21-generic #32-Ubuntu SMP Fri Apr 16 08:10:02 UTC
2010 i686 GNU/Linux

======== Excerpt from SMART log ========

No logfile created
======== End of Excerpt from SMART log ========
```

	Assertion and Expected Result	Actual Result
Results:		
	AM-01 Source acquired using interface AI.	as expected
	AM-02 Source is type DS.	as expected
	AM-03 Execution environment is XE.	as expected
	AM-05 An image is created on file system type FS.	as expected
	AO-04 User notified if space exhausted.	as expected
	AO-23 Logged information is correct.	as expected
	AO-24 Source is unchanged by acquisition.	not checked
Analysis:	Expected results achieved	

5.2.63   DA-13

Test Case DA-13 Smart Version 2010/11/03	
Case Summary:	DA-13 Create an image file where there is insufficient space on a single volume, and use destination device switching to continue on another volume.
Assertions:	AM-01 The tool uses access interface SRC-AI to access the digital source. AM-02 The tool acquires digital source DS. AM-03 The tool executes in execution environment XE. AM-05 If image file creation is specified, the tool creates an image file on file system type FS. AM-06 All visible sectors are acquired from the digital source. AM-08 All sectors acquired from the digital source are acquired accurately. AO-01 If the tool creates an image file, the data represented by the image file is the same as the data acquired by the tool. AO-04 If the tool is creating an image file and there is insufficient space on the image destination device to contain the image file, the tool shall notify the user. AO-05 If the tool creates a multifile image of a requested size then all the individual files shall be no larger than the requested size. AO-10 If there is insufficient space to contain all files of a multifile image and if destination device switching is supported, the image is continued on another device. AO-22 If requested, the tool calculates block hashes for a specified block size during an acquisition for each block acquired from the digital source. AO-23 If the tool logs any log significant information, the information is accurately recorded in the log file. AO-24 If the tool executes in a forensically safe execution environment, the digital source is unchanged by the acquisition process.
Tester Name:	brl
Test Host:	Max
Test Date:	Tue Feb 22 11:29:16 2011
Drives:	src(E0) dst (none) other (74-SATA-SSD)
Source Setup:	src hash (SHA1): < 4A6941F1337A8A22B10FC844B4D7FA6158BECB82 > src hash (MD5): < A97C8F36B7AC9D5233B90AC09284F938 > Reference SHA1 hashes, Win size: 14666304 (sectors) 7509147648 (bytes) 1 0 - 14666303 204B987D28A503DCD6AF42171FC057A3F1187D66 - 2 14666304 - 17938984 D025E559C154AD712EDF0BDC46DC81B84311A59A - 17938985 total sectors (9184760320 bytes) Model (ATLAS10K2-TY092J) serial # (169028142436)
Log Highlights:	====== Tool Settings: ====== segmentation Transport Media OS: Linux ubuntu 2.6.32-21-generic #32-Ubuntu SMP Fri Apr 16 08:10:02 UTC 2010 i686 GNU/Linux ====== Image file segments (First destination) ====== 1 1024 2011-02-22 13:18 da-13 2 7509147648 2011-02-22 13:00 da-13.image.001 ====== Image file segments (Final destination) ====== 1 1675612672 2011-02-22 13:12 da-13.image.002 2 3373 2011-02-22 13:12 da-13.image.info ======== Excerpt from SMART log ======== SHA1 Span Hashes total span hash: 4a6941f1 337a8a22 b10fc844 b4d7fa61 58becb82 SHA1 Segment-Delimited Span Hashes 1 0 - 7509147647: 204b987d 28a503dc d6af4217 1fc057a3 f1187d66 2 7509147648 - 9184760319: d025e559 c154ad71 2edf0bdc 46dc81b8 4311a59a

Test Case DA-13 Smart Version 2010/11/03		
	IO Summary:(Time: Tue Feb 22 13:12:17 2011) Bytes Read: 9,184,760,320 9,184,760,320 bytes written to image "da-13" ======== End of Excerpt from SMART log ======== ====== Source drive rehash ====== Rehash (SHA1) of source: 4A6941F1337A8A22B10FC844B4D7FA6158BECB82	
Results:		
	Assertion and Expected Result	**Actual Result**
	AM-01 Source acquired using interface AI.	as expected
	AM-02 Source is type DS.	as expected
	AM-03 Execution environment is XE.	as expected
	AM-05 An image is created on file system type FS.	as expected
	AM-06 All visible sectors acquired.	as expected
	AM-08 All sectors accurately acquired.	as expected
	AO-01 Image file is complete and accurate.	as expected
	AO-04 User notified if space exhausted.	as expected
	AO-05 Multifile image created.	as expected
	AO-10 Image file continued on new device.	as expected
	AO-22 Tool calculates hashes by block.	as expected
	AO-23 Logged information is correct.	as expected
	AO-24 Source is unchanged by acquisition.	as expected
Analysis:	Expected results achieved	

5.2.64   DA-14-ATA28

Test Case DA-14-ATA28 Smart Version 2010/11/03	
Case Summary:	DA-14 Create an unaligned clone from an image file.
Assertions:	AM-03 The tool executes in execution environment XE. AO-12 If requested, a clone is created from an image file. AO-13 A clone is created using access interface DST-AI to write to the clone device. AO-14 If an unaligned clone is created, each sector written to the clone is accurately written to the same disk address on the clone that the sector occupied on the digital source. AO-17 If requested, any excess sectors on a clone destination device are not modified. AO-23 If the tool logs any log significant information, the information is accurately recorded in the log file.
Tester Name:	brl
Test Host:	McGarrett
Test Date:	Thu Feb 10 10:23:48 2011
Drives:	src(01-IDE) dst (08-IDE) other (3C-SATA)
Source Setup:	src hash (SHA1): < A48BB5665D6DC57C22DB68E2F723DA9AA8DF82B9 > src hash (MD5): < F458F673894753FA6A0EC8B8EC63848E > 78165360 total sectors (40020664320 bytes) Model (0BB-00JHC0) serial # (WD-WMAMC74171) N Start LBA Length Start C/H/S End C/H/S boot Partition type 1 P 000000063 020980827 0000/001/01 1023/254/63 0C Fat32X 2 X 020980890 057175335 1023/000/01 1023/254/63 0F extended 3 S 000000063 000032067 1023/001/01 1023/254/63 01 Fat12 4 x 000032130 002104515 1023/000/01 1023/254/63 05 extended 5 S 000000063 002104452 1023/001/01 1023/254/63 06 Fat16 6 x 002136645 004192965 1023/000/01 1023/254/63 05 extended 7 S 000000063 004192902 1023/001/01 1023/254/63 16 other 8 x 006329610 008401995 1023/000/01 1023/254/63 05 extended 9 S 000000063 008401932 1023/001/01 1023/254/63 0B Fat32 10 x 014731605 010490445 1023/000/01 1023/254/63 05 extended 11 S 000000063 010490382 1023/001/01 1023/254/63 83 Linux 12 x 025222050 004209030 1023/000/01 1023/254/63 05 extended 13 S 000000063 004208967 1023/001/01 1023/254/63 82 Linux swap 14 x 029431080 027744255 1023/000/01 1023/254/63 05 extended 15 S 000000063 027744192 1023/001/01 1023/254/63 07 NTFS 16 S 000000000 000000000 0000/000/00 0000/000/00 00 empty entry 17 P 000000000 000000000 0000/000/00 0000/000/00 00 empty entry 18 P 000000000 000000000 0000/000/00 0000/000/00 00 empty entry 1 020980827 sectors 10742183424 bytes 3 000032067 sectors 16418304 bytes 5 002104452 sectors 1077479424 bytes 7 004192902 sectors 2146765824 bytes 9 008401932 sectors 4301789184 bytes 11 010490382 sectors 5371075584 bytes 13 004208967 sectors 2154991104 bytes 15 027744192 sectors 14205026304 bytes
Log Highlights:	====== Destination drive setup ====== 78165360 sectors wiped with 8 ====== Comparison of original to clone drive ====== Sectors compared: 78165360 Sectors match: 78165272 Sectors differ: 88 Bytes differ: 44735 Diffs range 56572401-56572488 0 source read errors, 0 destination read errors ====== Tool Settings: ====== dst-interface ata28

Test Case DA-14-ATA28 Smart Version 2010/11/03

```
OS: Linux ubuntu 2.6.32-21-generic #32-Ubuntu SMP Fri Apr 16 08:10:02 UTC
2010 i686 GNU/Linux

======== Excerpt from SMART log ========

Copy: da-06-ata28

SHA1 Span Hashes
 total span hash: a96a7193 e1d9c270 587b2be7 098638ac 048221d1

IO Summary:(Time: Thu Feb 10 12:01:57 2011)
Bytes Read: 40,020,664,320
40,020,664,320 bytes written to /dev/sdb
======== End of Excerpt from SMART log ========
```

Results:

Assertion and Expected Result	Actual Result
AM-03 Execution environment is XE.	as expected
AO-12 A clone is created from an image file.	as expected
AO-13 Clone created using interface AI.	as expected
AO-14 An unaligned clone is created.	as expected
AO-17 Excess sectors are unchanged.	as expected
AO-23 Logged information is correct.	as expected

Analysis: Expected results achieved

5.2.65 DA-14-ATA28-WB

Test Case DA-14-ATA28-WB Smart Version 2010/11/03	
Case Summary:	DA-14 Create an unaligned clone from an image file.
Assertions:	AM-03 The tool executes in execution environment XE. AO-12 If requested, a clone is created from an image file. AO-13 A clone is created using access interface DST-AI to write to the clone device. AO-14 If an unaligned clone is created, each sector written to the clone is accurately written to the same disk address on the clone that the sector occupied on the digital source. AO-17 If requested, any excess sectors on a clone destination device are not modified. AO-23 If the tool logs any log significant information, the information is accurately recorded in the log file.
Tester Name:	brl
Test Host:	WoFat
Test Date:	Mon Mar 14 15:10:55 2011
Drives:	src (01-IDE) dst (79-SATA-SSD) other (3C-SATA)
Source Setup:	src hash (SHA1): < A48BB5665D6DC57C22DB68E2F723DA9AA8DF82B9 > src hash (MD5): < F458F673894753FA6A0EC8B8EC63848E > 78165360 total sectors (40020664320 bytes) Model (0BB-00JHC0) serial # (WD-WMAMC74171) N Start LBA Length Start C/H/S End C/H/S boot Partition type 1 P 000000063 020980827 0000/001/01 1023/254/63 0C Fat32X 2 X 020980890 057175335 1023/000/01 1023/254/63 0F extended 3 S 000000063 000032067 1023/001/01 1023/254/63 01 Fat12 4 x 000032130 002104515 1023/000/01 1023/254/63 05 extended 5 S 000000063 002104452 1023/001/01 1023/254/63 06 Fat16 6 x 002136645 004192965 1023/000/01 1023/254/63 05 extended 7 S 000000063 004192902 1023/001/01 1023/254/63 16 other 8 x 006329610 008401995 1023/000/01 1023/254/63 05 extended 9 S 000000063 008401932 1023/001/01 1023/254/63 0B Fat32 10 x 014731605 010490445 1023/000/01 1023/254/63 05 extended 11 S 000000063 010490382 1023/001/01 1023/254/63 83 Linux 12 x 025222050 004209030 1023/000/01 1023/254/63 05 extended 13 S 000000063 004208967 1023/001/01 1023/254/63 82 Linux swap 14 x 029431080 027744255 1023/000/01 1023/254/63 05 extended 15 S 000000063 027744192 1023/001/01 1023/254/63 07 NTFS 16 S 000000000 000000000 0000/000/00 0000/000/00 00 empty entry 17 P 000000000 000000000 0000/000/00 0000/000/00 00 empty entry 18 P 000000000 000000000 0000/000/00 0000/000/00 00 empty entry 1 020980827 sectors 10742183424 bytes 3 000032067 sectors 16418304 bytes 5 002104452 sectors 1077479424 bytes 7 004192902 sectors 2146765824 bytes 9 008401932 sectors 4301789184 bytes 11 010490382 sectors 5371075584 bytes 13 004208967 sectors 2154991104 bytes 15 027744192 sectors 14205026304 bytes
Log Highlights:	====== Destination drive setup ====== 125045424 sectors wiped with 79 ====== Comparison of original to clone drive ====== Sectors compared: 78165360 Sectors match: 78165360 Sectors differ: 0 Bytes differ: 0 Diffs range Source (78165360) has 46880064 fewer sectors than destination (125045424) Zero fill: 0 Src Byte fill (01): 0 Dst Byte fill (79): 46880064 Other fill: 0 Other no fill: 0

```
Zero fill range:
Src fill range:
Dst fill range: 78165360-125045423
Other fill range:
Other not filled range:
0 source read errors, 0 destination read errors


====== Tool Settings: ======
dst-interface ESATA

OS: Linux ubuntu 2.6.32-21-generic #32-Ubuntu SMP Fri Apr 16 08:10:02 UTC
2010 i686 GNU/Linux

======== Excerpt from SMART log ========

Copy: da-06-ata28-wb

SHA1 Span Hashes
 total span hash: a48bb566 5d6dc57c 22db68e2 f723da9a a8df82b9

IO Summary:(Time: Thu Mar 17 12:41:22 2011)
Bytes Read: 40,020,664,320
40,020,664,320 bytes written to /dev/sdb
======== End of Excerpt from SMART log ========
```

Results:		
	Assertion and Expected Result	**Actual Result**
	AM-03 Execution environment is XE.	as expected
	AO-12 A clone is created from an image file.	as expected
	AO-13 Clone created using interface AI.	as expected
	AO-14 An unaligned clone is created.	as expected
	AO-17 Excess sectors are unchanged.	as expected
	AO-23 Logged information is correct.	as expected

Analysis:	Expected results achieved

5.2.66   DA-14-ATA48

Test Case DA-14-ATA48 Smart Version 2010/11/03	
Case Summary:	DA-14 Create an unaligned clone from an image file.
Assertions:	AM-03 The tool executes in execution environment XE. AO-12 If requested, a clone is created from an image file. AO-13 A clone is created using access interface DST-AI to write to the clone device. AO-14 If an unaligned clone is created, each sector written to the clone is accurately written to the same disk address on the clone that the sector occupied on the digital source. AO-17 If requested, any excess sectors on a clone destination device are not modified. AO-23 If the tool logs any log significant information, the information is accurately recorded in the log file.
Tester Name:	brl
Test Host:	WoFat
Test Date:	Wed Feb 9 11:21:39 2011
Drives:	src(4C) dst (46-SATA) other (67-SATA)
Source Setup:	src hash (SHA1): < 8FF620D2BEDCCAFE8412EDAAD56C8554F872EFBF > src hash (MD5): < D10F763B56D4CEBA2D1311C61F9FB382 > 390721968 total sectors (200049647616 bytes) 24320/254/63 (max cyl/hd values) 24321/255/63 (number of cyl/hd) IDE disk: Model (WDC WD2000JB-00KFA0) serial # (WD-WMAMR1031111) N Start LBA Length Start C/H/S End C/H/S boot Partition type 1 P 000000063 390700737 0000/001/01 1023/254/63 Boot 07 NTFS 2 P 000000000 000000000 0000/000/00 0000/000/00 00 empty entry 3 P 000000000 000000000 0000/000/00 0000/000/00 00 empty entry 4 P 000000000 000000000 0000/000/00 0000/000/00 00 empty entry 1 390700737 sectors 200038777344 bytes
Log Highlights:	====== Destination drive setup ====== 488397168 sectors wiped with 46 ====== Comparison of original to clone drive ====== Sectors compared: 390721968 Sectors match: 390721968 Sectors differ: 0 Bytes differ: 0 Diffs range Source (390721968) has 97675200 fewer sectors than destination (488397168) Zero fill: 0 Src Byte fill (4C): 0 Dst Byte fill (46): 97675200 Other fill: 0 Other no fill: 0 Zero fill range: Src fill range: Dst fill range: 390721968-488397167 Other fill range: Other not filled range: 0 source read errors, 0 destination read errors ====== Tool Settings: ====== dst-interface SATA48 OS: Linux ubuntu 2.6.32-21-generic #32-Ubuntu SMP Fri Apr 16 08:10:02 UTC 2010 i686 GNU/Linux ======== Excerpt from SMART log ======== Copy: da-06-ata48 SHA1 Span Hashes

```
    total span hash: 8ff620d2 bedccafe 8412edaa d56c8554 f872efbf

IO Summary:(Time: Wed Feb 9 15:30:03 2011)
Bytes Read: 200,049,647,616
200,049,647,616 bytes written to /dev/sdb
======== End of Excerpt from SMART log ========
```

Results:

Assertion and Expected Result	Actual Result
AM-03 Execution environment is XE.	as expected
AO-12 A clone is created from an image file.	as expected
AO-13 Clone created using interface AI.	as expected
AO-14 An unaligned clone is created.	as expected
AO-17 Excess sectors are unchanged.	as expected
AO-23 Logged information is correct.	as expected

Analysis: Expected results achieved

5.2.67   DA-14-BZIP2

Case Summary:	DA-14 Create an unaligned clone from an image file.
Assertions:	AM-03 The tool executes in execution environment XE. AO-12 If requested, a clone is created from an image file. AO-13 A clone is created using access interface DST-AI to write to the clone device. AO-14 If an unaligned clone is created, each sector written to the clone is accurately written to the same disk address on the clone that the sector occupied on the digital source. AO-17 If requested, any excess sectors on a clone destination device are not modified. AO-23 If the tool logs any log significant information, the information is accurately recorded in the log file.
Tester Name:	brl
Test Host:	McGarrett
Test Date:	Thu Feb 17 13:11:55 2011
Drives:	src(41) dst (02-IDE) other (68-SATA)
Source Setup:	src hash (SHA1): < 15CAA1A307271160D8372668BF8A03FC45A51CC9 > src hash (MD5): < 0A6A8EF78BDC14E2026710D8CCB5607C > 78125000 total sectors (40000000000 bytes) 65534/015/63 (max cyl/hd values) 65535/016/63 (number of cyl/hd) IDE disk: Model (WDC WD400BB-75JHC0) serial # (WD-WMAMC4658355) N Start LBA Length Start C/H/S End C/H/S boot Partition type 1 P 000000063 078107967 0000/001/01 1023/254/63 Boot 07 NTFS 2 P 000000000 000000000 0000/000/00 0000/000/00 00 empty entry 3 P 000000000 000000000 0000/000/00 0000/000/00 00 empty entry 4 P 000000000 000000000 0000/000/00 0000/000/00 00 empty entry 1 078107967 sectors 39991279104 bytes
Log Highlights:	====== Destination drive setup ====== 78165360 sectors wiped with 2 ====== Comparison of original to clone drive ====== Sectors compared: 78125000 Sectors match: 78125000 Sectors differ: 0 Bytes differ: 0 Diffs range Source (78125000) has 40360 fewer sectors than destination (78165360) Zero fill: 0 Src Byte fill (41): 0 Dst Byte fill (02): 40360 Other fill: 0 Other no fill: 0 Zero fill range: Src fill range: Dst fill range: 78125000-78165359 Other fill range: Other not filled range: 0 source read errors, 0 destination read errors ====== Tool Settings: ====== dst-interface ATA28 OS: Linux ubuntu 2.6.32-21-generic #32-Ubuntu SMP Fri Apr 16 08:10:02 UTC 2010 i686 GNU/Linux ======== Excerpt from SMART log ======== Copy: da-10-bzip2 SHA1 Span Hashes

```
          total span hash: 15caa1a3 07271160 d8372668 bf8a03fc 45a51cc9

          IO Summary:(Time: Thu Feb 17 13:59:54 2011)
          Bytes Read: 40,000,000,000
          40,000,000,000 bytes written to /dev/sda
          ======== End of Excerpt from SMART log ========
```

Results:

Assertion and Expected Result	Actual Result
AM-03 Execution environment is XE.	as expected
AO-12 A clone is created from an image file.	as expected
AO-13 Clone created using interface AI.	as expected
AO-14 An unaligned clone is created.	as expected
AO-17 Excess sectors are unchanged.	as expected
AO-23 Logged information is correct.	as expected

Analysis: | Expected results achieved

5.2.68   DA-14-CF

Test Case DA-14-CF Smart Version 2010/11/03	
Case Summary:	DA-14 Create an unaligned clone from an image file.
Assertions:	AM-03 The tool executes in execution environment XE. AO-12 If requested, a clone is created from an image file. AO-13 A clone is created using access interface DST-AI to write to the clone device. AO-14 If an unaligned clone is created, each sector written to the clone is accurately written to the same disk address on the clone that the sector occupied on the digital source. AO-17 If requested, any excess sectors on a clone destination device are not modified. AO-23 If the tool logs any log significant information, the information is accurately recorded in the log file.
Tester Name:	brl
Test Host:	Max
Test Date:	Tue Feb 15 11:43:50 2011
Drives:	src(C1-CF) dst (C2-CF) other (3A-SATA)
Source Setup:	src hash (SHA1): < 5B8235178DF99FA307430C088F81746606638A0B > src hash (MD5): < 776DF8B4D2589E21DEBCF589EDC16D78 > 503808 total sectors (257949696 bytes) Model (CF) serial # () N Start LBA Length Start C/H/S End C/H/S boot Partition type 1 P 778135908 1141509631 0357/116/40 0357/032/45 Boot 72 other 2 P 168689522 1936028240 0288/115/43 0367/114/50 Boot 65 other 3 P 1869881465 1936028192 0366/032/33 0357/032/43 Boot 79 other 4 P 2885681152 000055499 0372/097/50 0000/010/00 Boot 0D other 1 1141509631 sectors 584452931072 bytes 2 1936028240 sectors 991246458880 bytes 3 1936028192 sectors 991246434304 bytes 4 000055499 sectors 28415488 bytes
Log Highlights:	====== Destination drive setup ====== 503808 sectors wiped with C1 ====== Comparison of original to clone drive ====== Sectors compared: 503808 Sectors match: 503808 Sectors differ: 0 Bytes differ: 0 Diffs range 0 source read errors, 0 destination read errors ====== Tool Settings: ====== dst-interface USB OS: Linux ubuntu 2.6.32-21-generic #32-Ubuntu SMP Fri Apr 16 08:10:02 UTC 2010 i686 GNU/Linux ======== Excerpt from SMART log ======== Copy: da-07-cf MD5 Span Hashes total span hash: 776df8b4d2589e21debcf589edc16d78 IO Summary:(Time: Tue Feb 15 12:09:30 2011) Bytes Read: 257,949,696 257,949,696 bytes written to /dev/sdb ======== End of Excerpt from SMART log ========
Results:	

Assertion and Expected Result	Actual Result
AM-03 Execution environment is XE.	as expected

Test Case DA-14-CF Smart Version 2010/11/03		
	AO-12 A clone is created from an image file.	as expected
	AO-13 Clone created using interface AI.	as expected
	AO-14 An unaligned clone is created.	as expected
	AO-17 Excess sectors are unchanged.	as expected
	AO-23 Logged information is correct.	as expected
Analysis:	Expected results achieved	

5.2.69   DA-14-ESATA

Test Case DA-14-ESATA Smart Version 2010/11/03	
Case Summary:	DA-14 Create an unaligned clone from an image file.
Assertions:	AM-03 The tool executes in execution environment XE. AO-12 If requested, a clone is created from an image file. AO-13 A clone is created using access interface DST-AI to write to the clone device. AO-14 If an unaligned clone is created, each sector written to the clone is accurately written to the same disk address on the clone that the sector occupied on the digital source. AO-17 If requested, any excess sectors on a clone destination device are not modified. AO-23 If the tool logs any log significant information, the information is accurately recorded in the log file.
Tester Name:	brl
Test Host:	McGarrett
Test Date:	Wed Feb 9 09:28:55 2011
Drives:	src(07-SATA) dst (04-SATA) other (68-SATA)
Source Setup:	src hash (SHA1): < 655E9BDDB36A3F9C5C4CC8BF32B8C5B41AF9F52E > src hash (MD5): < 2EAF712DAD80F66E30DEA00365B4579B > 156301488 total sectors (80026361856 bytes) Model (WDC WD800JD-32HK) serial # (WD-WMAJ91510044) N Start LBA Length Start C/H/S End C/H/S boot Partition type 1 P 000000063 156280257 0000/001/01 1023/254/63 Boot 07 NTFS 2 P 000000000 000000000 0000/000/00 0000/000/00 00 empty entry 3 P 000000000 000000000 0000/000/00 0000/000/00 00 empty entry 4 P 000000000 000000000 0000/000/00 0000/000/00 00 empty entry 1 156280257 sectors 80015491584 bytes
Log Highlights:	====== Destination drive setup ====== 156301488 sectors wiped with 4 ====== Comparison of original to clone drive ====== Sectors compared: 156301488 Sectors match: 156301488 Sectors differ: 0 Bytes differ: 0 Diffs range 0 source read errors, 0 destination read errors ====== Tool Settings: ====== dst-interface SATA28 OS: Linux ubuntu 2.6.32-21-generic #32-Ubuntu SMP Fri Apr 16 08:10:02 UTC 2010 i686 GNU/Linux ======== Excerpt from SMART log ======== Copy: da-06-esata SHA1 Span Hashes total span hash: 655e9bdd b36a3f9c 5c4cc8bf 32b8c5b4 1af9f52e IO Summary:(Time: Wed Feb 9 11:31:30 2011) Bytes Read: 80,026,361,856 80,026,361,856 bytes written to /dev/sdb ======== End of Excerpt from SMART log ========
Results:	

Assertion and Expected Result	Actual Result
AM-03 Execution environment is XE.	as expected
AO-12 A clone is created from an image file.	as expected
AO-13 Clone created using interface AI.	as expected
AO-14 An unaligned clone is created.	as expected

Test Case DA-14-ESATA Smart Version 2010/11/03		
	AO-17 Excess sectors are unchanged.	as expected
	AO-23 Logged information is correct.	as expected
Analysis:	Expected results achieved	

5.2.70   DA-14-EWCOMPRESS

Test Case DA-14-EWCOMPRESS Smart Version 2010/11/03	
Case Summary:	DA-14 Create an unaligned clone from an image file.
Assertions:	AM-03 The tool executes in execution environment XE. AO-12 If requested, a clone is created from an image file. AO-13 A clone is created using access interface DST-AI to write to the clone device. AO-14 If an unaligned clone is created, each sector written to the clone is accurately written to the same disk address on the clone that the sector occupied on the digital source. AO-17 If requested, any excess sectors on a clone destination device are not modified. AO-23 If the tool logs any log significant information, the information is accurately recorded in the log file.
Tester Name:	brl
Test Host:	WoFat
Test Date:	Thu Feb 17 13:43:05 2011
Drives:	src(43) dst (04-IDE) other (67-SATA)
Source Setup:	src hash (SHA1): < 888E2E7F7AD237DC7A732281DD93F325065E5871 > src hash (MD5): < BC39C3F7EE7A50E77B9BA1E65A5AEEF7 > 78125000 total sectors (40000000000 bytes) Model (0BB-75JHC0) serial # (WD-WMAMC46588) N Start LBA Length Start C/H/S End C/H/S boot Partition type 1 P 000000063 020980827 0000/001/01 1023/254/63 0C Fat32X 2 X 020980890 057143205 1023/000/01 1023/254/63 0F extended 3 S 000000063 000032067 1023/001/01 1023/254/63 01 Fat12 4 x 000032130 002104515 1023/000/01 1023/254/63 05 extended 5 S 000000063 002104452 1023/001/01 1023/254/63 06 Fat16 6 x 002136645 004192965 1023/000/01 1023/254/63 05 extended 7 S 000000063 004192902 1023/001/01 1023/254/63 16 other 8 x 006329610 008401995 1023/000/01 1023/254/63 05 extended 9 S 000000063 008401932 1023/001/01 1023/254/63 0B Fat32 10 x 014731605 010490445 1023/000/01 1023/254/63 05 extended 11 S 000000063 010490382 1023/001/01 1023/254/63 83 Linux 12 x 025222050 004209030 1023/000/01 1023/254/63 05 extended 13 S 000000063 004208967 1023/001/01 1023/254/63 82 Linux swap 14 x 029431080 027712125 1023/000/01 1023/254/63 05 extended 15 S 000000063 027712062 1023/001/01 1023/254/63 07 NTFS 16 S 000000000 000000000 0000/000/00 0000/000/00 00 empty entry 17 P 000000000 000000000 0000/000/00 0000/000/00 00 empty entry 18 P 000000000 000000000 0000/000/00 0000/000/00 00 empty entry 1 020980827 sectors 10742183424 bytes 3 000032067 sectors 16418304 bytes 5 002104452 sectors 1077479424 bytes 7 004192902 sectors 2146765824 bytes 9 008401932 sectors 4301789184 bytes 11 010490382 sectors 5371075584 bytes 13 004208967 sectors 2154991104 bytes 15 027712062 sectors 14188575744 bytes
Log Highlights:	====== Destination drive setup ====== 78165360 sectors wiped with 4 ====== Comparison of original to clone drive ====== Sectors compared: 78125000 Sectors match: 78125000 Sectors differ: 0 Bytes differ: 0 Diffs range Source (78125000) has 40360 fewer sectors than destination (78165360) Zero fill: 0 Src Byte fill (43): 0 Dst Byte fill (04): 40360 Other fill: 0 Other no fill: 0

```
Zero fill range:
Src fill range:
Dst fill range: 78125000-78165359
Other fill range:
Other not filled range:
0 source read errors, 0 destination read errors


====== Tool Settings: ======
dst-interface ATA28

OS: Linux ubuntu 2.6.32-21-generic #32-Ubuntu SMP Fri Apr 16 08:10:02 UTC
2010 i686 GNU/Linux

======== Excerpt from SMART log ========

Copy: da-10-ewcompress

SHA1 Span Hashes
 total span hash: 888e2e7f 7ad237dc 7a732281 dd93f325 065e5871

IO Summary:(Time: Thu Feb 17 14:37:20 2011)
Bytes Read: 40,000,000,000
40,000,000,000 bytes written to /dev/sda
======== End of Excerpt from SMART log ========
```

Results:

Assertion and Expected Result	Actual Result
AM-03 Execution environment is XE.	as expected
AO-12 A clone is created from an image file.	as expected
AO-13 Clone created using interface AI.	as expected
AO-14 An unaligned clone is created.	as expected
AO-17 Excess sectors are unchanged.	as expected
AO-23 Logged information is correct.	as expected

Analysis: Expected results achieved

5.2.71 DA-14-EXT2

Test Case DA-14-EXT2 Smart Version 2010/11/03	
Case Summary:	DA-14 Create an unaligned clone from an image file.
Assertions:	AM-03 The tool executes in execution environment XE. AO-12 If requested, a clone is created from an image file. AO-13 A clone is created using access interface DST-AI to write to the clone device. AO-14 If an unaligned clone is created, each sector written to the clone is accurately written to the same disk address on the clone that the sector occupied on the digital source. AO-17 If requested, any excess sectors on a clone destination device are not modified. AO-23 If the tool logs any log significant information, the information is accurately recorded in the log file.
Tester Name:	brl
Test Host:	McGarrett
Test Date:	Tue Mar 1 09:02:01 2011
Drives:	src(43) dst (4E-SATA) other (3A-SATA)
Source Setup:	src hash (SHA1): < 888E2E7F7AD237DC7A732281DD93F325065E5871 > src hash (MD5): < BC39C3F7EE7A50E77B9BA1E65A5AEEF7 > 78125000 total sectors (40000000000 bytes) Model (0BB-75JHC0) serial # (WD-WMAMC46588) N Start LBA Length Start C/H/S End C/H/S boot Partition type 1 P 000000063 020980827 0000/001/01 1023/254/63 0C Fat32X 2 X 020980890 057143205 1023/000/01 1023/254/63 0F extended 3 S 000000063 000032067 1023/001/01 1023/254/63 01 Fat12 4 x 000032130 002104515 1023/000/01 1023/254/63 05 extended 5 S 000000063 002104452 1023/001/01 1023/254/63 06 Fat16 6 x 002136645 004192965 1023/000/01 1023/254/63 05 extended 7 S 000000063 004192902 1023/001/01 1023/254/63 16 other 8 x 006329610 008401995 1023/000/01 1023/254/63 05 extended 9 S 000000063 008401932 1023/001/01 1023/254/63 0B Fat32 10 x 014731605 010490445 1023/000/01 1023/254/63 05 extended 11 S 000000063 010490382 1023/001/01 1023/254/63 83 Linux 12 x 025222050 004209030 1023/000/01 1023/254/63 05 extended 13 S 000000063 004208967 1023/001/01 1023/254/63 82 Linux swap 14 x 029431080 027712125 1023/000/01 1023/254/63 05 extended 15 S 000000063 027712062 1023/001/01 1023/254/63 07 NTFS 16 S 000000000 000000000 0000/000/00 0000/000/00 00 empty entry 17 P 000000000 000000000 0000/000/00 0000/000/00 00 empty entry 18 P 000000000 000000000 0000/000/00 0000/000/00 00 empty entry 1 020980827 sectors 10742183424 bytes 3 000032067 sectors 16418304 bytes 5 002104452 sectors 1077479424 bytes 7 004192902 sectors 2146765824 bytes 9 008401932 sectors 4301789184 bytes 11 010490382 sectors 5371075584 bytes 13 004208967 sectors 2154991104 bytes 15 027712062 sectors 14188575744 bytes 43ext2-md5sum 5371075583 C7A84DE9ACBCB05463604CE8823D0874 43ext2-sha1sum 5371075583 283BCC32DE892C12C37698AF7E38703619E57F57
Log Highlights:	====== Destination drive setup ====== 156301488 sectors wiped with 4E ====== Comparison of original to clone drive ====== Sectors compared: 10490382 Sectors match: 10490382 Sectors differ: 0 Bytes differ: 0 Diffs range: run start Tue Mar 1 09:43:26 2011 run finish Tue Mar 1 09:47:00 2011 elapsed time 0:3:34 Normal exit

```
OS: Linux ubuntu 2.6.32-21-generic #32-Ubuntu SMP Fri Apr 16 08:10:02 UTC
2010 i686 GNU/Linux

======== Excerpt from SMART log ========

Copy: da-07-ext2

SHA1 Span Hashes
 total span hash: 283bcc32 de892c12 c37698af 7e387036 19e57f57

IO Summary:(Time: Tue Mar 1 09:20:27 2011)
Bytes Read: 5,371,075,584
5,371,075,584 bytes written to /dev/sdb9
======== End of Excerpt from SMART log ========
```

Results:

Assertion and Expected Result	Actual Result
AM-03 Execution environment is XE.	as expected
AO-12 A clone is created from an image file.	as expected
AO-13 Clone created using interface AI.	as expected
AO-14 An unaligned clone is created.	as expected
AO-17 Excess sectors are unchanged.	as expected
AO-23 Logged information is correct.	as expected

Analysis: Expected results achieved

5.2.72   DA-14-F12

Test Case DA-14-F12 Smart Version 2010/11/03	
Case Summary:	DA-14 Create an unaligned clone from an image file.
Assertions:	AM-03 The tool executes in execution environment XE. AO-12 If requested, a clone is created from an image file. AO-13 A clone is created using access interface DST-AI to write to the clone device. AO-14 If an unaligned clone is created, each sector written to the clone is accurately written to the same disk address on the clone that the sector occupied on the digital source. AO-17 If requested, any excess sectors on a clone destination device are not modified. AO-23 If the tool logs any log significant information, the information is accurately recorded in the log file.
Tester Name:	brl
Test Host:	McGarrett
Test Date:	Thu Mar 3 12:01:51 2011
Drives:	src(43) dst (4E-SATA) other (3A-SATA)
Source Setup:	src hash (SHA1): < 888E2E7F7AD237DC7A732281DD93F325065E5871 > src hash (MD5): < BC39C3F7EE7A50E77B9BA1E65A5AEEF7 > 78125000 total sectors (40000000000 bytes) Model (0BB-75JHC0) serial # (WD-WMAMC46588) N Start LBA Length Start C/H/S End C/H/S boot Partition type 1 P 000000063 020980827 0000/001/01 1023/254/63 0C Fat32X 2 X 020980890 057143205 1023/000/01 1023/254/63 0F extended 3 S 000000063 000032067 1023/001/01 1023/254/63 01 Fat12 4 x 000032130 002104515 1023/000/01 1023/254/63 05 extended 5 S 000000063 002104452 1023/001/01 1023/254/63 06 Fat16 6 x 002136645 004192965 1023/000/01 1023/254/63 05 extended 7 S 000000063 004192902 1023/001/01 1023/254/63 16 other 8 x 006329610 008401995 1023/000/01 1023/254/63 05 extended 9 S 000000063 008401932 1023/001/01 1023/254/63 0B Fat32 10 x 014731605 010490445 1023/000/01 1023/254/63 05 extended 11 S 000000063 010490382 1023/001/01 1023/254/63 83 Linux 12 x 025222050 004209030 1023/000/01 1023/254/63 05 extended 13 S 000000063 004208967 1023/001/01 1023/254/63 82 Linux swap 14 x 029431080 027712125 1023/000/01 1023/254/63 05 extended 15 S 000000063 027712062 1023/001/01 1023/254/63 07 NTFS 16 S 000000000 000000000 0000/000/00 0000/000/00 00 empty entry 17 P 000000000 000000000 0000/000/00 0000/000/00 00 empty entry 18 P 000000000 000000000 0000/000/00 0000/000/00 00 empty entry 1 020980827 sectors 10742183424 bytes 3 000032067 sectors 16418304 bytes 5 002104452 sectors 1077479424 bytes 7 004192902 sectors 2146765824 bytes 9 008401932 sectors 4301789184 bytes 11 010490382 sectors 5371075584 bytes 13 004208967 sectors 2154991104 bytes 15 027712062 sectors 14188575744 bytes 43F12-md5sum 16418303 CBA0C9984F51778E89DEF0C6BED06864 43F12-sha1sum 16418303 6853B517F50BF3CCADED3DB5FEAE08C18C62FCA0
Log Highlights:	====== Destination drive setup ====== 156301488 sectors wiped with 4E ====== Comparison of original to clone drive ====== Sectors compared: 32067 Sectors match: 32067 Sectors differ: 0 Bytes differ: 0 Diffs range: run start Thu Mar 3 14:37:36 2011 run finish Thu Mar 3 14:37:37 2011 elapsed time 0:0:1 Normal exit

```
OS: Linux ubuntu 2.6.32-21-generic #32-Ubuntu SMP Fri Apr 16 08:10:02 UTC
2010 i686 GNU/Linux

======== Excerpt from SMART log ========

Copy: da-07-f12

SHA1 Span Hashes
 total span hash: 6853b517 f50bf3cc aded3db5 feae08c1 8c62fca0

IO Summary:(Time: Thu Mar 3 14:20:44 2011)
Bytes Read: 16,418,304
16,418,304 bytes written to /dev/sdb5
======== End of Excerpt from SMART log ========
```

Results:

Assertion and Expected Result	Actual Result
AM-03 Execution environment is XE.	as expected
AO-12 A clone is created from an image file.	as expected
AO-13 Clone created using interface AI.	as expected
AO-14 An unaligned clone is created.	as expected
AO-17 Excess sectors are unchanged.	as expected
AO-23 Logged information is correct.	as expected

Analysis: Expected results achieved

5.2.73 DA-14-F16

Test Case DA-14-F16 Smart Version 2010/11/03	
Case Summary:	DA-14 Create an unaligned clone from an image file.
Assertions:	AM-03 The tool executes in execution environment XE. AO-12 If requested, a clone is created from an image file. AO-13 A clone is created using access interface DST-AI to write to the clone device. AO-14 If an unaligned clone is created, each sector written to the clone is accurately written to the same disk address on the clone that the sector occupied on the digital source. AO-17 If requested, any excess sectors on a clone destination device are not modified. AO-23 If the tool logs any log significant information, the information is accurately recorded in the log file.
Tester Name:	brl
Test Host:	McGarrett
Test Date:	Thu Mar 3 16:02:37 2011
Drives:	src(01-IDE) dst (4E-SATA) other (3A-SATA)
Source Setup:	src hash (SHA1): < A48BB5665D6DC57C22DB68E2F723DA9AA8DF82B9 > src hash (MD5): < F458F673894753FA6A0EC8B8EC63848E > 78165360 total sectors (40020664320 bytes) Model (0BB-00JHC0) serial # (WD-WMAMC74171) N Start LBA Length Start C/H/S End C/H/S boot Partition type 1 P 000000063 020980827 0000/001/01 1023/254/63 0C Fat32X 2 X 020980890 057175335 1023/000/01 1023/254/63 0F extended 3 S 000000063 000032067 1023/001/01 1023/254/63 01 Fat12 4 x 000032130 002104515 1023/000/01 1023/254/63 05 extended 5 S 000000063 002104452 1023/001/01 1023/254/63 06 Fat16 6 x 002136645 004192965 1023/000/01 1023/254/63 05 extended 7 S 000000063 004192902 1023/001/01 1023/254/63 16 other 8 x 006329610 008401995 1023/000/01 1023/254/63 05 extended 9 S 000000063 008401932 1023/001/01 1023/254/63 0B Fat32 10 x 014731605 010490445 1023/000/01 1023/254/63 05 extended 11 S 000000063 010490382 1023/001/01 1023/254/63 83 Linux 12 x 025222050 004209030 1023/000/01 1023/254/63 05 extended 13 S 000000063 004208967 1023/001/01 1023/254/63 82 Linux swap 14 x 029431080 027744255 1023/000/01 1023/254/63 05 extended 15 S 000000063 027744192 1023/001/01 1023/254/63 07 NTFS 16 S 000000000 000000000 0000/000/00 0000/000/00 00 empty entry 17 P 000000000 000000000 0000/000/00 0000/000/00 00 empty entry 18 P 000000000 000000000 0000/000/00 0000/000/00 00 empty entry 1 020980827 sectors 10742183424 bytes 3 000032067 sectors 16418304 bytes 5 002104452 sectors 1077479424 bytes 7 004192902 sectors 2146765824 bytes 9 008401932 sectors 4301789184 bytes 11 010490382 sectors 5371075584 bytes 13 004208967 sectors 2154991104 bytes 15 027744192 sectors 14205026304 bytes 01F16-md5 1077479423 8B24F3D793188AF2473F69B267AFDA42 01F16-sha1 1077479423 074BA831B10132F4BF9F86AFAB37CB7FEF482C7D
Log Highlights:	====== Destination drive setup ====== 156301488 sectors wiped with 4E ====== Comparison of original to clone drive ====== Sectors compared: 2104452 Sectors match: 2104452 Sectors differ: 0 Bytes differ: 0 Diffs range: run start Thu Mar 3 16:33:42 2011 run finish Thu Mar 3 16:34:25 2011 elapsed time 0:0:43 Normal exit

```
OS: Linux ubuntu 2.6.32-21-generic #32-Ubuntu SMP Fri Apr 16 08:10:02 UTC
2010 i686 GNU/Linux

======== Excerpt from SMART log ========

Copy: da-07-fat16

SHA1 Span Hashes
 total span hash: 074ba831 b10132f4 bf9f86af ab37cb7f ef482c7d

IO Summary:(Time: Thu Mar 3 16:08:50 2011)
Bytes Read: 1,077,479,424
1,077,479,424 bytes written to /dev/sdb6
======== End of Excerpt from SMART log ========
```

Results:

Assertion and Expected Result	Actual Result
AM-03 Execution environment is XE.	as expected
AO-12 A clone is created from an image file.	as expected
AO-13 Clone created using interface AI.	as expected
AO-14 An unaligned clone is created.	as expected
AO-17 Excess sectors are unchanged.	as expected
AO-23 Logged information is correct.	as expected

Analysis: Expected results achieved

5.2.74   DA-14-F32

Test Case DA-14-F32 Smart Version 2010/11/03	
Case Summary:	DA-14 Create an unaligned clone from an image file.
Assertions:	AM-03 The tool executes in execution environment XE. AO-12 If requested, a clone is created from an image file. AO-13 A clone is created using access interface DST-AI to write to the clone device. AO-14 If an unaligned clone is created, each sector written to the clone is accurately written to the same disk address on the clone that the sector occupied on the digital source. AO-17 If requested, any excess sectors on a clone destination device are not modified. AO-23 If the tool logs any log significant information, the information is accurately recorded in the log file.
Tester Name:	brl
Test Host:	McGarrett
Test Date:	Fri Mar 4 09:03:41 2011
Drives:	src(43) dst (4E-SATA) other (3A-SATA)
Source Setup:	src hash (SHA1): < 888E2E7F7AD237DC7A732281DD93F325065E5871 > src hash (MD5): < BC39C3F7EE7A50E77B9BA1E65A5AEEF7 > 78125000 total sectors (40000000000 bytes) Model (0BB-75JHC0) serial # (WD-WMAMC46588) N Start LBA Length Start C/H/S End C/H/S boot Partition type 1 P 000000063 020980827 0000/001/01 1023/254/63 0C Fat32X 2 X 020980890 057143205 1023/000/01 1023/254/63 0F extended 3 S 000000063 000032067 1023/001/01 1023/254/63 01 Fat12 4 x 000032130 002104515 1023/000/01 1023/254/63 05 extended 5 S 000000063 002104452 1023/001/01 1023/254/63 06 Fat16 6 x 002136645 004192965 1023/000/01 1023/254/63 05 extended 7 S 000000063 004192902 1023/001/01 1023/254/63 16 other 8 x 006329610 008401995 1023/000/01 1023/254/63 05 extended 9 S 000000063 008401932 1023/001/01 1023/254/63 0B Fat32 10 x 014731605 010490445 1023/000/01 1023/254/63 05 extended 11 S 000000063 010490382 1023/001/01 1023/254/63 83 Linux 12 x 025222050 004209030 1023/000/01 1023/254/63 05 extended 13 S 000000063 004208967 1023/001/01 1023/254/63 82 Linux swap 14 x 029431080 027712125 1023/000/01 1023/254/63 05 extended 15 S 000000063 027712062 1023/001/01 1023/254/63 07 NTFS 16 S 000000000 000000000 0000/000/00 0000/000/00 00 empty entry 17 P 000000000 000000000 0000/000/00 0000/000/00 00 empty entry 18 P 000000000 000000000 0000/000/00 0000/000/00 00 empty entry 1 020980827 sectors 10742183424 bytes 3 000032067 sectors 16418304 bytes 5 002104452 sectors 1077479424 bytes 7 004192902 sectors 2146765824 bytes 9 008401932 sectors 4301789184 bytes 11 010490382 sectors 5371075584 bytes 13 004208967 sectors 2154991104 bytes 15 027712062 sectors 14188575744 bytes 43F32-md5sum 4301789183 2C4D8D450E5AD28329F616D87114CCFE 43F32-sha1sum 4301789183 72462489BCF79A98B59B6A8CD938FEB46FA2A781
Log Highlights:	====== Destination drive setup ====== 156301488 sectors wiped with 4E ====== Comparison of original to clone drive ====== Sectors compared: 8401932 Sectors match: 8401932 Sectors differ: 0 Bytes differ: 0 Diffs range: run start Fri Mar 4 10:20:23 2011 run finish Fri Mar 4 10:23:16 2011 elapsed time 0:2:53 Normal exit

	OS: Linux ubuntu 2.6.32-21-generic #32-Ubuntu SMP Fri Apr 16 08:10:02 UTC 2010 i686 GNU/Linux ======== Excerpt from SMART log ======== Copy: da-07-f32 SHA1 Span Hashes total span hash: 72462489 bcf79a98 b59b6a8c d938feb4 6fa2a781 IO Summary:(Time: Fri Mar 4 09:21:06 2011) Bytes Read: 4,301,789,184 4,301,789,184 bytes written to /dev/sdb8 ======== End of Excerpt from SMART log ========
Results:	

Assertion and Expected Result	Actual Result
AM-03 Execution environment is XE.	as expected
AO-12 A clone is created from an image file.	as expected
AO-13 Clone created using interface AI.	as expected
AO-14 An unaligned clone is created.	as expected
AO-17 Excess sectors are unchanged.	as expected
AO-23 Logged information is correct.	as expected

Analysis:	Expected results achieved

5.2.75 DA-14-F32X

Test Case DA-14-F32X Smart Version 2010/11/03	
Case Summary:	DA-14 Create an unaligned clone from an image file.
Assertions:	AM-03 The tool executes in execution environment XE. AO-12 If requested, a clone is created from an image file. AO-13 A clone is created using access interface DST-AI to write to the clone device. AO-14 If an unaligned clone is created, each sector written to the clone is accurately written to the same disk address on the clone that the sector occupied on the digital source. AO-17 If requested, any excess sectors on a clone destination device are not modified. AO-23 If the tool logs any log significant information, the information is accurately recorded in the log file.
Tester Name:	brl
Test Host:	McGarrett
Test Date:	Fri Mar 4 16:05:07 2011
Drives:	src(01-IDE) dst (2A-SATA) other (3A-SATA)
Source Setup:	src hash (SHA1): < A48BB5665D6DC57C22DB68E2F723DA9AA8DF82B9 > src hash (MD5): < F458F673894753FA6A0EC8B8EC63848E > 78165360 total sectors (40020664320 bytes) Model (0BB-00JHC0) serial # (WD-WMAMC74171) N Start LBA Length Start C/H/S End C/H/S boot Partition type 1 P 000000063 020980827 0000/001/01 1023/254/63 0C Fat32X 2 X 020980890 057175335 1023/000/01 1023/254/63 0F extended 3 S 000000063 000032067 1023/001/01 1023/254/63 01 Fat12 4 x 000032130 002104515 1023/000/01 1023/254/63 05 extended 5 S 000000063 002104452 1023/001/01 1023/254/63 06 Fat16 6 x 002136645 004192965 1023/000/01 1023/254/63 05 extended 7 S 000000063 004192902 1023/001/01 1023/254/63 16 other 8 x 006329610 008401995 1023/000/01 1023/254/63 05 extended 9 S 000000063 008401932 1023/001/01 1023/254/63 0B Fat32 10 x 014731605 010490445 1023/000/01 1023/254/63 05 extended 11 S 000000063 010490382 1023/001/01 1023/254/63 83 Linux 12 x 025222050 004209030 1023/000/01 1023/254/63 05 extended 13 S 000000063 004208967 1023/001/01 1023/254/63 82 Linux swap 14 x 029431080 027744255 1023/000/01 1023/254/63 05 extended 15 S 000000063 027744192 1023/001/01 1023/254/63 07 NTFS 16 S 000000000 000000000 0000/000/00 0000/000/00 00 empty entry 17 P 000000000 000000000 0000/000/00 0000/000/00 00 empty entry 18 P 000000000 000000000 0000/000/00 0000/000/00 00 empty entry 1 020980827 sectors 10742183424 bytes 3 000032067 sectors 16418304 bytes 5 002104452 sectors 1077479424 bytes 7 004192902 sectors 2146765824 bytes 9 008401932 sectors 4301789184 bytes 11 010490382 sectors 5371075584 bytes 13 004208967 sectors 2154991104 bytes 15 027744192 sectors 14205026304 bytes 01F32X-md5 10742183423 B5BFD9CE3990C577EF89C5AFB925F947 01F32X-sha1 10742183423 30BA6CF583A176C5DB533E3A2F57BFD5A4A870C1
Log Highlights:	====== Destination drive setup ====== 156250000 sectors wiped with 2A ====== Comparison of original to clone drive ====== Sectors compared: 20980827 Sectors match: 20980827 Sectors differ: 0 Bytes differ: 0 Diffs range: Source (20980827) has 1558305 fewer sectors than destination (22539132) Zero fill: 0 Src Byte fill (01): 0 Dst Byte fill (2A): 1558305

```
Other fill: 0
Other no fill: 0
Zero fill range:
Src fill range:
Dst fill range: 20980827-22539131
Other fill range:
Other not filled range:
run start Fri Mar 4 16:27:53 2011
run finish Fri Mar 4 16:35:05 2011
elapsed time 0:7:12
Normal exit

OS: Linux ubuntu 2.6.32-21-generic #32-Ubuntu SMP Fri Apr 16 08:10:02 UTC
2010 i686 GNU/Linux

======== Excerpt from SMART log ========

Copy: da-07-f32x

SHA1 Span Hashes
 total span hash: 30ba6cf5 83a176c5 db533e3a 2f57bfd5 a4a870c1

IO Summary:(Time: Fri Mar 4 16:14:21 2011)
Bytes Read: 10,742,183,424
10,742,183,424 bytes written to /dev/sdb1
======== End of Excerpt from SMART log ========
```

Results:

Assertion and Expected Result	Actual Result
AM-03 Execution environment is XE.	as expected
AO-12 A clone is created from an image file.	as expected
AO-13 Clone created using interface AI.	as expected
AO-14 An unaligned clone is created.	as expected
AO-17 Excess sectors are unchanged.	as expected
AO-23 Logged information is correct.	as expected

Analysis: Expected results achieved

5.2.76 DA-14-FW

Test Case DA-14-FW Smart Version 2010/11/03	
Case Summary:	DA-14 Create an unaligned clone from an image file.
Assertions:	AM-03 The tool executes in execution environment XE. AO-12 If requested, a clone is created from an image file. AO-13 A clone is created using access interface DST-AI to write to the clone device. AO-14 If an unaligned clone is created, each sector written to the clone is accurately written to the same disk address on the clone that the sector occupied on the digital source. AO-17 If requested, any excess sectors on a clone destination device are not modified. AO-23 If the tool logs any log significant information, the information is accurately recorded in the log file.
Tester Name:	brl
Test Host:	Max
Test Date:	Thu Feb 10 10:12:50 2011
Drives:	src(63-FU2) dst (24) other (3A-SATA)
Source Setup:	src hash (SHA1): < F7069EDCBEAC863C88DECED82159F22DA96BE99B > src hash (MD5): < EE217BC4FA4F3D1B4021D29B065AA9EC > 117304992 total sectors (60060155904 bytes) Model (SP0612N) serial # () N Start LBA Length Start C/H/S End C/H/S boot Partition type 1 P 000000063 004192902 0000/001/01 0260/254/63 Boot 06 Fat16 2 X 004192965 113097600 0261/000/01 1023/254/63 0F extended 3 S 000000063 113097537 0261/001/01 1023/254/63 0B Fat32 4 S 000000000 000000000 0000/000/00 0000/000/00 00 empty entry 5 P 000000000 000000000 0000/000/00 0000/000/00 00 empty entry 6 P 000000000 000000000 0000/000/00 0000/000/00 00 empty entry 1 004192902 sectors 2146765824 bytes 3 113097537 sectors 57905938944 bytes
Log Highlights:	====== Destination drive setup ====== 143374741 sectors wiped with 24 ====== Comparison of original to clone drive ====== Sectors compared: 117304992 Sectors match: 117304992 Sectors differ: 0 Bytes differ: 0 Diffs range Source (117304992) has 26069749 fewer sectors than destination (143374741) Zero fill: 0 Src Byte fill (63): 0 Dst Byte fill (24): 26069749 Other fill: 0 Other no fill: 0 Zero fill range: Src fill range: Dst fill range: 117304992-143374740 Other fill range: Other not filled range: 0 source read errors, 0 destination read errors ====== Tool Settings: ====== dst-interface SCSI OS: Linux ubuntu 2.6.32-21-generic #32-Ubuntu SMP Fri Apr 16 08:10:02 UTC 2010 i686 GNU/Linux ======== Excerpt from SMART log ======== Copy: da-06-fw

Test Case DA-14-FW Smart Version 2010/11/03	
	SHA1 Span Hashes total span hash: f7069edc beac863c 88deced8 2159f22d a96be99b IO Summary:(Time: Thu Feb 10 12:17:20 2011) Bytes Read: 60,060,155,904 60,060,155,904 bytes written to /dev/sdf ======== End of Excerpt from SMART log ========
Results:	

Assertion and Expected Result	Actual Result
AM-03 Execution environment is XE.	as expected
AO-12 A clone is created from an image file.	as expected
AO-13 Clone created using interface AI.	as expected
AO-14 An unaligned clone is created.	as expected
AO-17 Excess sectors are unchanged.	as expected
AO-23 Logged information is correct.	as expected

Analysis:	Expected results achieved

5.2.77   DA-14-GZIP

Test Case DA-14-GZIP Smart Version 2010/11/03	
Case Summary:	DA-14 Create an unaligned clone from an image file.
Assertions:	AM-03 The tool executes in execution environment XE. AO-12 If requested, a clone is created from an image file. AO-13 A clone is created using access interface DST-AI to write to the clone device. AO-14 If an unaligned clone is created, each sector written to the clone is accurately written to the same disk address on the clone that the sector occupied on the digital source. AO-17 If requested, any excess sectors on a clone destination device are not modified. AO-23 If the tool logs any log significant information, the information is accurately recorded in the log file.
Tester Name:	brl
Test Host:	McGarrett
Test Date:	Fri Feb 18 09:37:45 2011
Drives:	src(41) dst (02-IDE) other (68-SATA)
Source Setup:	src hash (SHA1): < 15CAA1A307271160D8372668BF8A03FC45A51CC9 > src hash (MD5): < 0A6A8EF78BDC14E2026710D8CCB5607C > 78125000 total sectors (40000000000 bytes) 65534/015/63 (max cyl/hd values) 65535/016/63 (number of cyl/hd) IDE disk: Model (WDC WD400BB-75JHC0) serial # (WD-WMAMC4658355) N Start LBA Length Start C/H/S End C/H/S boot Partition type 1 P 000000063 078107967 0000/001/01 1023/254/63 Boot 07 NTFS 2 P 000000000 000000000 0000/000/00 0000/000/00 00 empty entry 3 P 000000000 000000000 0000/000/00 0000/000/00 00 empty entry 4 P 000000000 000000000 0000/000/00 0000/000/00 00 empty entry 1 078107967 sectors 39991279104 bytes
Log Highlights:	====== Destination drive setup ====== 78165360 sectors wiped with 2 ====== Comparison of original to clone drive ====== Sectors compared: 78125000 Sectors match: 78125000 Sectors differ: 0 Bytes differ: 0 Diffs range Source (78125000) has 40360 fewer sectors than destination (78165360) Zero fill: 0 Src Byte fill (41): 0 Dst Byte fill (02): 40360 Other fill: 0 Other no fill: 0 Zero fill range: Src fill range: Dst fill range: 78125000-78165359 Other fill range: Other not filled range: 0 source read errors, 0 destination read errors ====== Tool Settings: ====== dst-interface ATA28 OS: Linux ubuntu 2.6.32-21-generic #32-Ubuntu SMP Fri Apr 16 08:10:02 UTC 2010 i686 GNU/Linux ======== Excerpt from SMART log ======== Copy: da-10-gzip SHA1 Span Hashes

Test Case DA-14-GZIP Smart Version 2010/11/03	
	total span hash: 15caa1a3 07271160 d8372668 bf8a03fc 45a51cc9 IO Summary:(Time: Fri Feb 18 10:12:44 2011) Bytes Read: 40,000,000,000 40,000,000,000 bytes written to /dev/sdb ======== End of Excerpt from SMART log ========
Results:	

Assertion and Expected Result	Actual Result
AM-03 Execution environment is XE.	as expected
AO-12 A clone is created from an image file.	as expected
AO-13 Clone created using interface AI.	as expected
AO-14 An unaligned clone is created.	as expected
AO-17 Excess sectors are unchanged.	as expected
AO-23 Logged information is correct.	as expected

Analysis:	Expected results achieved

5.2.78 DA-14-HOT

Test Case DA-14-HOT Smart Version 2010/11/03	
Case Summary:	DA-14 Create an unaligned clone from an image file.
Assertions:	AM-03 The tool executes in execution environment XE.
	AO-12 If requested, a clone is created from an image file.
	AO-13 A clone is created using access interface DST-AI to write to the clone device.
	AO-14 If an unaligned clone is created, each sector written to the clone is accurately written to the same disk address on the clone that the sector occupied on the digital source.
	AO-17 If requested, any excess sectors on a clone destination device are not modified.
	AO-23 If the tool logs any log significant information, the information is accurately recorded in the log file.
Tester Name:	brl
Test Host:	Max
Test Date:	Tue Feb 22 14:11:54 2011
Drives:	src(E0) dst (25-IDE) other (74-SATA-SSD)
Source Setup:	src hash (SHA1): < 4A6941F1337A8A22B10FC844B4D7FA6158BECB82 >
	src hash (MD5): < A97C8F36B7AC9D5233B90AC09284F938 >
	17938985 total sectors (9184760320 bytes)
	Model (ATLAS10K2-TY092J) serial # (169028142436)
Log Highlights:	====== Destination drive setup ======
	58633344 sectors wiped with 25
	====== Comparison of original to clone drive ======
	Sectors compared: 17938985
	Sectors match: 17938985
	Sectors differ: 0
	Bytes differ: 0
	Diffs range
	Source (17938985) has 40694359 fewer sectors than destination (58633344)
	Zero fill: 0
	Src Byte fill (E0): 0
	Dst Byte fill (25): 40694359
	Other fill: 0
	Other no fill: 0
	Zero fill range:
	Src fill range:
	Dst fill range: 17938985-58633343
	Other fill range:
	Other not filled range:
	0 source read errors, 0 destination read errors
	====== Tool Settings: ======
	dst-interface ATA28
	OS: Linux ubuntu 2.6.32-21-generic #32-Ubuntu SMP Fri Apr 16 08:10:02 UTC 2010 i686 GNU/Linux
	======== Excerpt from SMART log ========
	Copy: da-13
	SHA1 Span Hashes
	total span hash: 4a6941f1 337a8a22 b10fc844 b4d7fa61 58becb82
	IO Summary:(Time: Tue Feb 22 15:12:34 2011)
	Bytes Read: 9,184,760,320
	9,184,760,320 bytes written to /dev/sda
	======== End of Excerpt from SMART log ========
Results:	

Test Case DA-14-HOT Smart Version 2010/11/03		
	Assertion and Expected Result	**Actual Result**
	AM-03 Execution environment is XE.	as expected
	AO-12 A clone is created from an image file.	as expected
	AO-13 Clone created using interface AI.	as expected
	AO-14 An unaligned clone is created.	as expected
	AO-17 Excess sectors are unchanged.	as expected
	AO-23 Logged information is correct.	as expected
Analysis:	Expected results achieved	

5.2.79 DA-14-NTFS

Test Case DA-14-NTFS Smart Version 2010/11/03	
Case Summary:	DA-14 Create an unaligned clone from an image file.
Assertions:	AM-03 The tool executes in execution environment XE. AO-12 If requested, a clone is created from an image file. AO-13 A clone is created using access interface DST-AI to write to the clone device. AO-14 If an unaligned clone is created, each sector written to the clone is accurately written to the same disk address on the clone that the sector occupied on the digital source. AO-17 If requested, any excess sectors on a clone destination device are not modified. AO-23 If the tool logs any log significant information, the information is accurately recorded in the log file.
Tester Name:	brl
Test Host:	McGarrett
Test Date:	Fri Mar 4 09:11:33 2011
Drives:	src(43) dst (4E-SATA) other (3A-SATA)
Source Setup:	src hash (SHA1): < 888E2E7F7AD237DC7A732281DD93F325065E5871 > src hash (MD5): < BC39C3F7EE7A50E77B9BA1E65A5AEEF7 > 78125000 total sectors (40000000000 bytes) Model (0BB-75JHC0) serial # (WD-WMAMC46588) N Start LBA Length Start C/H/S End C/H/S boot Partition type 1 P 000000063 020980827 0000/001/01 1023/254/63 0C Fat32X 2 X 020980890 057143205 1023/000/01 1023/254/63 0F extended 3 S 000000063 000032067 1023/001/01 1023/254/63 01 Fat12 4 x 000032130 002104515 1023/000/01 1023/254/63 05 extended 5 S 000000063 002104452 1023/001/01 1023/254/63 06 Fat16 6 x 002136645 004192965 1023/000/01 1023/254/63 05 extended 7 S 000000063 004192902 1023/001/01 1023/254/63 16 other 8 x 006329610 008401995 1023/000/01 1023/254/63 05 extended 9 S 000000063 008401932 1023/001/01 1023/254/63 0B Fat32 10 x 014731605 010490445 1023/000/01 1023/254/63 05 extended 11 S 000000063 010490382 1023/001/01 1023/254/63 83 Linux 12 x 025222050 004209030 1023/000/01 1023/254/63 05 extended 13 S 000000063 004208967 1023/001/01 1023/254/63 82 Linux swap 14 x 029431080 027712125 1023/000/01 1023/254/63 05 extended 15 S 000000063 027712062 1023/001/01 1023/254/63 07 NTFS 16 S 000000000 000000000 0000/000/00 0000/000/00 00 empty entry 17 P 000000000 000000000 0000/000/00 0000/000/00 00 empty entry 18 P 000000000 000000000 0000/000/00 0000/000/00 00 empty entry 1 020980827 sectors 10742183424 bytes 3 000032067 sectors 16418304 bytes 5 002104452 sectors 1077479424 bytes 7 004192902 sectors 2146765824 bytes 9 008401932 sectors 4301789184 bytes 11 010490382 sectors 5371075584 bytes 13 004208967 sectors 2154991104 bytes 15 027712062 sectors 14188575744 bytes 43ntfs-md5sum 14188575744 5D42FA317C802ACFEF2D313092D7411E 43ntfs-sha1sum 14188575744 73eb2d27564b060db796efb78694a10e6b43d23f
Log Highlights:	====== Destination drive setup ====== 156301488 sectors wiped with 4E ====== Comparison of original to clone drive ====== Sectors compared: 27712062 Sectors match: 27712062 Sectors differ: 0 Bytes differ: 0 Diffs range: run start Fri Mar 4 10:24:36 2011 run finish Fri Mar 4 10:34:04 2011 elapsed time 0:9:28 Normal exit

```
Test Case DA-14-NTFS Smart Version 2010/11/03
```

```
        OS: Linux ubuntu 2.6.32-21-generic #32-Ubuntu SMP Fri Apr 16 08:10:02 UTC
        2010 i686 GNU/Linux

        ======== Excerpt from SMART log ========

        Copy: da-07-ntfs

        SHA1 Span Hashes
         total span hash: 73eb2d27 564b060d b796efb7 8694a10e 6b43d23f

        IO Summary:(Time: Fri Mar 4 09:37:15 2011)
        Bytes Read: 14,188,575,744
        14,188,575,744 bytes written to /dev/sdb11
        ======== End of Excerpt from SMART log ========
```

Results:

Assertion and Expected Result	Actual Result
AM-03 Execution environment is XE.	as expected
AO-12 A clone is created from an image file.	as expected
AO-13 Clone created using interface AI.	as expected
AO-14 An unaligned clone is created.	as expected
AO-17 Excess sectors are unchanged.	as expected
AO-23 Logged information is correct.	as expected

Analysis: Expected results achieved

5.2.80   DA-14-OSX

Test Case DA-14-OSX Smart Version 2010/11/03	
Case Summary:	DA-14 Create an unaligned clone from an image file.
Assertions:	AM-03 The tool executes in execution environment XE. AO-12 If requested, a clone is created from an image file. AO-13 A clone is created using access interface DST-AI to write to the clone device. AO-14 If an unaligned clone is created, each sector written to the clone is accurately written to the same disk address on the clone that the sector occupied on the digital source. AO-17 If requested, any excess sectors on a clone destination device are not modified. AO-23 If the tool logs any log significant information, the information is accurately recorded in the log file.
Tester Name:	brl
Test Host:	WoFat
Test Date:	Mon Feb 28 15:10:10 2011
Drives:	src(4B-SATA) dst (58-SATA) other (67-SATA)
Source Setup:	src hash (SHA1): < 70CC62B43F6A41CA4D6760AA0B9B4C415D3F48E2 > src hash (MD5): < 746B4C06CDD5FBD67C0820DB4325B40C > 156301488 total sectors (80026361856 bytes) Model (ST380815AS) serial # (6QZ5C9V5) N Start LBA Length Start C/H/S End C/H/S boot Partition type 1 P 000000063 020971520 0000/001/01 1023/254/63 AF other 2 P 020971629 010485536 1023/254/63 1023/254/63 AF other 3 P 031457223 006291456 1023/254/63 1023/254/63 A8 other 4 X 037748679 008388694 1023/254/63 1023/254/63 05 extended 5 S 000000039 004194304 1023/254/63 1023/254/63 AF other 6 x 004194343 004194351 1023/254/63 1023/254/63 05 extended 7 S 000000047 004194304 1023/254/63 1023/254/63 AF other 8 S 000000000 000000000 0000/000/00 0000/000/00 00 empty entry 1 020971520 sectors 10737418240 bytes 2 010485536 sectors 5368594432 bytes 3 006291456 sectors 3221225472 bytes 5 004194304 sectors 2147483648 bytes 7 004194304 sectors 2147483648 bytes 4BOSX-sha1 5368594432 3DE70998AD136E66CD09B9B4F2F5164E77B3B705 Excess destination partition sectors hash: SHA1 5368594432 - 5368709119 = DAE359ECCBFC5A24528469B7E2075B76D6E48891 -
Log Highlights:	====== Destination drive setup ====== 312581808 sectors wiped with 58 ====== Comparison of original to clone drive ====== Sectors compared: 10485536 Sectors match: 10485536 Sectors differ: 0 Bytes differ: 0 Diffs range: Source (10485536) has 224 fewer sectors than destination (10485760) Zero fill: 7 Src Byte fill (4B): 0 Dst Byte fill (58): 216 Other fill: 0 Other no fill: 1 Zero fill range: 10485752-10485757, 10485759 Src fill range: Dst fill range: 10485536-10485751 Other fill range: Other not filled range: 10485758 run start Tue Mar 1 08:27:24 2011 run finish Tue Mar 1 08:30:21 2011 elapsed time 0:2:57 Normal exit

OS: Linux ubuntu 2.6.32-21-generic #32-Ubuntu SMP Fri Apr 16 08:10:02 UTC
2010 i686 GNU/Linux

======== Excerpt from SMART log ========

Copy: da-07-osx

SHA1 Span Hashes
 total span hash: 3de70998 ad136e66 cd09b9b4 f2f5164e 77b3b705

IO Summary:(Time: Mon Feb 28 16:04:33 2011)
Bytes Read: 5,368,594,432
5,368,594,432 bytes written to /dev/sdb2
======== End of Excerpt from SMART log ========

Excess destination partition sectors hash:
SHA1 5368594432 - 5368709119 = DAE359ECCBFC5A24528469B7E2075B76D6E48891 -

Results:

Assertion and Expected Result	Actual Result
AM-03 Execution environment is XE.	as expected
AO-12 A clone is created from an image file.	as expected
AO-13 Clone created using interface AI.	as expected
AO-14 An unaligned clone is created.	as expected
AO-17 Excess sectors are unchanged.	as expected
AO-23 Logged information is correct.	as expected

Analysis: Expected results achieved

5.2.81 DA-14-OSXC

Test Case DA-14-OSXC Smart Version 2010/11/03	
Case Summary:	DA-14 Create an unaligned clone from an image file.
Assertions:	AM-03 The tool executes in execution environment XE. AO-12 If requested, a clone is created from an image file. AO-13 A clone is created using access interface DST-AI to write to the clone device. AO-14 If an unaligned clone is created, each sector written to the clone is accurately written to the same disk address on the clone that the sector occupied on the digital source. AO-17 If requested, any excess sectors on a clone destination device are not modified. AO-23 If the tool logs any log significant information, the information is accurately recorded in the log file.
Tester Name:	brl
Test Host:	WoFat
Test Date:	Fri Mar 4 10:38:30 2011
Drives:	src(4B-SATA) dst (58-SATA) other (67-SATA)
Source Setup:	src hash (SHA1): < 70CC62B43F6A41CA4D6760AA0B9B4C415D3F48E2 > src hash (MD5): < 746B4C06CDD5FBD67C0820DB4325B40C > 156301488 total sectors (80026361856 bytes) Model (ST380815AS) serial # (6QZ5C9V5) N Start LBA Length Start C/H/S End C/H/S boot Partition type 1 P 000000063 020971520 0000/001/01 1023/254/63 AF other 2 P 020971629 010485536 1023/254/63 1023/254/63 AF other 3 P 031457223 006291456 1023/254/63 1023/254/63 A8 other 4 X 037748679 008388694 1023/254/63 1023/254/63 05 extended 5 S 000000039 004194304 1023/254/63 1023/254/63 AF other 6 x 004194343 004194351 1023/254/63 1023/254/63 05 extended 7 S 000000047 004194304 1023/254/63 1023/254/63 AF other 8 S 000000000 000000000 0000/000/00 0000/000/00 00 empty entry 1 020971520 sectors 10737418240 bytes 2 010485536 sectors 5368594432 bytes 3 006291456 sectors 3221225472 bytes 5 004194304 sectors 2147483648 bytes 7 004194304 sectors 2147483648 bytes 4BOSXC-sha1 2147483648 2D6303D74F9EDE617639643DCCF41EC2091D5F37
Log Highlights:	====== Destination drive setup ====== 312581808 sectors wiped with 58 ====== Comparison of original to clone drive ====== Sectors compared: 4194304 Sectors match: 4194304 Sectors differ: 0 Bytes differ: 0 Diffs range: run start Fri Mar 4 10:58:14 2011 run finish Fri Mar 4 10:59:24 2011 elapsed time 0:1:10 Normal exit OS: Linux ubuntu 2.6.32-21-generic #32-Ubuntu SMP Fri Apr 16 08:10:02 UTC 2010 i686 GNU/Linux ======== Excerpt from SMART log ======== Copy: da-07-osxc SHA1 Span Hashes total span hash: 2d6303d7 4f9ede61 7639643d ccf41ec2 091d5f37 IO Summary:(Time: Fri Mar 4 10:46:54 2011) Bytes Read: 2,147,483,648 2,147,483,648 bytes written to /dev/sdb5

Test Case DA-14-OSXC Smart Version 2010/11/03
======== End of Excerpt from SMART log ========

Results:		
	Assertion and Expected Result	**Actual Result**
	AM-03 Execution environment is XE.	as expected
	AO-12 A clone is created from an image file.	as expected
	AO-13 Clone created using interface AI.	as expected
	AO-14 An unaligned clone is created.	as expected
	AO-17 Excess sectors are unchanged.	as expected
	AO-23 Logged information is correct.	as expected
Analysis:	Expected results achieved	

5.2.82   DA-14-OSXCJ

Test Case DA-14-OSXCJ Smart Version 2010/11/03	
Case Summary:	DA-14 Create an unaligned clone from an image file.
Assertions:	AM-03 The tool executes in execution environment XE. AO-12 If requested, a clone is created from an image file. AO-13 A clone is created using access interface DST-AI to write to the clone device. AO-14 If an unaligned clone is created, each sector written to the clone is accurately written to the same disk address on the clone that the sector occupied on the digital source. AO-17 If requested, any excess sectors on a clone destination device are not modified. AO-23 If the tool logs any log significant information, the information is accurately recorded in the log file.
Tester Name:	brl
Test Host:	WoFat
Test Date:	Fri Mar 4 14:55:21 2011
Drives:	src(4B-SATA) dst (58-SATA) other (67-SATA)
Source Setup:	src hash (SHA1): < 70CC62B43F6A41CA4D6760AA0B9B4C415D3F48E2 > src hash (MD5): < 746B4C06CDD5FBD67C0820DB4325B40C > 156301488 total sectors (80026361856 bytes) Model (ST380815AS) serial # (6QZ5C9V5) N Start LBA Length Start C/H/S End C/H/S boot Partition type 1 P 000000063 020971520 0000/001/01 1023/254/63 AF other 2 P 020971629 010485536 1023/254/63 1023/254/63 AF other 3 P 031457223 006291456 1023/254/63 1023/254/63 A8 other 4 X 037748679 008388694 1023/254/63 1023/254/63 05 extended 5 S 000000039 004194304 1023/254/63 1023/254/63 AF other 6 x 004194343 004194351 1023/254/63 1023/254/63 05 extended 7 S 000000047 004194304 1023/254/63 1023/254/63 AF other 8 S 000000000 000000000 0000/000/00 0000/000/00 00 empty entry 1 020971520 sectors 10737418240 bytes 2 010485536 sectors 5368594432 bytes 3 006291456 sectors 3221225472 bytes 5 004194304 sectors 2147483648 bytes 7 004194304 sectors 2147483648 bytes 4BOSXCJ-sha1 2147483648 29EA089958EF2A695081712FFBA68BA5164C980B
Log Highlights:	====== Destination drive setup ====== 312581808 sectors wiped with 58 ====== Comparison of original to clone drive ====== Sectors compared: 4194304 Sectors match: 4194304 Sectors differ: 0 Bytes differ: 0 Diffs range: run start Fri Mar 4 15:11:39 2011 run finish Fri Mar 4 15:12:49 2011 elapsed time 0:1:10 Normal exit OS: Linux ubuntu 2.6.32-21-generic #32-Ubuntu SMP Fri Apr 16 08:10:02 UTC 2010 i686 GNU/Linux ======== Excerpt from SMART log ======== Copy: da-07-osxcj SHA1 Span Hashes total span hash: 29ea0899 58ef2a69 5081712f fba68ba5 164c980b IO Summary:(Time: Fri Mar 4 14:59:08 2011) Bytes Read: 2,147,483,648 2,147,483,648 bytes written to /dev/sdb6

Test Case DA-14-OSXCJ Smart Version 2010/11/03

======== End of Excerpt from SMART log ========

Results:

Assertion and Expected Result	Actual Result
AM-03 Execution environment is XE.	as expected
AO-12 A clone is created from an image file.	as expected
AO-13 Clone created using interface AI.	as expected
AO-14 An unaligned clone is created.	as expected
AO-17 Excess sectors are unchanged.	as expected
AO-23 Logged information is correct.	as expected

Analysis: Expected results achieved

5.2.83 DA-14-OSXJ

Test Case DA-14-OSXJ Smart Version 2010/11/03	
Case Summary:	DA-14 Create an unaligned clone from an image file.
Assertions:	AM-03 The tool executes in execution environment XE. AO-12 If requested, a clone is created from an image file. AO-13 A clone is created using access interface DST-AI to write to the clone device. AO-14 If an unaligned clone is created, each sector written to the clone is accurately written to the same disk address on the clone that the sector occupied on the digital source. AO-17 If requested, any excess sectors on a clone destination device are not modified. AO-23 If the tool logs any log significant information, the information is accurately recorded in the log file.
Tester Name:	brl
Test Host:	WoFat
Test Date:	Mon Feb 28 10:31:15 2011
Drives:	src(4B-SATA) dst (58-SATA) other (67-SATA)
Source Setup:	src hash (SHA1): < 70CC62B43F6A41CA4D6760AA0B9B4C415D3F48E2 > src hash (MD5): < 746B4C06CDD5FBD67C0820DB4325B40C > 156301488 total sectors (80026361856 bytes) Model (ST380815AS) serial # (6QZ5C9V5) N Start LBA Length Start C/H/S End C/H/S boot Partition type 1 P 000000063 020971520 0000/001/01 1023/254/63 AF other 2 P 020971629 010485536 1023/254/63 1023/254/63 AF other 3 P 031457223 006291456 1023/254/63 1023/254/63 A8 other 4 X 037748679 008388694 1023/254/63 1023/254/63 05 extended 5 S 000000039 004194304 1023/254/63 1023/254/63 AF other 6 x 004194343 004194351 1023/254/63 1023/254/63 05 extended 7 S 000000047 004194304 1023/254/63 1023/254/63 AF other 8 S 000000000 000000000 0000/000/00 0000/000/00 00 empty entry 1 020971520 sectors 10737418240 bytes 2 010485536 sectors 5368594432 bytes 3 006291456 sectors 3221225472 bytes 5 004194304 sectors 2147483648 bytes 7 004194304 sectors 2147483648 bytes 4BOSXJ-sha1 10737418240 37311859444BD914EDAD43D93F2862E76B279A87
Log Highlights:	====== Destination drive setup ====== 312581808 sectors wiped with 58 ====== Comparison of original to clone drive ====== Sectors compared: 20971520 Sectors match: 20971520 Sectors differ: 0 Bytes differ: 0 Diffs range: run start Mon Feb 28 10:53:54 2011 run finish Mon Feb 28 10:59:45 2011 elapsed time 0:5:51 Normal exit OS: Linux ubuntu 2.6.32-21-generic #32-Ubuntu SMP Fri Apr 16 08:10:02 UTC 2010 i686 GNU/Linux ======== Excerpt from SMART log ======== Copy: da-07-osxj SHA1 Span Hashes total span hash: 37311859 444bd914 edad43d9 3f2862e7 6b279a87 IO Summary:(Time: Mon Feb 28 10:40:33 2011) Bytes Read: 10,737,418,240 10,737,418,240 bytes written to /dev/sdb1

Test Case DA-14-OSXJ Smart Version 2010/11/03	
	======== End of Excerpt from SMART log ========
Results:	

Assertion and Expected Result	Actual Result
AM-03 Execution environment is XE.	as expected
AO-12 A clone is created from an image file.	as expected
AO-13 Clone created using interface AI.	as expected
AO-14 An unaligned clone is created.	as expected
AO-17 Excess sectors are unchanged.	as expected
AO-23 Logged information is correct.	as expected

Analysis:	Expected results achieved

5.2.84 DA-14-OSXU

Test Case DA-14-OSXU Smart Version 2010/11/03	
Case Summary:	DA-14 Create an unaligned clone from an image file.
Assertions:	AM-03 The tool executes in execution environment XE. AO-12 If requested, a clone is created from an image file. AO-13 A clone is created using access interface DST-AI to write to the clone device. AO-14 If an unaligned clone is created, each sector written to the clone is accurately written to the same disk address on the clone that the sector occupied on the digital source. AO-17 If requested, any excess sectors on a clone destination device are not modified. AO-23 If the tool logs any log significant information, the information is accurately recorded in the log file.
Tester Name:	brl
Test Host:	WoFat
Test Date:	Fri Mar 4 15:37:07 2011
Drives:	src(4B-SATA) dst (58-SATA) other (67-SATA)
Source Setup:	src hash (SHA1): < 70CC62B43F6A41CA4D6760AA0B9B4C415D3F48E2 > src hash (MD5): < 746B4C06CDD5FBD67C0820DB4325B40C > 156301488 total sectors (80026361856 bytes) Model (ST380815AS) serial # (6QZ5C9V5) N Start LBA Length Start C/H/S End C/H/S boot Partition type 1 P 000000063 020971520 0000/001/01 1023/254/63 AF other 2 P 020971629 010485536 1023/254/63 1023/254/63 AF other 3 P 031457223 006291456 1023/254/63 1023/254/63 A8 other 4 X 037748679 008388694 1023/254/63 1023/254/63 05 extended 5 S 000000039 004194304 1023/254/63 1023/254/63 AF other 6 x 004194343 004194351 1023/254/63 1023/254/63 05 extended 7 S 000000047 004194304 1023/254/63 1023/254/63 AF other 8 S 000000000 000000000 0000/000/00 0000/000/00 00 empty entry 1 020971520 sectors 10737418240 bytes 2 010485536 sectors 5368594432 bytes 3 006291456 sectors 3221225472 bytes 5 004194304 sectors 2147483648 bytes 7 004194304 sectors 2147483648 bytes 4BOSXU-sha1 3221225472 D102A01562C82533C052CE6CFBB1D467EC9B5BC6
Log Highlights:	====== Destination drive setup ====== 312581808 sectors wiped with 58 ====== Comparison of original to clone drive ====== Sectors compared: 6291456 Sectors match: 6291456 Sectors differ: 0 Bytes differ: 0 Diffs range: run start Fri Mar 4 16:13:11 2011 run finish Fri Mar 4 16:14:58 2011 elapsed time 0:1:47 Normal exit OS: Linux ubuntu 2.6.32-21-generic #32-Ubuntu SMP Fri Apr 16 08:10:02 UTC 2010 i686 GNU/Linux ======== Excerpt from SMART log ======== Copy: da-07-osxu SHA1 Span Hashes total span hash: d102a015 62c82533 c052ce6c fbb1d467 ec9b5bc6 IO Summary:(Time: Fri Mar 4 15:43:40 2011) Bytes Read: 3,221,225,472 3,221,225,472 bytes written to /dev/sdb3

Test Case DA-14-OSXU Smart Version 2010/11/03	
	======== End of Excerpt from SMART log ========
Results:	

Assertion and Expected Result	Actual Result
AM-03 Execution environment is XE.	as expected
AO-12 A clone is created from an image file.	as expected
AO-13 Clone created using interface AI.	as expected
AO-14 An unaligned clone is created.	as expected
AO-17 Excess sectors are unchanged.	as expected
AO-23 Logged information is correct.	as expected

Analysis:	Expected results achieved

5.2.85   DA-14-SATA28

Test Case DA-14-SATA28 Smart Version 2010/11/03	
Case Summary:	DA-14 Create an unaligned clone from an image file.
Assertions:	AM-03 The tool executes in execution environment XE. AO-12 If requested, a clone is created from an image file. AO-13 A clone is created using access interface DST-AI to write to the clone device. AO-14 If an unaligned clone is created, each sector written to the clone is accurately written to the same disk address on the clone that the sector occupied on the digital source. AO-17 If requested, any excess sectors on a clone destination device are not modified. AO-23 If the tool logs any log significant information, the information is accurately recorded in the log file.
Tester Name:	brl
Test Host:	McGarrett
Test Date:	Mon Feb 14 10:22:56 2011
Drives:	src(4B-SATA) dst (24-SATA) other (68-SATA)
Source Setup:	src hash (SHA1): < 70CC62B43F6A41CA4D6760AA0B9B4C415D3F48E2 > src hash (MD5): < 746B4C06CDD5FBD67C0820DB4325B40C > 156301488 total sectors (80026361856 bytes) Model (ST380815AS) serial # (6QZ5C9V5) N Start LBA Length Start C/H/S End C/H/S boot Partition type 1 P 000000063 020971520 0000/001/01 1023/254/63 AF other 2 P 020971629 010485536 1023/254/63 1023/254/63 AF other 3 P 031457223 006291456 1023/254/63 1023/254/63 A8 other 4 X 037748679 008388694 1023/254/63 1023/254/63 05 extended 5 S 000000039 004194304 1023/254/63 1023/254/63 AF other 6 x 004194343 004194351 1023/254/63 1023/254/63 05 extended 7 S 000000047 004194304 1023/254/63 1023/254/63 AF other 8 S 000000000 000000000 0000/000/00 0000/000/00 00 empty entry 1 020971520 sectors 10737418240 bytes 2 010485536 sectors 5368594432 bytes 3 006291456 sectors 3221225472 bytes 5 004194304 sectors 2147483648 bytes 7 004194304 sectors 2147483648 bytes
Log Highlights:	====== Destination drive setup ====== 156301488 sectors wiped with 24 ====== Comparison of original to clone drive ====== Sectors compared: 156301488 Sectors match: 156301488 Sectors differ: 0 Bytes differ: 0 Diffs range 0 source read errors, 0 destination read errors ====== Tool Settings: ====== dst-interface SATA28 OS: Linux ubuntu 2.6.32-21-generic #32-Ubuntu SMP Fri Apr 16 08:10:02 UTC 2010 i686 GNU/Linux ======== Excerpt from SMART log ======== Copy: da-06-sata28 SHA1 Span Hashes total span hash: 70cc62b4 3f6a41ca 4d6760aa 0b9b4c41 5d3f48e2 IO Summary:(Time: Mon Feb 14 14:09:47 2011) Bytes Read: 80,026,361,856 80,026,361,856 bytes written to /dev/sdb

Test Case DA-14-SATA28 Smart Version 2010/11/03	
	======== End of Excerpt from SMART log ========
Results:	

Assertion and Expected Result	Actual Result
AM-03 Execution environment is XE.	as expected
AO-12 A clone is created from an image file.	as expected
AO-13 Clone created using interface AI.	as expected
AO-14 An unaligned clone is created.	as expected
AO-17 Excess sectors are unchanged.	as expected
AO-23 Logged information is correct.	as expected

Analysis:	Expected results achieved

5.2.86   DA-14-SATA28-IMAGE2

Test Case DA-14-SATA28-IMAGE2 Smart Version 2010/11/03	
Case Summary:	DA-14 Create an unaligned clone from an image file.
Assertions:	AM-03 The tool executes in execution environment XE. AO-12 If requested, a clone is created from an image file. AO-13 A clone is created using access interface DST-AI to write to the clone device. AO-14 If an unaligned clone is created, each sector written to the clone is accurately written to the same disk address on the clone that the sector occupied on the digital source. AO-17 If requested, any excess sectors on a clone destination device are not modified. AO-23 If the tool logs any log significant information, the information is accurately recorded in the log file.
Tester Name:	brl
Test Host:	McGarrett
Test Date:	Mon Feb 14 10:24:07 2011
Drives:	src(4B-SATA) dst (25-SATA) other (5A-SATA)
Source Setup:	src hash (SHA1): < 70CC62B43F6A41CA4D6760AA0B9B4C415D3F48E2 > src hash (MD5): < 746B4C06CDD5FBD67C0820DB4325B40C > 156301488 total sectors (80026361856 bytes) Model (ST380815AS) serial # (6QZ5C9V5) N Start LBA Length Start C/H/S End C/H/S boot Partition type 1 P 000000063 020971520 0000/001/01 1023/254/63 AF other 2 P 020971629 010485536 1023/254/63 1023/254/63 AF other 3 P 031457223 006291456 1023/254/63 1023/254/63 A8 other 4 X 037748679 008388694 1023/254/63 1023/254/63 05 extended 5 S 000000039 004194304 1023/254/63 1023/254/63 AF other 6 x 004194343 004194351 1023/254/63 1023/254/63 05 extended 7 S 000000047 004194304 1023/254/63 1023/254/63 AF other 8 S 000000000 000000000 0000/000/00 0000/000/00 00 empty entry 1 020971520 sectors 10737418240 bytes 2 010485536 sectors 5368594432 bytes 3 006291456 sectors 3221225472 bytes 5 004194304 sectors 2147483648 bytes 7 004194304 sectors 2147483648 bytes
Log Highlights:	====== Destination drive setup ====== 156301488 sectors wiped with 25 ====== Comparison of original to clone drive ====== Sectors compared: 156301488 Sectors match: 156301488 Sectors differ: 0 Bytes differ: 0 Diffs range 0 source read errors, 0 destination read errors ====== Tool Settings: ====== dst-interface SATA28 OS: Linux ubuntu 2.6.32-21-generic #32-Ubuntu SMP Fri Apr 16 08:10:02 UTC 2010 i686 GNU/Linux ======== Excerpt from SMART log ======== Copy: da-06-sata28-image2 SHA1 Span Hashes total span hash: 70cc62b4 3f6a41ca 4d6760aa 0b9b4c41 5d3f48e2 IO Summary:(Time: Mon Feb 14 14:12:59 2011) Bytes Read: 80,026,361,856 80,026,361,856 bytes written to /dev/sdc

Test Case DA-14-SATA28-IMAGE2 Smart Version 2010/11/03	
	======== End of Excerpt from SMART log ========
Results:	

Assertion and Expected Result	Actual Result
AM-03 Execution environment is XE.	as expected
AO-12 A clone is created from an image file.	as expected
AO-13 Clone created using interface AI.	as expected
AO-14 An unaligned clone is created.	as expected
AO-17 Excess sectors are unchanged.	as expected
AO-23 Logged information is correct.	as expected

Analysis:	Expected results achieved

5.2.87 DA-14-SATA48

Test Case DA-14-SATA48 Smart Version 2010/11/03	
Case Summary:	DA-14 Create an unaligned clone from an image file.
Assertions:	AM-03 The tool executes in execution environment XE. AO-12 If requested, a clone is created from an image file. AO-13 A clone is created using access interface DST-AI to write to the clone device. AO-14 If an unaligned clone is created, each sector written to the clone is accurately written to the same disk address on the clone that the sector occupied on the digital source. AO-17 If requested, any excess sectors on a clone destination device are not modified. AO-23 If the tool logs any log significant information, the information is accurately recorded in the log file.
Tester Name:	brl
Test Host:	WoFat
Test Date:	Fri Feb 11 08:24:02 2011
Drives:	src(0D-SATA) dst (46-SATA) other (67-SATA)
Source Setup:	src hash (SHA1): < BAAD80E8781E55F2E3EF528CA73BD41D228C1377 > src hash (MD5): < 1FA7C3CBE60EB9E89863DED2411E40C9 > 488397168 total sectors (250059350016 bytes) 30400/254/63 (max cyl/hd values) 30401/255/63 (number of cyl/hd) Model (WDC WD2500JD-22F) serial # (WD-WMAEH2678216) N Start LBA Length Start C/H/S End C/H/S boot Partition type 1 P 000000063 488375937 0000/001/01 1023/254/63 Boot 07 NTFS 2 P 000000000 000000000 0000/000/00 0000/000/00 00 empty entry 3 P 000000000 000000000 0000/000/00 0000/000/00 00 empty entry 4 P 000000000 000000000 0000/000/00 0000/000/00 00 empty entry 1 488375937 sectors 250048479744 bytes
Log Highlights:	====== Destination drive setup ====== 488397168 sectors wiped with 46 ====== Comparison of original to clone drive ====== Sectors compared: 488397168 Sectors match: 488397168 Sectors differ: 0 Bytes differ: 0 Diffs range 0 source read errors, 0 destination read errors ====== Tool Settings: ====== dst-interface SATA48 OS: Linux ubuntu 2.6.32-21-generic #32-Ubuntu SMP Fri Apr 16 08:10:02 UTC 2010 i686 GNU/Linux ======== Excerpt from SMART log ======== Copy: da-06-sata48 SHA1 Span Hashes total span hash: baad80e8 781e55f2 e3ef528c a73bd41d 228c1377 IO Summary:(Time: Fri Feb 11 10:42:01 2011) Bytes Read: 250,059,350,016 250,059,350,016 bytes written to /dev/sdb ======== End of Excerpt from SMART log ========
Results:	

Assertion and Expected Result	Actual Result
AM-03 Execution environment is XE.	as expected
AO-12 A clone is created from an image file.	as expected

Test Case DA-14-SATA48 Smart Version 2010/11/03		
AO-13 Clone created using interface AI.	as expected	
AO-14 An unaligned clone is created.	as expected	
AO-17 Excess sectors are unchanged.	as expected	
AO-23 Logged information is correct.	as expected	
Analysis:	Expected results achieved	

5.2.88 DA-14-SCSI

Test Case DA-14-SCSI Smart Version 2010/11/03	
Case Summary:	DA-14 Create an unaligned clone from an image file.
Assertions:	AM-03 The tool executes in execution environment XE. AO-12 If requested, a clone is created from an image file. AO-13 A clone is created using access interface DST-AI to write to the clone device. AO-14 If an unaligned clone is created, each sector written to the clone is accurately written to the same disk address on the clone that the sector occupied on the digital source. AO-17 If requested, any excess sectors on a clone destination device are not modified. AO-23 If the tool logs any log significant information, the information is accurately recorded in the log file.
Tester Name:	brl
Test Host:	Max
Test Date:	Wed Feb 9 09:11:09 2011
Drives:	src(E0) dst (CC) other (3A-SATA)
Source Setup:	src hash (SHA1): < 4A6941F1337A8A22B10FC844B4D7FA6158BECB82 > src hash (MD5): < A97C8F36B7AC9D5233B90AC09284F938 > 17938985 total sectors (9184760320 bytes) Model (ATLAS10K2-TY092J) serial # (169028142436)
Log Highlights:	====== Destination drive setup ====== 71687370 sectors wiped with CC ====== Comparison of original to clone drive ====== Sectors compared: 17938985 Sectors match: 17938985 Sectors differ: 0 Bytes differ: 0 Diffs range Source (17938985) has 53748385 fewer sectors than destination (71687370) Zero fill: 0 Src Byte fill (E0): 0 Dst Byte fill (CC): 53748385 Other fill: 0 Other no fill: 0 Zero fill range: Src fill range: Dst fill range: 17938985-71687369 Other fill range: Other not filled range: 0 source read errors, 0 destination read errors ====== Tool Settings: ====== dst-interface SCSI OS: Linux ubuntu 2.6.32-21-generic #32-Ubuntu SMP Fri Apr 16 08:10:02 UTC 2010 i686 GNU/Linux ======== Excerpt from SMART log ======== Copy: da-06-scsi SHA1 Span Hashes total span hash: 4a6941f1 337a8a22 b10fc844 b4d7fa61 58becb82 IO Summary:(Time: Wed Feb 9 10:15:15 2011) Bytes Read: 9,184,760,320 9,184,760,320 bytes written to /dev/sdf ======== End of Excerpt from SMART log ========
Results:	

Test Case DA-14-SCSI Smart Version 2010/11/03		
	Assertion and Expected Result	**Actual Result**
	AM-03 Execution environment is XE.	as expected
	AO-12 A clone is created from an image file.	as expected
	AO-13 Clone created using interface AI.	as expected
	AO-14 An unaligned clone is created.	as expected
	AO-17 Excess sectors are unchanged.	as expected
	AO-23 Logged information is correct.	as expected
Analysis:	Expected results achieved	

5.2.89 DA-14-SWAP

Test Case DA-14-SWAP Smart Version 2010/11/03	
Case Summary:	DA-14 Create an unaligned clone from an image file.
Assertions:	AM-03 The tool executes in execution environment XE. AO-12 If requested, a clone is created from an image file. AO-13 A clone is created using access interface DST-AI to write to the clone device. AO-14 If an unaligned clone is created, each sector written to the clone is accurately written to the same disk address on the clone that the sector occupied on the digital source. AO-17 If requested, any excess sectors on a clone destination device are not modified. AO-23 If the tool logs any log significant information, the information is accurately recorded in the log file.
Tester Name:	brl
Test Host:	McGarrett
Test Date:	Fri Mar 4 09:12:51 2011
Drives:	src(43) dst (4E-SATA) other (3A-SATA)
Source Setup:	src hash (SHA1): < 888E2E7F7AD237DC7A732281DD93F325065E5871 > src hash (MD5): < BC39C3F7EE7A50E77B9BA1E65A5AEEF7 > 78125000 total sectors (40000000000 bytes) Model (0BB-75JHC0) serial # (WD-WMAMC46588) N Start LBA Length Start C/H/S End C/H/S boot Partition type 1 P 000000063 020980827 0000/001/01 1023/254/63 0C Fat32X 2 X 020980890 057143205 1023/000/01 1023/254/63 0F extended 3 S 000000063 000032067 1023/001/01 1023/254/63 01 Fat12 4 x 000032130 002104515 1023/000/01 1023/254/63 05 extended 5 S 000000063 002104452 1023/001/01 1023/254/63 06 Fat16 6 x 002136645 004192965 1023/000/01 1023/254/63 05 extended 7 S 000000063 004192902 1023/001/01 1023/254/63 16 other 8 x 006329610 008401995 1023/000/01 1023/254/63 05 extended 9 S 000000063 008401932 1023/001/01 1023/254/63 0B Fat32 10 x 014731605 010490445 1023/000/01 1023/254/63 05 extended 11 S 000000063 010490382 1023/001/01 1023/254/63 83 Linux 12 x 025222050 004209030 1023/000/01 1023/254/63 05 extended 13 S 000000063 004208967 1023/001/01 1023/254/63 82 Linux swap 14 x 029431080 027712125 1023/000/01 1023/254/63 05 extended 15 S 000000063 027712062 1023/001/01 1023/254/63 07 NTFS 16 S 000000000 000000000 0000/000/00 0000/000/00 00 empty entry 17 P 000000000 000000000 0000/000/00 0000/000/00 00 empty entry 18 P 000000000 000000000 0000/000/00 0000/000/00 00 empty entry 1 020980827 sectors 10742183424 bytes 3 000032067 sectors 16418304 bytes 5 002104452 sectors 1077479424 bytes 7 004192902 sectors 2146765824 bytes 9 008401932 sectors 4301789184 bytes 11 010490382 sectors 5371075584 bytes 13 004208967 sectors 2154991104 bytes 15 027712062 sectors 14188575744 bytes 43swap-md5sum 2154991103 4B602964A30FE20D1B22B046A7375A7C 43swap-sha1sum 2154991103 F5B062CC31DA088DF7FAF8F7A47E500BF4244BCF
Log Highlights:	====== Destination drive setup ====== 156301488 sectors wiped with 4E ====== Comparison of original to clone drive ====== Sectors compared: 4208967 Sectors match: 4208960 Sectors differ: 7 Bytes differ: 3493 Diffs range: 4208960-4208966 run start Fri Mar 4 10:52:10 2011 run finish Fri Mar 4 10:53:34 2011 elapsed time 0:1:24 Normal exit

Test Case DA-14-SWAP Smart Version 2010/11/03	
	OS: Linux ubuntu 2.6.32-21-generic #32-Ubuntu SMP Fri Apr 16 08:10:02 UTC 2010 i686 GNU/Linux ======== Excerpt from SMART log ======== Copy: da-07-swap task aborted. IO Summary: Discrepancy! (Time: Fri Mar 4 10:04:29 2011) Bytes Read: 2,154,991,104 2,154,987,520 bytes written to /dev/sdb10 ======== End of Excerpt from SMART log ========
Results:	

Assertion and Expected Result	Actual Result
AM-03 Execution environment is XE.	as expected
AO-12 A clone is created from an image file.	task aborted
AO-13 Clone created using interface AI.	as expected
AO-14 An unaligned clone is created.	last seven sectors skipped
AO-17 Excess sectors are unchanged.	as expected
AO-23 Logged information is correct.	as expected

Analysis:	Expected results not achieved

5.2.90 DA-14-SWAP-ALT

Test Case DA-14-SWAP-ALT Smart Version 2010/11/03	
Case Summary:	DA-14 Create an unaligned clone from an image file.
Assertions:	AM-03 The tool executes in execution environment XE. AO-12 If requested, a clone is created from an image file. AO-13 A clone is created using access interface DST-AI to write to the clone device. AO-14 If an unaligned clone is created, each sector written to the clone is accurately written to the same disk address on the clone that the sector occupied on the digital source. AO-17 If requested, any excess sectors on a clone destination device are not modified. AO-23 If the tool logs any log significant information, the information is accurately recorded in the log file.
Tester Name:	brl
Test Host:	McGarrett
Test Date:	Fri Mar 11 10:38:12 2011
Drives:	src(43) dst (45-SATA) other (3A-SATA)
Source Setup:	src hash (SHA1): < 888E2E7F7AD237DC7A732281DD93F325065E5871 > src hash (MD5): < BC39C3F7EE7A50E77B9BA1E65A5AEEF7 > 78125000 total sectors (40000000000 bytes) Model (0BB-75JHC0) serial # (WD-WMAMC46588) N Start LBA Length Start C/H/S End C/H/S boot Partition type 1 P 000000063 020980827 0000/001/01 1023/254/63 0C Fat32X 2 X 020980890 057143205 1023/000/01 1023/254/63 0F extended 3 S 000000063 000032067 1023/001/01 1023/254/63 01 Fat12 4 x 000032130 002104515 1023/000/01 1023/254/63 05 extended 5 S 000000063 002104452 1023/001/01 1023/254/63 06 Fat16 6 x 002136645 004192965 1023/000/01 1023/254/63 05 extended 7 S 000000063 004192902 1023/001/01 1023/254/63 16 other 8 x 006329610 008401995 1023/000/01 1023/254/63 05 extended 9 S 000000063 008401932 1023/001/01 1023/254/63 0B Fat32 10 x 014731605 010490445 1023/000/01 1023/254/63 05 extended 11 S 000000063 010490382 1023/001/01 1023/254/63 83 Linux 12 x 025222050 004209030 1023/000/01 1023/254/63 05 extended 13 S 000000063 004208967 1023/001/01 1023/254/63 82 Linux swap 14 x 029431080 027712125 1023/000/01 1023/254/63 05 extended 15 S 000000063 027712062 1023/001/01 1023/254/63 07 NTFS 16 S 000000000 000000000 0000/000/00 0000/000/00 00 empty entry 17 P 000000000 000000000 0000/000/00 0000/000/00 00 empty entry 18 P 000000000 000000000 0000/000/00 0000/000/00 00 empty entry 1 020980827 sectors 10742183424 bytes 3 000032067 sectors 16418304 bytes 5 002104452 sectors 1077479424 bytes 7 004192902 sectors 2146765824 bytes 9 008401932 sectors 4301789184 bytes 11 010490382 sectors 5371075584 bytes 13 004208967 sectors 2154991104 bytes 15 027712062 sectors 14188575744 bytes 43swap-md5sum 2154991103 4B602964A30FE20D1B22B046A7375A7C 43swap-sha1sum 2154991103 F5B062CC31DA088DF7FAF8F7A47E500BF4244BCF
Log Highlights:	====== Destination drive setup ====== 10000001 sectors wiped with 45 ====== Comparison of original to clone drive ====== Sectors compared: 4208967 Sectors match: 4208960 Sectors differ: 7 Bytes differ: 3577 Diffs range: 4208960-4208966 Source (4208967) has 1028097 fewer sectors than destination (5237064) Zero fill: 0 Src Byte fill (43): 0 Dst Byte fill (45): 1028097

```
Other fill: 0
Other no fill: 0
Zero fill range:
Src fill range:
Dst fill range: 4208967-5237063
Other fill range:
Other not filled range:
run start Fri Mar 11 11:42:43 2011
run finish Fri Mar 11 11:44:46 2011
elapsed time 0:2:3
Normal exit

OS: Linux ubuntu 2.6.32-21-generic #32-Ubuntu SMP Fri Apr 16 08:10:02 UTC
2010 i686 GNU/Linux

======== Excerpt from SMART log ========

Copy: da-07-swap

SHA1 Span Hashes
 total span hash: 18b73d89 2d772b88 437ce039 2e1732ca 8fe2a2f4

IO Summary:(Time: Fri Mar 11 11:27:51 2011)
Bytes Read: 2,154,991,104
2,154,991,104 bytes written to /dev/sda5
======== End of Excerpt from SMART log ========
```

Results:		
	Assertion and Expected Result	**Actual Result**
	AM-03 Execution environment is XE.	as expected
	AO-12 A clone is created from an image file.	as expected
	AO-13 Clone created using interface AI.	as expected
	AO-14 An unaligned clone is created.	as expected
	AO-17 Excess sectors are unchanged.	as expected
	AO-23 Logged information is correct.	as expected

Analysis:	Expected results achieved

5.2.91 DA-14-THUMB

Test Case DA-14-THUMB Smart Version 2010/11/03	
Case Summary:	DA-14 Create an unaligned clone from an image file.
Assertions:	AM-03 The tool executes in execution environment XE.
	AO-12 If requested, a clone is created from an image file.
	AO-13 A clone is created using access interface DST-AI to write to the clone device.
	AO-14 If an unaligned clone is created, each sector written to the clone is accurately written to the same disk address on the clone that the sector occupied on the digital source.
	AO-17 If requested, any excess sectors on a clone destination device are not modified.
	AO-23 If the tool logs any log significant information, the information is accurately recorded in the log file.
Tester Name:	brl
Test Host:	Max
Test Date:	Tue Feb 15 14:38:47 2011
Drives:	src(D5-THUMB) dst (D6-THUMB) other (3A-SATA)
Source Setup:	src hash (SHA1): < D68520EF74A336E49DCCF83815B7B08FDC53E38A >
	src hash (MD5): < C843593624B2B3B878596D8760B19954 >
	505856 total sectors (258998272 bytes)
	Model (usb2.0Flash Disk) serial # ()
Log Highlights:	====== Destination drive setup ======
	4001760 sectors wiped with D6
	====== Comparison of original to clone drive ======
	Sectors compared: 505856
	Sectors match: 505856
	Sectors differ: 0
	Bytes differ: 0
	Diffs range
	Source (505856) has 3495904 fewer sectors than destination (4001760)
	Zero fill: 0
	Src Byte fill (D5): 0
	Dst Byte fill (D6): 3495904
	Other fill: 0
	Other no fill: 0
	Zero fill range:
	Src fill range:
	Dst fill range: 505856-4001759
	Other fill range:
	Other not filled range:
	0 source read errors, 0 destination read errors
	====== Tool Settings: ======
	dst-interface USB
	OS: Linux ubuntu 2.6.32-21-generic #32-Ubuntu SMP Fri Apr 16 08:10:02 UTC 2010 i686 GNU/Linux
	======== Excerpt from SMART log ========
	Copy: da-07-thumb
	SHA1 Span Hashes
	total span hash: d68520ef 74a336e4 9dccf838 15b7b08f dc53e38a
	IO Summary:(Time: Tue Feb 15 15:00:44 2011)
	Bytes Read: 258,998,272
	258,998,272 bytes written to /dev/sdg
	======== End of Excerpt from SMART log ========
Results:	

Test Case DA-14-THUMB Smart Version 2010/11/03		
	Assertion and Expected Result	**Actual Result**
	AM-03 Execution environment is XE.	as expected
	AO-12 A clone is created from an image file.	as expected
	AO-13 Clone created using interface AI.	as expected
	AO-14 An unaligned clone is created.	as expected
	AO-17 Excess sectors are unchanged.	as expected
	AO-23 Logged information is correct.	as expected
Analysis:	Expected results achieved	

5.2.92   DA-14-USB

Test Case DA-14-USB Smart Version 2010/11/03	
Case Summary:	DA-14 Create an unaligned clone from an image file.
Assertions:	AM-03 The tool executes in execution environment XE. AO-12 If requested, a clone is created from an image file. AO-13 A clone is created using access interface DST-AI to write to the clone device. AO-14 If an unaligned clone is created, each sector written to the clone is accurately written to the same disk address on the clone that the sector occupied on the digital source. AO-17 If requested, any excess sectors on a clone destination device are not modified. AO-23 If the tool logs any log significant information, the information is accurately recorded in the log file.
Tester Name:	brl
Test Host:	Max
Test Date:	Fri Feb 11 12:54:07 2011
Drives:	src(63-FU2) dst (24) other (3A-SATA)
Source Setup:	src hash (SHA1): < F7069EDCBEAC863C88DECED82159F22DA96BE99B > src hash (MD5): < EE217BC4FA4F3D1B4021D29B065AA9EC > 117304992 total sectors (60060155904 bytes) Model (SP0612N) serial # () N Start LBA Length Start C/H/S End C/H/S boot Partition type 1 P 000000063 004192902 0000/001/01 0260/254/63 Boot 06 Fat16 2 X 004192965 113097600 0261/000/01 1023/254/63 0F extended 3 S 000000063 113097537 0261/001/01 1023/254/63 0B Fat32 4 S 000000000 000000000 0000/000/00 0000/000/00 00 empty entry 5 P 000000000 000000000 0000/000/00 0000/000/00 00 empty entry 6 P 000000000 000000000 0000/000/00 0000/000/00 00 empty entry 1 004192902 sectors 2146765824 bytes 3 113097537 sectors 57905938944 bytes
Log Highlights:	====== Destination drive setup ====== 143374741 sectors wiped with 24 ====== Comparison of original to clone drive ====== Sectors compared: 117304992 Sectors match: 117304992 Sectors differ: 0 Bytes differ: 0 Diffs range Source (117304992) has 26069749 fewer sectors than destination (143374741) Zero fill: 0 Src Byte fill (63): 0 Dst Byte fill (24): 26069749 Other fill: 0 Other no fill: 0 Zero fill range: Src fill range: Dst fill range: 117304992-143374740 Other fill range: Other not filled range: 0 source read errors, 0 destination read errors ====== Tool Settings: ====== dst-interface SCSI OS: Linux ubuntu 2.6.32-21-generic #32-Ubuntu SMP Fri Apr 16 08:10:02 UTC 2010 i686 GNU/Linux ======== Excerpt from SMART log ======== Copy: da-06-usb

	SHA1 Span Hashes total span hash: f7069edc beac863c 88deced8 2159f22d a96be99b IO Summary:(Time: Mon Feb 14 11:12:53 2011) Bytes Read: 60,060,155,904 60,060,155,904 bytes written to /dev/sdf ======== End of Excerpt from SMART log ========
Results:	

Assertion and Expected Result	Actual Result
AM-03 Execution environment is XE.	as expected
AO-12 A clone is created from an image file.	as expected
AO-13 Clone created using interface AI.	as expected
AO-14 An unaligned clone is created.	as expected
AO-17 Excess sectors are unchanged.	as expected
AO-23 Logged information is correct.	as expected

Analysis:	Expected results achieved

5.2.93 DA-16

Test Case DA-16 Smart Version 2010/11/03	
Case Summary:	DA-16 Create a clone from a subset of an image file.
Assertions:	AM-03 The tool executes in execution environment XE. AO-12 If requested, a clone is created from an image file. AO-13 A clone is created using access interface DST-AI to write to the clone device. AO-16 If a subset of an image or acquisition is specified, all the subset is cloned. AO-17 If requested, any excess sectors on a clone destination device are not modified. AO-23 If the tool logs any log significant information, the information is accurately recorded in the log file.
Tester Name:	brl
Test Host:	Max
Test Date:	Wed Feb 23 15:27:53 2011
Drives:	src(E0) dst (25-IDE) other (3A-SATA)
Source Setup:	src hash (SHA1): < 4A6941F1337A8A22B10FC844B4D7FA6158BECB82 > src hash (MD5): < A97C8F36B7AC9D5233B90AC09284F938 > 17938985 total sectors (9184760320 bytes) Model (ATLAS10K2-TY092J) serial # (169028142436) Excess destination partition sectors hash: @(#) winhash.csh Version 1.4 Created 04/25/08 at 11:28:17 SHA1 0 - 16775167 83722BE316F75C95CEF0E5DC0D0BC9B00B3E8D84 - SHA1 16775168 - 33550335 AACEF840D1C70A07B6F0C7462B68AE164065D2D3 - SHA1 33550336 - 50325503 9C072363D41686AF51AB19ECB9B4BC53B238D271 - SHA1 50325504 - 58633343 C4F5D56895B9C6815A41FDA2B6137E8B70400253 -
Log Highlights:	====== Destination drive setup ====== 58633344 sectors wiped with 25 ====== Comparison of original to clone drive ====== Sectors compared: 17938985 Sectors match: 1163817 Sectors differ: 16775168 Bytes differ: 8152731648 Diffs range 0-16775167 Source (17938985) has 40694359 fewer sectors than destination (58633344) Zero fill: 0 Src Byte fill (E0): 0 Dst Byte fill (25): 40694359 Other fill: 0 Other no fill: 0 Zero fill range: Src fill range: Dst fill range: 17938985-58633343 Other fill range: Other not filled range: 0 source read errors, 0 destination read errors ====== Tool Settings: ====== dst-interface ATA28 OS: Linux ubuntu 2.6.32-21-generic #32-Ubuntu SMP Fri Apr 16 08:10:02 UTC 2010 i686 GNU/Linux ======== Excerpt from SMART log ======== Copy: da-06-scsi SHA1 Span Hashes total span hash: f0a0f715 c3e17726 4ab36bde 9580cd40 b58dc89a IO Summary:(Time: Thu Feb 24 13:56:20 2011)

Test Case DA-16 Smart Version 2010/11/03	
	Bytes Read: 595,874,304 595,874,304 bytes written to ======== End of Excerpt from SMART log ======== Excess destination partition sectors hash: @(#) winhash.csh Version 1.4 Created 04/25/08 at 11:28:17 SHA1 0 - 16775167 83722BE316F75C95CEF0E5DC0D0BC9B00B3E8D84 - SHA1 16775168 - 33550335 91BDAB284F11FD6DD54A26C7BFC7356002A47E97 - SHA1 33550336 - 50325503 9C072363D41686AF51AB19ECB9B4BC53B238D271 - SHA1 50325504 - 58633343 C4F5D56895B9C6815A41FDA2B6137E8B70400253 -
Results:	

Assertion and Expected Result	Actual Result
AM-03 Execution environment is XE.	as expected
AO-12 A clone is created from an image file.	as expected
AO-13 Clone created using interface AI.	as expected
AO-16 Clone is created from a subset of an image.	as expected
AO-17 Excess sectors are unchanged.	as expected
AO-23 Logged information is correct.	as expected

Analysis:	Expected results achieved

5.2.94 DA-17

Test Case DA-17 Smart Version 2010/11/03	
Case Summary:	DA-17 Create a truncated clone from an image file.
Assertions :	AM-03 The tool executes in execution environment XE. AO-12 If requested, a clone is created from an image file. AO-13 A clone is created using access interface DST-AI to write to the clone device. AO-19 If there is insufficient space to create a complete clone, a truncated clone is created using all available sectors of the clone device. AO-20 If a truncated clone is created, the tool notifies the user. AO-23 If the tool logs any log significant information, the information is accurately recorded in the log file.
Tester Name:	brl
Test Host:	McGarrett
Test Date:	Mon Feb 28 10:09:06 2011
Drives:	src(63-FU2) dst (02-IDE) other (3A-SATA)
Source Setup:	src hash (SHA1): < F7069EDCBEAC863C88DECED82159F22DA96BE99B > src hash (MD5): < EE217BC4FA4F3D1B4021D29B065AA9EC > 117304992 total sectors (60060155904 bytes) Model (SP0612N) serial # () N Start LBA Length Start C/H/S End C/H/S boot Partition type 1 P 000000063 004192902 0000/001/01 0260/254/63 Boot 06 Fat16 2 X 004192965 113097600 0261/000/01 1023/254/63 0F extended 3 S 000000063 113097537 0261/001/01 1023/254/63 0B Fat32 4 S 000000000 000000000 0000/000/00 0000/000/00 00 empty entry 5 P 000000000 000000000 0000/000/00 0000/000/00 00 empty entry 6 P 000000000 000000000 0000/000/00 0000/000/00 00 empty entry 1 004192902 sectors 2146765824 bytes 3 113097537 sectors 57905938944 bytes
Log Highlights :	====== Destination drive setup ====== 78165360 sectors wiped with 2 ====== Screen Message: ====== 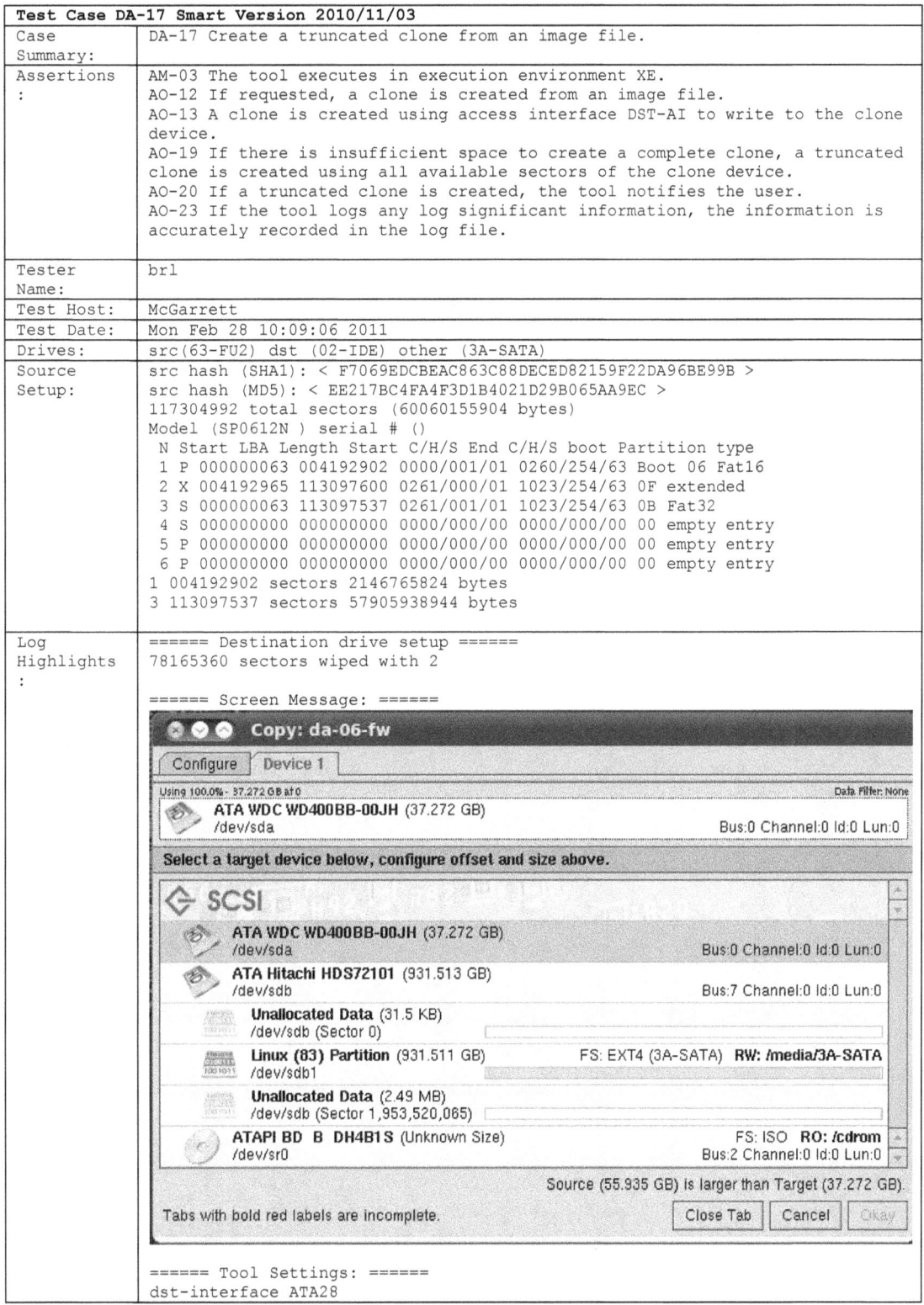 ====== Tool Settings: ====== dst-interface ATA28

```
Test Case DA-17 Smart Version 2010/11/03
```

	OS: Linux ubuntu 2.6.32-21-generic #32-Ubuntu SMP Fri Apr 16 08:10:02 UTC 2010 i686 GNU/Linux ======== Excerpt from SMART log ======== No logfile created ======== End of Excerpt from SMART log ========
Results:	

Assertion and Expected Result	Actual Result
AM-03 Execution environment is XE.	as expected
AO-12 A clone is created from an image file.	as expected
AO-13 Clone created using interface AI.	as expected
AO-19 Truncated clone is created.	as expected
AO-20 User notified that clone is truncated.	as expected
AO-23 Logged information is correct.	as expected

Analysis:	Expected results achieved

5.2.95   DA-24

Test Case DA-24 Smart Version 2010/11/03	
Case Summary:	DA-24 Verify a valid image.
Assertions:	AM-03 The tool executes in execution environment XE. AO-06 If the tool performs an image file integrity check on an image file that has not been changed since the file was created, the tool shall notify the user that the image file has not been changed. AO-23 If the tool logs any log significant information, the information is accurately recorded in the log file.
Tester Name:	brl
Test Host:	Max
Test Date:	Fri Feb 25 10:03:23 2011
Drives:	src(E0) dst (none) other (3A-SATA)
Source Setup:	src hash (SHA1): < 4A6941F1337A8A22B10FC844B4D7FA6158BECB82 > src hash (MD5): < A97C8F36B7AC9D5233B90AC09284F938 > 17938985 total sectors (9184760320 bytes) Model (ATLAS10K2-TY092J) serial # (169028142436)
Log Highlights:	====== Screen Message: ====== ======== Excerpt from SMART log ======== Authenticate: da-06-scsi (PASSED) Current Hash Summary SHA1 Span Hashes total span hash: 4a6941f1 337a8a22 b10fc844 b4d7fa61 58becb82 Stored Hashes SHA1 Span Hashes total span hash: 4a6941f1 337a8a22 b10fc844 b4d7fa61 58becb82 ======== End of Excerpt from SMART log ========
Results:	

Assertion and Expected Result	Actual Result
AM-03 Execution environment is XE.	as expected
AO-06 Tool verifies image file unchanged.	as expected
AO-23 Logged information is correct.	as expected

Analysis:	Expected results achieved

5.2.96   DA-24-DEVICE

Test Case DA-24-DEVICE Smart Version 2010/11/03	
Case Summary:	DA-24 Verify a valid image.
Assertions:	AM-03 The tool executes in execution environment XE. AO-06 If the tool performs an image file integrity check on an image file that has not been changed since the file was created, the tool shall notify the user that the image file has not been changed. AO-23 If the tool logs any log significant information, the information is accurately recorded in the log file.
Tester Name:	brl
Test Host:	Max
Test Date:	Fri Feb 25 10:22:51 2011
Drives:	src(E0) dst (none) other (3A-SATA)
Source Setup:	src hash (SHA1): < 4A6941F1337A8A22B10FC844B4D7FA6158BECB82 > src hash (MD5): < A97C8F36B7AC9D5233B90AC09284F938 > 17938985 total sectors (9184760320 bytes) Model (ATLAS10K2-TY092J) serial # (169028142436)
Log Highlights:	====== Screen Message: ====== ⚠ Okay ======== Excerpt from SMART log ======== Authenticate: da-06-scsi (PASSED) Image Hash Summary SHA1 Span Hashes total span hash: 4a6941f1 337a8a22 b10fc844 b4d7fa61 58becb82 Device Hash Summary SHA1 Span Hashes total span hash: 4a6941f1 337a8a22 b10fc844 b4d7fa61 58becb82 ======== End of Excerpt from SMART log ========
Results:	

Assertion and Expected Result	Actual Result
AM-03 Execution environment is XE.	as expected
AO-06 Tool verifies image file unchanged.	as expected
AO-23 Logged information is correct.	as expected

Analysis:	Expected results achieved

5.2.97 DA-25

Test Case DA-25 Smart Version 2010/11/03	
Case Summary:	DA-25 Detect a corrupted image.
Assertions:	AM-03 The tool executes in execution environment XE. AO-07 If the tool performs an image file integrity check on an image file that has been changed since the file was created, the tool shall notify the user that the image file has been changed. AO-08 If the tool performs an image file integrity check on an image file that has been changed since the file was created, the tool shall notify the user of the affected locations. AO-23 If the tool logs any log significant information, the information is accurately recorded in the log file.
Tester Name:	brl
Test Host:	Max
Test Date:	Fri Feb 25 13:46:52 2011
Drives:	src(E0) dst (none) other (3A-SATA)
Source Setup:	src hash (SHA1): < 4A6941F1337A8A22B10FC844B4D7FA6158BECB82 > src hash (MD5): < A97C8F36B7AC9D5233B90AC09284F938 > 17938985 total sectors (9184760320 bytes) Model (ATLAS10K2-TY092J) serial # (169028142436)
Log Highlights:	====== Image file corrupted for test run: ====== Change byte 2059 of file /media/3A-SATA/da-06-scsi/da-06-scsi.image.001 from 0x35 to 0x00 ======== Excerpt from SMART log ======== Authenticate: da-06-scsi (FAILED) Current Hash Summary SHA1 Span Hashes total span hash: c233b031 3d626b4d 390e40bf 7065a30b 6fb48bde Stored Hashes SHA1 Span Hashes total span hash: 4a6941f1 337a8a22 b10fc844 b4d7fa61 58becb82 ======== End of Excerpt from SMART log ========
Results:	<table><tr><th>Assertion and Expected Result</th><th>Actual Result</th></tr><tr><td>AM-03 Execution environment is XE.</td><td>as expected</td></tr><tr><td>AO-07 User notified if image file has changed.</td><td>as expected</td></tr><tr><td>AO-08 User notified of changed locations.</td><td>as expected</td></tr><tr><td>AO-23 Logged information is correct.</td><td>as expected</td></tr></table>
Analysis:	Expected results achieved

5.2.98   DA-25-DEVICE

Test Case DA-25-DEVICE Smart Version 2010/11/03	
Case Summary:	DA-25 Detect a corrupted image.
Assertions:	AM-03 The tool executes in execution environment XE. AO-07 If the tool performs an image file integrity check on an image file that has been changed since the file was created, the tool shall notify the user that the image file has been changed. AO-08 If the tool performs an image file integrity check on an image file that has been changed since the file was created, the tool shall notify the user of the affected locations. AO-23 If the tool logs any log significant information, the information is accurately recorded in the log file.
Tester Name:	brl
Test Host:	Max
Test Date:	Fri Feb 25 13:47:11 2011
Drives:	src(E0) dst (none) other (3A-SATA)
Source Setup:	src hash (SHA1): < 4A6941F1337A8A22B10FC844B4D7FA6158BECB82 > src hash (MD5): < A97C8F36B7AC9D5233B90AC09284F938 > 17938985 total sectors (9184760320 bytes) Model (ATLAS10K2-TY092J) serial # (169028142436)
Log Highlights:	====== Image file corrupted for test run: ====== Change byte 2059 of file /media/3A-SATA/da-06-scsi/da-06-scsi.image.001 from 0x35 to 0x00 ======== Excerpt from SMART log ======== Authenticate: da-06-scsi (FAILED) Image Hash Summary SHA1 Span Hashes total span hash: c233b031 3d626b4d 390e40bf 7065a30b 6fb48bde Device Hash Summary SHA1 Span Hashes total span hash: 4a6941f1 337a8a22 b10fc844 b4d7fa61 58becb82 ======== End of Excerpt from SMART log ========
Results:	

Assertion and Expected Result	Actual Result
AM-03 Execution environment is XE.	as expected
AO-07 User notified if image file has changed.	as expected
AO-08 User notified of changed locations.	as expected
AO-23 Logged information is correct.	as expected

Analysis:	Expected results achieved

5.2.99   DA-26-EWC2R

Test Case DA-26-EWC2R Smart Version 2010/11/03	
Case Summary:	DA-26 Convert an image to an alternate image file format.
Assertions:	AM-03 The tool executes in execution environment XE. AO-09 If the tool converts a source image file from one format to a target image file in another format, the acquired data represented in the target image file is the same as the acquired data in the source image file. AO-23 If the tool logs any log significant information, the information is accurately recorded in the log file.
Tester Name:	brl
Test Host:	WoFat
Test Date:	Wed Mar 2 16:11:23 2011
Drives:	src(43) dst (5A-SATA) other (67-SATA)
Source Setup:	src hash (SHA1): < 888E2E7F7AD237DC7A732281DD93F325065E5871 > src hash (MD5): < BC39C3F7EE7A50E77B9BA1E65A5AEEF7 > 78125000 total sectors (40000000000 bytes) Model (0BB-75JHC0) serial # (WD-WMAMC46588) N Start LBA Length Start C/H/S End C/H/S boot Partition type 1 P 000000063 020980827 0000/001/01 1023/254/63 0C Fat32X 2 X 020980890 057143205 1023/000/01 1023/254/63 0F extended 3 S 000000063 000032067 1023/001/01 1023/254/63 01 Fat12 4 x 000032130 002104515 1023/000/01 1023/254/63 05 extended 5 S 000000063 002104452 1023/001/01 1023/254/63 06 Fat16 6 x 002136645 004192965 1023/000/01 1023/254/63 05 extended 7 S 000000063 004192902 1023/001/01 1023/254/63 16 other 8 x 006329610 008401995 1023/000/01 1023/254/63 05 extended 9 S 000000063 008401932 1023/001/01 1023/254/63 0B Fat32 10 x 014731605 010490445 1023/000/01 1023/254/63 05 extended 11 S 000000063 010490382 1023/001/01 1023/254/63 83 Linux 12 x 025222050 004209030 1023/000/01 1023/254/63 05 extended 13 S 000000063 004208967 1023/001/01 1023/254/63 82 Linux swap 14 x 029431080 027712125 1023/000/01 1023/254/63 05 extended 15 S 000000063 027712062 1023/001/01 1023/254/63 07 NTFS 16 S 000000000 000000000 0000/000/00 0000/000/00 00 empty entry 17 P 000000000 000000000 0000/000/00 0000/000/00 00 empty entry 18 P 000000000 000000000 0000/000/00 0000/000/00 00 empty entry 1 020980827 sectors 10742183424 bytes 3 000032067 sectors 16418304 bytes 5 002104452 sectors 1077479424 bytes 7 004192902 sectors 2146765824 bytes 9 008401932 sectors 4301789184 bytes 11 010490382 sectors 5371075584 bytes 13 004208967 sectors 2154991104 bytes 15 027712062 sectors 14188575744 bytes
Log Highlights:	OS: Linux ubuntu 2.6.32-21-generic #32-Ubuntu SMP Fri Apr 16 08:10:02 UTC 2010 i686 GNU/Linux ====== Image file segments ====== 1 10793 2011-03-03 10:21 da-26-ewc2r 2 40000000000 2011-03-02 17:25 da-26-ewc2r.image.001 3 28143 2011-03-02 17:25 da-26-ewc2r.image.info ======== Excerpt from SMART log ======== Copy: da-10-ewcompress Authenticate: da-26-ewc2r (PASSED) Current Hash Summary SHA1 Span Hashes total span hash: 888e2e7f 7ad237dc 7a732281 dd93f325 065e5871 Stored Hashes SHA1 Span Hashes

Test Case DA-26-EWC2R Smart Version 2010/11/03	
	total span hash: 888e2e7f 7ad237dc 7a732281 dd93f325 065e5871 IO Summary:(Time: Wed Mar 2 17:25:21 2011) Bytes Read: 40,000,000,000 40,000,000,000 bytes written to image "da-26-ewc2r" ======== End of Excerpt from SMART log ========
Results:	

Assertion and Expected Result	Actual Result
AM-03 Execution environment is XE.	as expected
AO-09 Tool converts image file format.	as expected
AO-23 Logged information is correct.	as expected

Analysis:	Expected results achieved

5.2.100   DA-26-BZ2R

Test Case DA-26-BZ2R Smart Version 2010/11/03	
Case Summary:	DA-26 Convert an image to an alternate image file format.
Assertions:	AM-03 The tool executes in execution environment XE. AO-09 If the tool converts a source image file from one format to a target image file in another format, the acquired data represented in the target image file is the same as the acquired data in the source image file. AO-23 If the tool logs any log significant information, the information is accurately recorded in the log file.
Tester Name:	brl
Test Host:	WoFat
Test Date:	Thu Mar 3 10:44:43 2011
Drives:	src(41) dst (67-SATA) other (68-SATA)
Source Setup:	src hash (SHA1): < 15CAA1A307271160D8372668BF8A03FC45A51CC9 > src hash (MD5): < 0A6A8EF78BDC14E2026710D8CCB5607C > 78125000 total sectors (40000000000 bytes) 65534/015/63 (max cyl/hd values) 65535/016/63 (number of cyl/hd) IDE disk: Model (WDC WD400BB-75JHC0) serial # (WD-WMAMC4658355) N Start LBA Length Start C/H/S End C/H/S boot Partition type 1 P 000000063 078107967 0000/001/01 1023/254/63 Boot 07 NTFS 2 P 000000000 000000000 0000/000/00 0000/000/00 00 empty entry 3 P 000000000 000000000 0000/000/00 0000/000/00 00 empty entry 4 P 000000000 000000000 0000/000/00 0000/000/00 00 empty entry 1 078107967 sectors 39991279104 bytes
Log Highlights:	OS: Linux ubuntu 2.6.32-21-generic #32-Ubuntu SMP Fri Apr 16 08:10:02 UTC 2010 i686 GNU/Linux ====== Image file segments ====== 1 5530 2011-03-03 13:57 da-26-bz2r 2 40000000000 2011-03-03 11:43 da-26-bz2r.image.001 3 4568 2011-03-03 11:43 da-26-bz2r.image.info ======== Excerpt from SMART log ======== Copy: da-10-bzip2 Authenticate: da-26-bz2r (PASSED) Current Hash Summary SHA1 Span Hashes total span hash: 15caa1a3 07271160 d8372668 bf8a03fc 45a51cc9 Stored Hashes SHA1 Span Hashes total span hash: 15caa1a3 07271160 d8372668 bf8a03fc 45a51cc9 IO Summary:(Time: Thu Mar 3 11:43:06 2011) Bytes Read: 40,000,000,000 40,000,000,000 bytes written to image "da-26-bz2r" ======== End of Excerpt from SMART log ========
Results:	

Assertion and Expected Result	Actual Result
AM-03 Execution environment is XE.	as expected
AO-09 Tool converts image file format.	as expected
AO-23 Logged information is correct.	as expected

Analysis:	Expected results achieved

5.2.101   DA-26-G2R

Test Case DA-26-G2R Smart Version 2010/11/03	
Case Summary:	DA-26 Convert an image to an alternate image file format.
Assertions:	AM-03 The tool executes in execution environment XE. AO-09 If the tool converts a source image file from one format to a target image file in another format, the acquired data represented in the target image file is the same as the acquired data in the source image file. AO-23 If the tool logs any log significant information, the information is accurately recorded in the log file.
Tester Name:	brl
Test Host:	WoFat
Test Date:	Thu Mar 3 14:10:55 2011
Drives:	src(41) dst (67-SATA) other (68-SATA)
Source Setup:	src hash (SHA1): < 15CAA1A307271160D8372668BF8A03FC45A51CC9 > src hash (MD5): < 0A6A8EF78BDC14E2026710D8CCB5607C > 78125000 total sectors (40000000000 bytes) 65534/015/63 (max cyl/hd values) 65535/016/63 (number of cyl/hd) IDE disk: Model (WDC WD400BB-75JHC0) serial # (WD-WMAMC4658355) N Start LBA Length Start C/H/S End C/H/S boot Partition type 1 P 000000063 078107967 0000/001/01 1023/254/63 Boot 07 NTFS 2 P 000000000 000000000 0000/000/00 0000/000/00 00 empty entry 3 P 000000000 000000000 0000/000/00 0000/000/00 00 empty entry 4 P 000000000 000000000 0000/000/00 0000/000/00 00 empty entry 1 078107967 sectors 39991279104 bytes
Log Highlights:	OS: Linux ubuntu 2.6.32-21-generic #32-Ubuntu SMP Fri Apr 16 08:10:02 UTC 2010 i686 GNU/Linux ====== Image file segments ====== 1 5517 2011-03-03 16:16 da-26-g2r 2 40000000000 2011-03-03 15:07 da-26-g2r.image.001 3 4560 2011-03-03 15:07 da-26-g2r.image.info ======== Excerpt from SMART log ======== Copy: da-10-gzip Authenticate: da-26-g2r (PASSED) Current Hash Summary SHA1 Span Hashes total span hash: 15caa1a3 07271160 d8372668 bf8a03fc 45a51cc9 Stored Hashes SHA1 Span Hashes total span hash: 15caa1a3 07271160 d8372668 bf8a03fc 45a51cc9 IO Summary:(Time: Thu Mar 3 15:07:20 2011) Bytes Read: 40,000,000,000 40,000,000,000 bytes written to image "da-26-g2r" ======== End of Excerpt from SMART log ========
Results:	

Assertion and Expected Result	Actual Result
AM-03 Execution environment is XE.	as expected
AO-09 Tool converts image file format.	as expected
AO-23 Logged information is correct.	as expected

Analysis:	Expected results achieved

5.2.102   DA-26-R2BZ

Test Case DA-26-R2BZ Smart Version 2010/11/03	
Case Summary:	DA-26 Convert an image to an alternate image file format.
Assertions:	AM-03 The tool executes in execution environment XE. AO-09 If the tool converts a source image file from one format to a target image file in another format, the acquired data represented in the target image file is the same as the acquired data in the source image file. AO-23 If the tool logs any log significant information, the information is accurately recorded in the log file.
Tester Name:	brl
Test Host:	WoFat
Test Date:	Wed Mar 2 11:14:27 2011
Drives:	src(E0) dst (67-SATA) other (5A-SATA)
Source Setup:	src hash (SHA1): < 4A6941F1337A8A22B10FC844B4D7FA6158BECB82 > src hash (MD5): < A97C8F36B7AC9D5233B90AC09284F938 > 17938985 total sectors (9184760320 bytes) Model (ATLAS10K2-TY092J) serial # (169028142436)
Log Highlights:	OS: Linux ubuntu 2.6.32-21-generic #32-Ubuntu SMP Fri Apr 16 08:10:02 UTC 2010 i686 GNU/Linux ====== Image file segments ====== 1 6225 2011-03-02 12:01 da-26-r2bz 2 44121880 2011-03-02 11:43 da-26-r2bz.image.001.bz2 3 4634 2011-03-02 11:43 da-26-r2bz.image.info ======== Excerpt from SMART log ======== Copy: da-06-scsi Authenticate: da-26-r2bz (PASSED) Current Hash Summary SHA1 Span Hashes total span hash: 4a6941f1 337a8a22 b10fc844 b4d7fa61 58becb82 Stored Hashes SHA1 Span Hashes total span hash: 4a6941f1 337a8a22 b10fc844 b4d7fa61 58becb82 IO Summary:(Time: Wed Mar 2 11:43:48 2011) Bytes Read: 9,184,760,320 9,184,760,320 bytes written to image "da-26-r2bz" ======== End of Excerpt from SMART log ========
Results:	

Assertion and Expected Result	Actual Result
AM-03 Execution environment is XE.	as expected
AO-09 Tool converts image file format.	as expected
AO-23 Logged information is correct.	as expected

Analysis:	Expected results achieved

5.2.103　　DA-26-R2EWC

Test Case DA-26-R2EWC Smart Version 2010/11/03	
Case Summary:	DA-26 Convert an image to an alternate image file format.
Assertions:	AM-03 The tool executes in execution environment XE. AO-09 If the tool converts a source image file from one format to a target image file in another format, the acquired data represented in the target image file is the same as the acquired data in the source image file. AO-23 If the tool logs any log significant information, the information is accurately recorded in the log file.
Tester Name:	brl
Test Host:	WoFat
Test Date:	Wed Mar 2 13:31:24 2011
Drives:	src(E0) dst (67-SATA) other (5A-SATA)
Source Setup:	src hash (SHA1): < 4A6941F1337A8A22B10FC844B4D7FA6158BECB82 > src hash (MD5): < A97C8F36B7AC9D5233B90AC09284F938 > 17938985 total sectors (9184760320 bytes) Model (ATLAS10K2-TY092J) serial # (169028142436)
Log Highlights:	OS: Linux ubuntu 2.6.32-21-generic #32-Ubuntu SMP Fri Apr 16 08:10:02 UTC 2010 i686 GNU/Linux ====== Image file segments ====== 1 6234 2011-03-02 14:03 da-26-r2ewc 2 4631 2011-03-02 13:50 da-26-r2ewc.image.info 3 154210247 2011-03-02 13:50 da-26-r2ewc.image.s01 ======== Excerpt from SMART log ======== Copy: da-06-scsi Authenticate: da-26-r2ewc (PASSED) Current Hash Summary SHA1 Span Hashes total span hash: 4a6941f1 337a8a22 b10fc844 b4d7fa61 58becb82 Stored Hashes SHA1 Span Hashes total span hash: 4a6941f1 337a8a22 b10fc844 b4d7fa61 58becb82 IO Summary:(Time: Wed Mar 2 13:50:55 2011) Bytes Read: 9,184,760,320 9,184,760,320 bytes written to image "da-26-r2ewc" ======== End of Excerpt from SMART log ========
Results:	

Assertion and Expected Result	Actual Result
AM-03 Execution environment is XE.	as expected
AO-09 Tool converts image file format.	as expected
AO-23 Logged information is correct.	as expected

Analysis:	Expected results achieved

5.2.104   DA-26-R2G

Test Case DA-26-R2G Smart Version 2010/11/03	
Case Summary:	DA-26 Convert an image to an alternate image file format.
Assertions:	AM-03 The tool executes in execution environment XE. AO-09 If the tool converts a source image file from one format to a target image file in another format, the acquired data represented in the target image file is the same as the acquired data in the source image file. AO-23 If the tool logs any log significant information, the information is accurately recorded in the log file.
Tester Name:	brl
Test Host:	WoFat
Test Date:	Wed Mar 2 14:16:26 2011
Drives:	src(E0) dst (67-SATA) other (5A-SATA)
Source Setup:	src hash (SHA1): < 4A6941F1337A8A22B10FC844B4D7FA6158BECB82 > src hash (MD5): < A97C8F36B7AC9D5233B90AC09284F938 > 17938985 total sectors (9184760320 bytes) Model (ATLAS10K2-TY092J) serial # (169028142436)
Log Highlights:	OS: Linux ubuntu 2.6.32-21-generic #32-Ubuntu SMP Fri Apr 16 08:10:02 UTC 2010 i686 GNU/Linux ====== Image file segments ====== 1 3737 2011-03-02 14:49 da-26-r2g 2 131336524 2011-03-02 14:49 da-26-r2g.image.001.gz 3 4628 2011-03-02 14:49 da-26-r2g.image.info ======== Excerpt from SMART log ======== Copy: da-06-scsi Authenticate: da-26-r2g (PASSED) Current Hash Summary SHA1 Span Hashes total span hash: 4a6941f1 337a8a22 b10fc844 b4d7fa61 58becb82 Stored Hashes SHA1 Span Hashes total span hash: 4a6941f1 337a8a22 b10fc844 b4d7fa61 58becb82 IO Summary:(Time: Wed Mar 2 14:49:17 2011) Bytes Read: 9,184,760,320 9,184,760,320 bytes written to image "da-26-r2g" ======== End of Excerpt from SMART log ========
Results:	<table><tr><th>Assertion and Expected Result</th><th>Actual Result</th></tr><tr><td>AM-03 Execution environment is XE.</td><td>as expected</td></tr><tr><td>AO-09 Tool converts image file format.</td><td>as expected</td></tr><tr><td>AO-23 Logged information is correct.</td><td>as expected</td></tr></table>
Analysis:	Expected results achieved

About the National Institute of Justice

A component of the Office of Justice Programs, NIJ is the research, development and evaluation agency of the U.S. Department of Justice. NIJ's mission is to advance scientific research, development and evaluation to enhance the administration of justice and public safety. NIJ's principal authorities are derived from the Omnibus Crime Control and Safe Streets Act of 1968, as amended (see 42 U.S.C. §§ 3721–3723).

The NIJ Director is appointed by the President and confirmed by the Senate. The Director establishes the Institute's objectives, guided by the priorities of the Office of Justice Programs, the U.S. Department of Justice, and the needs of the field. The Institute actively solicits the views of criminal justice and other professionals and researchers to inform its search for the knowledge and tools to guide policy and practice.

Strategic Goals

NIJ has seven strategic goals grouped into three categories:

Creating relevant knowledge and tools

1. Partner with state and local practitioners and policymakers to identify social science research and technology needs.
2. Create scientific, relevant, and reliable knowledge—with a particular emphasis on terrorism, violent crime, drugs and crime, cost-effectiveness, and community-based efforts—to enhance the administration of justice and public safety.
3. Develop affordable and effective tools and technologies to enhance the administration of justice and public safety.

Dissemination

4. Disseminate relevant knowledge and information to practitioners and policymakers in an understandable, timely and concise manner.
5. Act as an honest broker to identify the information, tools and technologies that respond to the needs of stakeholders.

Agency management

6. Practice fairness and openness in the research and development process.
7. Ensure professionalism, excellence, accountability, cost-effectiveness and integrity in the management and conduct of NIJ activities and programs.

Program Areas

In addressing these strategic challenges, the Institute is involved in the following program areas: crime control and prevention, including policing; drugs and crime; justice systems and offender behavior, including corrections; violence and victimization; communications and information technologies; critical incident response; investigative and forensic sciences, including DNA; less-than-lethal technologies; officer protection; education and training technologies; testing and standards; technology assistance to law enforcement and corrections agencies; field testing of promising programs; and international crime control.

In addition to sponsoring research and development and technology assistance, NIJ evaluates programs, policies, and technologies. NIJ communicates its research and evaluation findings through conferences and print and electronic media.

To find out more about the National Institute of Justice, please visit:

www.nij.gov

or contact:

National Criminal Justice
 Reference Service
P.O. Box 6000
Rockville, MD 20849–6000
800–851–3420
http://www.ncjrs.gov